Food Culture in
France

France. Cartography by Bookcomp, Inc.

Food Culture in
France

JULIA ABRAMSON

Food Culture around the World
Ken Albala, Series Editor

GREENWOOD PRESS
Westport, Connecticut · London

Library of Congress Cataloging-in-Publication Data

Abramson, Julia.
 Food culture in France / Julia Abramson.
  p. cm.—(Food culture around the world, ISSN 1545–2638)
 Includes bibliographical references and index.
 ISBN 0–313–32797–1 (alk. paper)
 1. Cookery, French. 2. Food habits—France. I. Title.
 TX719.A237 2007
 641.5'944—dc22   2006031524

British Library Cataloguing in Publication Data is available.

Library of Congress Catalog Card Number: 2006031524
ISBN-10: 0–313–32797–1
ISBN-13: 978–0–313–32797–1
ISSN: 1545–2638

First published in 2007

Greenwood Press, 88 Post Road West, Westport, CT 06881
An imprint of Greenwood Publishing Group, Inc.
www.greenwood.com

Printed in the United States of America

The paper used in this book complies with the
Permanent Paper Standard issued by the National
Information Standards Organization (Z39.48–1984).

10 9 8 7 6 5 4 3 2 1

The publisher has done its best to make sure the instructions and/or recipes in this book
are correct. However, users should apply judgment and experience when preparing recipes,
especially parents and teachers working with young people. The publisher accepts no
responsibility for the outcome of any recipe included in this volume.

Contents

Series Foreword

The appearance of the Food Culture around the World series marks a definitive stage in the maturation of Food Studies as a discipline to reach a wider audience of students, general readers, and foodies alike. In comprehensive interdisciplinary reference volumes, each on the food culture of a country or region for which information is most in demand, a remarkable team of experts from around the world offers a deeper understanding and appreciation of the role of food in shaping human culture for a whole new generation. I am honored to have been associated with this project as series editor. Each volume follows a series format, with a chronology of food-related dates and narrative chapters entitled Introduction, Historical Overview, Major Foods and Ingredients, Cooking, Typical Meals, Eating Out, Special Occasions, and Diet and Health. Each also includes a glossary, bibliography, resource guide, and illustrations. Finding or growing food has of course been the major preoccupation of our species throughout history, but how various peoples around the world learn to exploit their natural resources, come to esteem or shun specific foods, and develop unique cuisines reveals much more about what it is to be human. There is perhaps no better way to understand a culture, its values, preoccupations, and fears, than by examining its attitudes toward food. Food provides the daily sustenance around which families and communities bond. It provides the material basis for rituals through which people celebrate the passage of life stages and their connection to divinity. Food preferences also serve to separate individuals and groups from each other, and as one of the most powerful factors in the construction of identity, we physically, emotionally and spiritually become what we eat. By studying the foodways of people different from ourselves we also grow to understand and tolerate the rich diversity of practices around the world. What seems strange or frightening among other people becomes perfectly rational when set in context. It is my hope that readers will gain from these volumes not only an aesthetic appreciation for the glories of the many culinary traditions described, but also ultimately a more profound respect for the peoples who devised them. Whether it is eating New Year's dumplings in China, folding tamales with friends in Mexico, or going out to a famous Michelin-starred restaurant in France, understanding these food traditions helps us to understand the people themselves. As globalization proceeds apace in the twenty-first century it is also more important than ever to preserve unique local and regional traditions. In many cases these books describe ways of eating that have already begun to disappear or have been seriously transformed by modernity. To know how and why these losses occur today also enables us to decide what traditions, whether from our own heritage or that of others, we wish to keep alive. These books are thus not only about the food and culture of peoples around the world, but also about ourselves and who we hope to be.

Ken Albala
University of the Pacific

Acknowledgments

For two decades and more, I have been traveling regularly to France to live and work, to research and write. In this time, many people have opened their doors to me and shared their meals and food lore, their conversation and friendship. I am profoundly grateful for this hospitality and for these many personalized introductions to the food cultures of France. Of all my debts, that to my cousin Charlotte Berger-Grenèche and to François Depoil is by far the greatest. Discerning eaters and accomplished cooks; convivial, generous hosts; and thoughtful participants in the culture of their own country, Charlotte and François more than anyone else have taught me what it means to eat *à la française*. This book is for them, and it is for my parents, who nourished my interest in food from the very beginning.

Thanks are due to the wonderfully supportive community of scholars interested in food history and in France. Beatrice Fink, Barbara Ketcham Wheaton, and Carolin C. Young shared with me their enthusiasm for French food and have steadfastly encouraged mine. Ken Albala, editor for the Greenwood Press world food culture series, and Wendi Schnaufer, senior editor at the Press, made it possible for me to write this book. I am grateful to Kyri Watson Claflin, Priscilla Parkhurst Ferguson, Alison Matthews-David, Norman Stillman, and Charles Walton, who read drafts of these chapters. Layla Roesler responded with grace, wit, and precision to what must have seemed like endless questions about her family life. Through her good humor this book has been much enriched.

For the photographs I am indebted to Philippe Bornier, Hervé Depoil, Janine Depoil, Nadine Leick, Arnold Matthews, and Christian Verdet. They have been generous beyond measure for the sake of friendship, food, and conversation across cultures. My warm thanks especially to Hervé Depoil for doing *le maxi*.

Finally, colleagues and students at the university where I have taught for the last seven years have supported my engagement in the study of food history and cultures. At the University of Oklahoma a special thank you goes to Paul Bell, Pamela Genova, Andy Horton, Helga Madland, Edward Sankowski, Zev Trachtenberg, and of course to Sarah Tracy. For their enthusiastic participation, hard work, and frank questions, I thank the undergraduate students who have taken my seminars on food and culture (Honors College) and on French food and film (Program in Film and Video Studies) and the graduate students in my course on French gastronomic literature (Department of Modern Languages, Literatures, and Linguistics). Many of the passages in this book were written with my students in mind. Their unfailing intellectual curiosity fueled my own enthusiasm for the topics covered in this volume, and their questions usually led us all directly to the heart of the matter.

Introduction

Nearly every American has some idea about French food. For those who dine out, the ideal for an elegant, glamorous restaurant meal is often a French one. For curious home cooks, the many French cookbooks published in the United States since the mid-twentieth century have guided experiments in the kitchen. Arm-chair travelers will have read the great American chronicles of life and food in France, such as Samuel Chamberlain's columns in the early issues of *Gourmet* magazine, M.F.K. Fisher's memoirs, and Ernest Hemingway's *A Moveable Feast*. The export of Champagne and adaptations of the breakfast *croissant* have made these items standard units in the international food currency. For those who have traveled abroad, a plate of silky *foie gras*, a bite of milky crisp fresh almond, or a fragrant piece of *baguette* still warm from the oven has perhaps been a gastronomic revelation. What interested eater would not be moved by French food? In poorer kitchens, generations of resourceful cooks have perfected ingenious yet practical ways of transforming the meanest bits of meat and aging root vegetables into rich stews, nourishing soups, and tantalizing sausages. The subtle coherence of flavors and the dignified unfolding of the several-course meals that are now standard are at once seductive, soothing, and stimulating. Of course, a few clichés persist, as well. Snails and frogs feature in the cuisine, however, it is an error to imagine that these murky creatures play a large role in everyday eating. Since the Second World War, affluence has reshaped the diet for much of the French population. Nonetheless, people are much more likely to shop for food at one of the many discount stores than at picturesque outdoor markets, although these are practically a national treasure. That the French drink only rarefied bottled spring waters (when not drinking wine) is in fact one of the new myths.

So what do the 60 million French of today really eat on a daily basis? Here is the essential question that this book addresses. To understand the full significance of the table customs, the book also treats the issues of why and how foods are eaten. Why is it that the different dishes in an everyday meal are eaten successively in separate courses, rather than appearing on the table all at once? How is it possible to eat this succession of foods without becoming uncomfortably full, from meal to meal, and desperately unhealthy, over time? How is it that the French cultivate pleasure rather than count calories, yet in fact enjoy an unusually high standard of health, as a nation? Why, at noon, does this population of productive, hard-working, secular individualists march practically in lockstep to the dining room, causing nearly everything from Dunkerque to Cannes to grind to a halt for the sacred lunch break? Why do the French themselves regard eating lunch in school and business cafeterias as an anomaly, when the country actually has the best-developed and most heavily used canteen system in Europe?

Food Culture in France answers these questions and many others. As the aim has been to provide a three-dimensional picture of food customs, the approach is inclusive. The chapters that follow draw on a wide range of sources, from cookbooks and personal experience, to recent studies by ethnologists and sociologists, to the writings of historians and cultural critics. Throughout, an attempt is made to provide both the historical information necessary to illuminate contemporary food culture and full descriptions of today's practices, including workday meals, celebration meals, attitudes toward health, public policy addressing food quality, trends in restaurant cooking, and changing views of wine. The recipes that appear in the text correspond to a few of the typical dishes that come under discussion. The bibliography at the end of the volume lists the references consulted for each chapter and includes a list of cookbooks. It is hoped that these resources as well as the selection of Web sites and films will provide the reader with a point of departure for further exploration.

Bonne lecture (happy reading) and *bon appétit!*

Timeline

ca. 30,000 B.C.E.	Old Stone Age nomads hunt big game and gather plants for food.
ca. 16,000–14,000 B.C.E.	Charcoal and ochre drawings of bulls and reindeer in the Lascaux Caves in the Dordogne show main Ice Age food sources.
10,000–9000 B.C.E.	Food sources change as glaciers recede. Reindeer retreat to colder northern regions. Forest animals such as deer and wild boar multiply.
8000 B.C.E.	The bow and arrow, and the companionship of domesticated dogs, make hunting easier. Forests provide berries, chestnuts, and hazelnuts. Humans eat mollusks, including snails.
6000 B.C.E.	New Stone Age people farm and tend herds. Domesticates include sheep, goats, cattle, corn, barley, and millet.
800 B.C.E.	Iron Age Celts fit iron cutting edges on ploughs used to till soil, improving farm production.
600 B.C.E.	Greek merchants from Phocaea establish a colony at Massilia (Marseille) where they plant olive trees for oil and grape vines for wine, elements in the Mediterranean diet.

51 B.C.E.	Julius Caesar annexes Gallic lands to the Empire. A Roman-style *forum* or market and public meeting space is added to each Gallic town.
19 B.C.E.	The Roman-engineered Pont-du-Gard aqueduct daily transports 20,000 cubic meters (about 26,000 cubic yards) of water to urban areas. Gallic regional specialties include grain (Beauce), sheep (Ardennes), geese (Artois), and wine (Roussillon, Languedoc).
481–511 C.E.	The Salic legal code issued in Paris under King Clovis specifies punishments for anyone who attacks a neighbor's grape vines.
585	Famine forces innovation in bread-making. In *The History of the Franks* (593–94), chronicler Gregory of Tours notes that people supplemented wheat flour with pounded grape seeds and ferns.
780	Saint William of Gellone, one of Charlemagne's paladins, forces Saracen warriors to retreat from the southern territories. Legend has it that he concealed his troops in wine barrels.
822	The abbot Adalhard of Corbie records that monks are adding hops flowers to their ale, making true beer.
1000–1300	People clear forest and drain marshland to cultivate grains for bread. The population grows.
1110	Louis VI (The Fat) allows fishmongers to set up stands outside his palace walls in Paris. The site becomes the market Les Halles.
1148, 1204	Knights and soldiers return from the First and Second Crusades bringing lemons and spices: saffron, cardamom, cinnamon, cloves, ginger, mace and nutmeg, cumin, and sugar.
1150–1310	City and monastic trade fairs in the Champagne region are international. Flemish and Italian merchants arrive with spices and other exotics.
1315, 1317	Cannibalism and crime follow widespread famines.
1341	The Valois monarch Philip VI (1293–1350) introduces the *grande gabelle* (salt tax) in the north.
1468	Renaissance elites are conspicuous consumers. The feast for Charles the Bold of Burgundy's wedding

	includes 200 oxen, 63 pigs, 1,000 pounds of lard, 2,500 calves, 2,500 sheep, 3,600 shoulders of mutton, 11,800 chickens, 18,640 pigeons, 3,640 swans, 2,100 peacocks, and 1,668 wolves.
1476	King Louis XI (1461–1483) decrees that butchers slaughter pigs and sell raw pork, but *chaircutiers* (charcutiers) sell cooked and cured pork and raw pork fat.
1486	The manuscript *Le Viandier* by Guillaume de Tirel (Taillevent) appears in print as an early cookbook.
1492–1494, 1502	Spanish explorer Christopher Columbus encounters foods hitherto unknown in the Old World: sweet potatoes, peppers, maize, chocolate, and vanilla.
1534	Physician and priest François Rabelais publishes the novel *Gargantua*, about a race of giants. Massive feasts are central to the social satire.
ca. 1600	Peasant families who survived the bubonic plague and Hundred Years War and Wars of Religion clear land to plant new crops: cold-hardy buckwheat and New World maize.
1606	Henri IV (1589–1610) declares his wish that "every peasant may have a chicken in the pot on Sundays." Hunger and poverty are widespread.
1651	François Pierre de La Varenne publishes the cookbook *Le Cuisinier françois*. For flavoring, he privileges herbs and onions over spices.
1667	Courtiers now use forks, but Louis XIV (1643–1715) uses his fingers to eat.
1669	Suleiman Aga, Turkish ambassador to the court of Louis XIV, serves coffee at Versailles.
1672	Coffee is sold at a temporary café at the St. Germain fair. Within the decade the Café Procope, the first successful café in France and still in business today, will open in Paris.
1681	Physicist Denys Papin, in residence in England, invents the pressure cooker. The "digester" efficiently reduces solid foods nearly to liquid.
1685	Louis XIV revokes the Edict of Nantes (1598), Protestants flee, and the country reverts to strict observance of Catholic feast and fast days.

1709	An unusually cold winter sets in early and kills crops. Famine and grain riots break out.
1735	Louis XV (1715–1774) favors small, intimate suppers over state banquets and personally makes omelets and coffee for selected guests.
1760s	Modern-style restaurants, with menus and private tables, open in Paris.
1775	Peasants and urban dwellers riot to protest grain shortages.
1785	With the help of Louis XVI, the naturalist Antoine-Auguste Parmentier promotes the still-unpopular potato as an alternative to grains.
1787	Most people subsist on bread, which costs nearly 60 percent of their income.
1789	Louis XVI sends troops against the newly formed National Assembly, and a mob retorts by attacking the Bastille prison. Rioting abounds during the Revolution and hunger is prevalent.
1790	The National Assembly abolishes the hated and much-abused salt tax, *la gabelle*.
1793	Louis XVI dies at the guillotine. In prison since late January 1791, he has been eating several-course meals while famine plagues France.
1803	Grimod de la Reynière publishes the first narrative restaurant guide for Paris. Two years later he modernizes the meal: he recommends serving dishes one by one in sequence, so that they can be enjoyed hot.
1804	Nicolas Appert opens a vacuum-bottling factory. He preserves meats, vegetables, and fruits to provision Napoleon's troops.
1808	Cadet de Gassicourt publishes a "gastronomic map." Pictures of apples and cider bottles in Normandy and ducks at Alençon visually connect taste to place.
1814–1815	At the Congress of Vienna after the Napoleonic wars, diplomat, bishop, and noted gourmand Charles-Maurice de Talleyrand-Périgord wines and dines European ministers. They concede to his demands for the restored Bourbon monarch, Louis XVIII. The

great chef Marie-Antoine Carême is Talleyrand's right-hand man for political strategy at table.

1830   French forces take Algiers. The colonial empire will expand to include Senegal (1857), Indochina (1859–1863), Tunisia (1881), and Morocco (1912).

1859   Ferdinand Carré demonstrates his ammonia absorbtion unit, the technology that was the basis for the first industrial refrigerators.

1861   Louis Pasteur applies heat and pressure to sterilize milk.

1870   Prussian troops occupy the capital, and desperate Parisians resort to eating zoo animals.

1870s   Grape phylloxerae devastate vines across France.

1883   The network of trains encourages peasants to farm beyond self-sufficiency and to specialize. The Orient Express makes its inaugural run from Paris to Constantinople, with several-course meals served in elegant restaurant cars.

1892   Jules Méline draws up protectionist tariffs for agricultural production.

1903   Chef Auguste Escoffier publishes Le guide culinaire, which simplifies and systematizes the sauces and cooking methods that compose elegant cuisine.

1905   A new federal law prohibits fraud in the sale of food. The law will stand until it is integrated into the European food safety code in 1993.

1919   Meat prices escalate. Import duties on sugar make it unaffordable to most.

1927   Parliament rules that only wine bottled within the demarcated Champagne area may be labeled as "Champagne."

1940   France capitulates to Germany during the Second World War. Food prices are at a premium. Bread is rationed. The black market for food flourishes.

1943   Under German occupation during the Vichy period, rationing allows for 1,200 calories per day per person. Life expectancy drops by eight years.

1949   Bread rationing is lifted. The weekly newspaper *Le Monde* runs a column on dining called "The Pleasures of the Table" signed "La Reynière." Robert Courtine's pseudonym evokes Grimod de la Reynière, the First Empire restaurant guide author.

1965   Half of all French households own a refrigerator.

1977   Chef Michel Guérard serves *cuisine minceur*—light or diet food—at his spa and restaurant. He emphasizes small portions, avoids salt and animal fats, and favors lean meats, vegetables, and fruits.

1990s   Press reports defend the national cuisine in a society marked by Europeanization, globalization, and the presence of immigrant cultures.

1999   To protest against junk food and the presence of foreign corporate interests in the local food chain, farmer José Bové vandalizes a partially constructed McDonald's restaurant in Millau.

2002   Chef Paul Bocuse and baker Lionel Poilâne unsuccessfully lobby Pope John Paul II to remove *gourmandise* (gluttony) from the list of the Seven Deadly Sins.

2003   The Tour d'Argent restaurant in Paris serves its one-millionth *canard à presse* (roasted pressed duck).

2004   Debate continues over whether genetically modified foods and advertising for fast food should be banned in France and Europe.

2005   All automatic vending machines are gone from public schools by the time the fall term begins. The law (of August 2004) that called for this measure aimed to reduce the consumption of sweets and sugared drinks associated with rising obesity levels among children and young people.

2006   Avian flu detected in chickens in Pas-de-Calais. Consumption of chicken drops in March, then rises again.

1

Historical Overview

ORIGINS

The earliest peoples in what is now France likely garnered the largest portion of their food from plants. About 500,000 years ago, nomadic forerunners of modern humans ranged north from Africa into western Europe. These hunter-gatherers foraged in field and forest for berries, nuts, roots, and leaves. When climate change caused the extinction of big game, they hunted horses and aurochs. Paleolithic or Old Stone Age (earliest times to 6000 B.C.E.) paintings on cave walls from about 35,000 to 15,000 B.C.E. at Lascaux, Font-de-Gaume, Cosquer, Chauvet, and Niaux show animal food sources and other creatures—lions, rhinoceros, mammoths—that probably had spiritual significance. Around 8000 B.C.E. Stone Age peoples domesticated dogs as hunting companions.

During the New Stone Age, people made a gradual transition from foraging for food to farming. The innovations of agriculture and pottery that define the Neolithic period came west from the Fertile Crescent to Europe in about 6000 B.C.E. People now cultivated emmer and einkorn (old types of wheat) and naked barley. During winter, they stored extra grain in pits dug into the ground and in pots. In cooler northern regions, rye and oats flourished, first as wild grasses, then as tended crops. Peas, chickpeas, and lentils came under cultivation. Neolithic populations managed animals, in addition to hunting. They herded cattle, sometimes grazing the herds seasonally in different locations. Pigs, sheep, and goats were also kept and may have been moved according to the same practice of transhumance.

Boar, beaver, hare, hedgehog, and quantities of snails added to the list of animal protein eaten in the Neolithic period. Populations living on the Mediterranean and Atlantic coasts and on rivers harvested shellfish and fish.

The invention of pottery changed cooking and storage in the New Stone Age. People made wide-mouthed vessels using bits of bone, shell, sand, flint, or grog (pulverized burnt clay) as a tempering medium. The additions strengthened the clay so that the pots could be placed directly on a fire. This added another technique to spit-roasting, drying, smoking, and heating mixtures by dropping in hot rocks. The end of the Neolithic period saw the incorporation of metals into the arsenal of tools, including cooking implements. The use of copper, bronze (about 1800–700 B.C.E.), and then iron (from about 700 B.C.E.) mark shifts toward technology that maintained more populous civilizations.

GREEKS ON THE CÔTE D'AZUR

In about 600 B.C.E. a few Phocaeans (Greeks from Asia Minor) looking for new territory established colonies that they called Massilia (Marseille) and Agde, bringing their eating customs and essential foods. During the Age of Metals, the Greeks had developed the civilization that underpins much of Western culture, including literary and philosophical traditions and both urban and pastoral ways of life. The ideal diet of classical antiquity was based on three cultivated foods: wheat, grapes, and olives. When the Phocaeans arrived in the new colonies with their vines and fruit, this was the earliest introduction of the Mediterranean diet based on bread, wine, and oil.

In the colonial centers of Greek civilization, elite diners participating in a *symposion* or convivial, shared banquet in a private home drank wine mixed with water only after eating, and valued conversation as an integral part of the meal. Wealthy Greeks loved meat (beef, lamb, pork), but it was not considered everyday fare, and the large domesticates were killed ceremonially. After the required sacrifices had been made to appease the gods, meat was carefully distributed or else sold off in portions equal in size, with little concern for cut or texture. Cheese featured frequently in meals. Fish, eels, and shellfish were eaten, along with the all-purpose salty flavoring sauce *garos* (Roman *garum* or *liquamen*) made of fermented fish.

For the common person, the building blocks for most meals were barley or wheat and pulses. The grains were eaten as porridge or baked into bread or unleavened biscuit if ovens were available. Pulses in the everyday diet included lentils, chickpeas, and fava or broad beans. Greeks brought with them knowledge of the all-important vegetables onion, garlic, and capers. They cultivated cabbages, carrots, gourds, and early forms of cauliflower and lettuce, which were made into salads and cooked dishes. Figs and grapes, apples, pears, plums, quinces, and pomegranates were the best-known fruits. As the cities grew, so did their institutions, including places for eating out such as *kapêleia* or taverns that served wine and inexpensive bar food.

CELTIC ANCESTORS

Tribes of Indo-Europeans that originated in Hallstadt (present-day Austria) and swept west by around 700 B.C.E. developed a diet based on meat, milk, and ale, as well as grains. The Greeks called these peoples *Galatai* or *Keltoi*, giving the name Celts; the Romans would name them Gauls. The city of Paris derives its name from the Celtic Parisii tribe that settled in the Île-de-France. The prehistoric Celts (their language was oral) have a special place in the collective imagination as the ancestors of the modern French.

Celtic civilization was based on farming and animal husbandry. Tribes occupied swathes of land that measured about 1,200 to 2,000 square kilometers (about 450 to 750 square miles). The land was left as open fields that members of the tribe worked in common. Many of the Celtic deities such as the matrons or mother-goddesses were associated with fertility and with flowers, fruits, and grains. Celts in northern Europe mined iron and lead, gold and silver, and developed advanced metalworking techniques such as soldering and the use of rivets. To support farming, they manufactured innovative iron ploughs, harrows, and reapers. They wrought a range of cooking and eating utensils, including flagons, cups, bowls, cauldrons, spits, grills, and serving platters. At their most populous, the Celts in Gaul probably numbered between 6 and 9 million. They did not construct a unified empire or kingdom. Rather, governance was decentralized within tribes headed by a warrior elite and the families that composed each tribe.

Celts ate meat primarily from domesticated oxen or cattle and pigs. Sheep, goats, horses, and dogs were less common. It appears that they domesticated the hare and species of ducks and geese. There is a popular idea that Celts feasted constantly on roast wild boar. Children know this story from the famous cartoons that Goscinny and Uderzo published beginning in the early 1960s about the rotund character Astérix the Gaul and friends, including a benevolent druid. It is certainly true that wild boar roamed the forests, and Celts hunted them in self-defense, but hunting was restricted to elites. For food, the tribes relied on their fields and barnyards. They mined salt and developed techniques for preserving meat and fish through salting, drying, and smoking. Butchers specialized in making hams and sausages and were greatly admired for their facility with curing pork. They made cheeses, drank milk from their herds, and brewed ale (beer without hops) from grain. Meats, fat from meat and milk (lard, butter), and cool-weather grains associated with the Celts typified the diet in what later became northern France.

Ties between the Celtic and the Mediterranean civilizations enlarged the diets. Celts traded metal jewelry, coins, ingots, and tools; amber and salt; hides from their animals; meat products; and slaves with neighboring tribes and with other populations. They cultivated some grapes in the north, but they could not get enough of the heady southern wines that they traded up from Massilia and Rome. Athenaeus, the Greek writer from Naucratis (Egypt) who moved to Rome at the end of the first century, remarked in his *Deipnosophistae* (*Professors at Dinner*, ca. 200–230) that the Celts were heavy drinkers who tossed back their wine undiluted with water. Where the Greeks and Romans kept wine in amphorae (clay jars), Celts used wooden barrels for more convenient storage and transport. Stored in amphorae, wine took on the pitchy or resinous flavor of the jar seal. Exposed to wooden barrels, wine drunk by the Celts must have developed some flavors like those prized by today's oenophiles. The familiarity bred by commerce between the different populations also prepared the way for Rome's annexation of Celtic lands to the Empire in 51 B.C.E.

ROMAN GAUL

The fertile, productive Celtic territories were a temptation not to be resisted by the Romans. Since the inception of the republic in the fifth century B.C.E., Rome ballooned, subsuming far-off Dacia (Romania), North Africa, Syria, and Arabia as provinces; the first imperial dynasty was established in 27 B.C.E. Urban Romans were consumers in need of provisions, and the constantly campaigning legions of the vast military machine required a solid diet of wheat bread, wine, olive oil, meat, cheese, and vegetables. Celts, for their part, provoked ravenous Rome, as they periodically migrated in search of land. Bellicose Cisalpine (from "this side of the Alps," nearest Rome) populations sacked Rome in 387 (or 390) B.C.E. and made incursions elsewhere. The legions butted heads with the tribes for two centuries before the general Julius Caesar was sent to quell them. In 52 B.C.E., he won a decisive victory against the Gallic leader Vercingétorix. A year later, the "three Gauls" or large divisions of Celtic territories had become provinces, with the usual military outposts throughout. Rivers demarcated *Gallia Belgica* from *Celtica* (later *Gallia Lugdunensis*) and *Aquitania*. Beyond the Rhine lay *Germania* and to the south *Provincia* (later *Narbonnensis*) and *Cisalpina*.

The Romans did much to unify and urbanize Celtic lands. Using the old tribal divisions of land as a basis for *latifundia* or large farms with attached estates, and the *oppida* or hill-forts for *civitates* or administrative structures, they centralized political conduits. The Romans built roads for their military but also to the benefit of traders. They undertook huge public projects in durable stone for the cities. Amphitheatres at Orange, Nîmes, and Arles are still used today for concerts, operas, plays, and bull-fighting. City walls, aqueducts (such as the Pont-du-Gard and those built to supply Vienne), and the remains of public baths also persist.

For Gallo-Romans, dining habits at their most luxurious drew on Greek manners, gastronomic specialties from across the Empire, and the agricultural riches of Gaul itself. Roman trade provided links even to India and China, and so a few people had knowledge of quite exotic foods. Greek ways were considered the most elegant and civilized. The colony at Massilia was a destination for Romans as for Romanized Celts—Gallo-Romans—who sought an education and cosmopolitan finish. Eating customs evolved from the Roman adaptations of Greek precedents. Wealthy citizens designed their houses to follow the Roman style, with a courtyard and *triclinium* or dining room. The food at a *convivium* or dinner party could be elaborate, with any-where from two to seven courses. The *gustatio* or *promulsis* (first course) featured vegetables, fish, and eggs. The *mensae primae* (main course or courses) offered meats and poultry and were accompanied by wine mixed with water. A *cena* (fancy dinner) finished with *mensae secundae* or fruits, nuts, and desserts. Elegant diners reclined rather than sat. Propped up on their left elbows, they politely touched food only with the right hand. Among the educated, attitudes toward diet and health were shaped by the prevailing theory of the humors, which were supposed to be balanced through diet. Continuing Hippocratic tradition, the Greek physician Galen, who worked in the Roman context during the second century, recommended choosing foods with qualities (hot, cold, dry, wet) appropriate for one's personal balance of the four bodily humors (blood, black bile, yellow bile, phlegm) as the way to maintain good health.

At least for the wealthiest eaters, trade enlarged the food choice provided by the local produce. Emmer, soft and hard wheats, and spelt were available in Gaul. Sophisticated wine drinkers tracked yearly variations in quality, and they sought vintages from the best locations across the provinces. For vegetables, there were leeks, lettuces, mallow, cucumbers, gourds, rocket, asparagus, turnips, and beets. The list of fruits and nuts grew ever longer as produce was imported from afar. Figs, apples, pears, grapes, and sun- or smoke-dried raisins were basics. Sorb apples (related to serviceberries), sour cherries, peaches (from Persia), arbutus fruits, dates, hazelnuts, walnuts, chestnuts, pistachios, and pine nuts (pine kernels) were eaten. The Mediterranean gave fish and shellfish including mackerel, wrasse, tuna, bass, octopus, sea urchin, and scallops; oysters from present-day Brittany and Normandy were esteemed a delicacy. *Garum* or fish sauce—made off the Atlantic coast from fermented mackerel and tuna—and *allec* or fish pickle were common. Snails were popular, and wild boar and deer caught on the hunt were prized. Domestic sheep, goats, and cows gave milk for cheese as well as meat. Guinea fowl (originally from Numidia), partridges, hens, and pheasant gave eggs and provided roasts. Spices were valued as flavorings in elite cooking; some were used in perfumes. Among the herbs and spices, lovage nearly always combined with black or long pepper, traded from India in exchange for gold. Other herbs included rosemary, myrtle, bay, saffron, rue, parsley, thyme, juniper berries (native to Gaul), cumin, caraway, celery seed, pennyroyal, mustard, mint, and coriander.

In the late third and fourth centuries, the Romans encouraged British Celts to migrate back to the Continent to defend depopulated Brittany. Today, the few remaining Breton speakers trace their culture back to the Celts. By about the fifth century, Latin penetrated even to rural areas, preparing the way for the development of French. In the modern language, the Celtic heritage echoes primarily in words that pertain to agriculture and in place names.

FRANKS FROM RHINELAND

As the exhausted, overextended Roman Empire crumbled during the fourth century, Germanic tribes crossed west over the Rhine River to settle in Gaul, bringing a new wave of northern influence on diet. Federations and alliances already existed among Germans, Celts, and Gallo-Romans. The Roman army that defeated Attila the Hun in 451 near Troyes was anchored by tribal Germans—Franks, Visigoths, and Burgundians. During the last imperial centuries, decadent emperors, crushing taxes, plague, and famine added to the general unrest and misery. Gallic elites left the cities, contributing to urban decline. During the fifth century, Germanic Visigoths crossed out of Italy and were settled in Gallic Aquitaine. The tribal leader Odoacer the Goth deposed the last Roman emperor in the

Shellfish merchant bringing coastal oysters and mussels to the Saint Antoine market in Lyon. Courtesy of Hervé Depoil.

West in 476. But it was the powerful Franks who exerted the most lasting influence within future French territory.

Although the Franks made periodic migrations, they farmed and herded in the intervening years, like the Celts. They fished, gathered berries and nuts from the forests, grew wheat and barley, and made ale, the favored beverage; some Germanic pagan rites required the conspicuous display of ale casks in the middle of dwellings. Hardy spelt, although lower in yield and in gluten than wheat, was the preferred grain. Franks made hard cider from apples and grew rye. They hunted game and ate domesticated meat, including poultry, which they thought gave them strength to wage war. They roasted meat and made stews, using barley or oats to thicken the mixture. They steadfastly preferred their own butter and lard over southern olive oil, and the men also used butter to condition their characteristic long hair and flowing beards. Both Romans and Christians complained about the reek of rancid butter that was said to announce a German.

Romanized Gauls considered themselves elegant and civilized, in contrast to the Germans. They took pride in Gallic particularities and in the classical heritage, as well as in their own discernment. This is clear in the fourth-century writings of Decimus Agnus Ausonius. His pastoral poem *Mosella* catalogues the edible fish in the tributary of the Rhine named in the title (the Moselle), and he wrote an encomium to the wines and oysters of his native Bordeaux. Romans characterized Germans as uncouth rustics and fickle, though formidable, fighters. The disparaging comments should be taken with a grain of salt. The moralist Salvian of Marseille, whose writings date to about 440, had no special liking for the Germans. Yet he observed that educated and well-born individuals around him were casting their lot with the Goths and Franks. In a time of unrest, they found humane treatment at the hands of the barbarians, while noble Rome had turned uncivilized.[1] A century later, the physician and ambassador Anthimus balanced the classical heritage with the Germanic present. His treatise *De observatione ciborum* (*On the Observance of Foods*), addressed to the Frankish king Theuderic (d. 534), draws on the cookbook author Apicius for recipes and on Galen for medical advice. Yet Anthimus makes concessions to the intended reader and the available food supply. Meats and beer are recommended; local river salmon and trout are indicated; Roman fish sauce is categorically forbidden.[2]

GALLO-CHRISTIANS

In Gaul Christian food practices that evolved from Judaic and Mediterranean traditions had the distinguishing cast of asceticism. In the first and second centuries, mystery religions involving the worship of a dying god (such as Isis or Mithras) who was then reborn became popular. Of these, Christianity had the greatest staying power. By the end of the fourth century under Theodosius, it became the official religion of the Roman Empire. Christianity penetrated first in the southern parts of Gaul where the Germanic traditions held less sway. Early Eucharistic (thanksgiving) meals borrowed from Jewish Passover seders and Greco-Roman banquets. Diners reclined. A variety of foods were eaten in courses. Ceremonial cups of wine were drunk throughout. Bread was preferred over meat. The practice of self-denial and also self-definition through the refusal of habits perceived as typical characterized the early Christian approach to food. The rejection of meats, like the recommendations for sexual abstinence, is an example of asceticism as well as a populist touch and concession to necessity. The meatless diet avoided sacrificial carnage, in particular of the lamb that Jews offered up in temples.

Bread and wine, instead of meat, acquired a powerful symbolic association to sacrifice in Christianity. Christian ritual was overlaid on pagan celebrations of grain and the harvest. As part of the Catholic rite of communion, a piece of bread, later the thin unleavened wafer known as the host, was ingested along with a sip of wine. By miraculous transubstantiation, the bread and wine ostensibly turned into the body and blood of Christ. The communicant directly incorporated his god. Outside of church ceremony, eating bread at daily meals recalled its blessed, Eucharistic counterpart. Bread and wine evoked the body and blood of Christ. Through symbolism, the rite of communion recast sacrifice on a supernatural level, avoiding actual bloodshed while fostering a penchant for the mystical. To eat a meal was to commune with fellow Christians and with the Christian god, to consume him, and to become him.

As the number of monasteries and nunneries increased and bishops consolidated power, institutional pronouncements set ideals for Gallo-Christian food practice. The virtuous fasted on Fridays. Starting in the fourth century, fasting was required for the period before Easter (Lent). Other days were added in rhythm with the natural seasons and older pagan holidays. In extreme cases, saintly figures miraculously abstained from food for long periods. More commonly, Christians fasted for short periods while charitably giving alms and donating food. In the early sixth century, the Rule of Benedict of Nursia (d. ca. 540), father of monasticism in the West, mandated hospitality to guests and to any pilgrim as a basic tenet of monastic life. The principles of inclusion and generosity were not always put into practice. In defiance of Jewish principles of fellowship, early Christian tolerance, and Greek and Gallo-Roman conviviality, the Council of Agde that met in 506 forbade Christians from sharing a meal with "Jews and heretics," on pain of excommunication. Benedict prescribed an acceptable diet for a monk as bread, servings from two cooked dishes, fruits or vegetables in season, wine in limited quantity; meals were to be taken twice daily in summer and once in winter.

If asceticism and fasting characterized early Christianity, indulgence featured in monastic feasting. Clerics could not bear arms, but they gave feasts to build up their reputations. To be sure, Gallic bishops financed banquets to alleviate the hunger of the poor, but the ability to host a feast also signaled power. Some won privileges for their monasteries to import luxury foods such as pepper, cinnamon, and foreign nuts. Despite the Christian principle of disdaining commerce, monasteries participated in trade networks, buying products imported through the Mediterranean ports. Having productive kitchen gardens and well-stocked larders, they could entertain elite visitors. Monks and nuns earned a reputation as food experts. In later centuries the stock figure of the gluttonous monk became a target for satirists. He remained so through the early eighteenth century, when the power of the Catholic Church in France began to decline.

Feasting and fasting traditions—extreme eating—reflect the natural alternation of cycles of plenty and shortage, tied to the seasons and the harvest cycle. They also reveal contradictions inherent to the Gallo-Christian cult of late antiquity. The problem was how to define moderation according to Christian principles. Greeks and Romans explained the need for moderation at table through principles of health. The Christian was burdened with original sin. For the Christian, the flesh was impure. How can the duties of the host to be generous reconcile with the obligation of the penitent to live sparingly?

CAROLINGIAN RENEWAL

After the Roman period, the Merovingian dynasty of Frankish tribal leaders converted to Christianity and shifted the capital from Romanized Lyon to northern, Frankish Paris. The Frankish kingships were military, personal, and quite ill managed. At length, a powerful palace mayor (administrator) to the king overthrew his employer, giving rise to the new dynasty of Carolingians, the most influential of whom was Charlemagne (r. 768–814). Charlemagne waged war to enlarge his dominions across Europe, set himself up as protector of the Church and of the faithful, and was crowned Emperor on Christmas day in the year 800 by Pope Leo III in Rome. The social hierarchy based on landholding, wealth, and rank would underpin the feudal castes of the next centuries. Unlike in the Roman era, no system of direct taxation was used. The acquisition of land cemented power for titled individuals such as counts and dukes, who then exacted tributes from the peasants working their terrain. Nobles, like the Saxons and other peoples conquered in war, made annual gifts to the emperor. Charlemagne made donations to the Church.

Sophisticated systems of exchange also flourished in the marketplace. Monastic fairs at Paris, Langres, Flavigny, Tournus, Cormery, St. Maixent, and St. Benoît de Cessieu brought in revenue, linked merchants to monasteries and the king, and encouraged international trade. Exotic products show the reach of the trade networks. The Frankish liturgy included the ceremonial use of chrism (balsam or balm mixed with oil), for instance. Carolingian documents describing the abbey at St. Gall (in present-day Switzerland) indicate a richly provisioned establishment. Spices were available, and the diet included imports such as lemons and dates.

In the Carolingian era, as in ancient times and up through the Revolution of 1789, most people relied on grains for food. Barley, wheat, and millet were the most common. Near the Rhine valley, oats and rye became important. Pulses complemented the grain. Beer and wine were the beverages of choice. Water was not dependably safe, so children also drank diluted alcohols. Hoarding and speculation on grain and wine aggravated shortages. Famine was common. Difficult conditions fostered tales about the supernatural provision of food and drink. In earlier centuries, spontaneous generation was said to have produced loaves, fish, communion wine, or holy oil. Frankish tastes color provisionary miracles of the Merovingian and Carolingian eras. According to the *vita* or life written in the ninth century, Saint Sadalberga (ca. 605–670), born near Langres, miraculously filled a vat with beer just in time for the visit of the abbot who assisted her to found a monastery.[3]

Attempting to counter hunger, Charlemagne fixed prices for bread, but this measure did not hold market rates steady. His *Capitulare de villis vel curtis imperii,* or decrees regarding the imperial domains, sought to remedy shortages by improving agriculture. The capitularies listed plants that Charlemagne wanted to be cultivated throughout the empire, such as cucumbers, artichokes, chickpeas, fava beans, mustard, radishes, turnips, beets, cabbages, lettuce, rocket, and various herbs.[4] He exhorted cooks, bakers, butchers, millers, and makers of *garum*, cheese, *cervoise* (ale), *hydromel* (fermented honey drink), and mustard to work carefully in a clean environment. It is thanks to Carolingian monastic scribes that many ancient texts are known today, including the oldest surviving copies of Apicius's cookbook *De re coquinaria* (*On Cookery*, ca. fourth century), taken during the ninth century. The plants and foods listed in the capitularies were familiar from antiquity. Encouraging agriculture and food production was part of the effort to renew the achievements of imperial Rome within the contemporary Christian empire. Charlemagne himself was said to have been a careful eater and a moderate drinker.[5] The narrative left by his biographer Einhard shows the effort to negotiate customs from Frankish warrior feasts (involving meat from hunted game and plenty of alcohol) with both classical moderation and Christian asceticism.

After the *Serment de Strasbourg* or Strasbourg Oath of 842, Carolingian territories were divided into three parts. West Francia covered much of the territory of contemporary France. In the feudal era, peasants would work land and trades in exchange for protection given by the landowner. A warrior class of *chevaliers* or knights who were supposed to aid the lords and monarch fought their way into that class to obtain their own hereditary titles and landowning rights. Dynastic competitions were keen in the Middle Ages. The Capetian kings (r. 987–1322) expanded their Parisian stronghold to include the counties of Flanders and Boulogne. In the ninth and tenth centuries, Normans or Norsemen ("northern" or Scandinavian warriors and sailors) descended in boats to plunder and scout for land. They settled in the northwest (today's Normandy), invaded Britain, then merged with Aquitaine and Britain to form the powerful Anglo-Norman or Angevin empire. In the south, the counts of Provence defended their territory.

GRAIN AND SWORDS

The agricultural and population expansion that lasted about 300 years until the mid-thirteenth century owed much to the absence of the military class. After Pope Urban II's call in 1095 from Clermont-Ferrand to take Jerusalem from the Turks, Christian warriors left in droves to crusade against the Muslim "infidel." Armed knights were apt to skirmish over small slights, posing a constant threat to peasants, priests, and the more peaceable nobles. With the knights conveniently gone on crusade, peasants reclaimed land through cutting forests and draining marshes. Grain farming increased to newly opened fields in the north and east. Three-crop rotations, with winter and spring plantings next to a fallow field that was sometimes grazed (and thus manured), improved use of the soil. New wheeled plows were more versatile and efficient. Heavy workhorses bred from Carolingian cavalry animals—the knights' battle chargers— pulled plows faster than the old-fashioned teams of oxen. Improved food production supported a larger population. From the start to the end of the Capetian dynasty, the population tripled to about 20 million.

During the era of the crusades, so productive at home, people imagined "France" as a place and an idea. Writing about the Capetians, the abbot Suger of St. Denis forsook the customary phrase "king of the Franks" for the new description "king of France." The Old French epic *Chanson de Roland* (*Song of Roland*) looks back in time to recount a battle against Moors in Spain that was fought during the era of Charlemagne. The contemporary language of the written version (ca. 1100), however, refers to the homeland as *la douce France* (sweet France).

From its association with pagan Rome and the god Bacchus, wine became the symbol of Christian France. During the Middle Ages, monks grew grapes and produced wine for medicinal use and to offer to travelers and pilgrims whom the laws of hospitality obliged them to host. Today, the link between Christian succor and wine is recalled by events such as the wine auction held every November at the Hôtel-Dieu or historic hospice in the town of Beaune in Burgundy. The auction is now commercial, but it was originally conceived to benefit the charity hospital, authorized by Pope Eugenius IV in 1441 and staffed by nuns.

There was literally little spice in the gustatory life of the peasant. The feudal era had been relatively prosperous. As a result of the ravages of the Hundred Years War (1337–1453) fought against England and the Black Death or bubonic plague (1348–1349), which killed 8 million people, the society was now in bad shape. Meat-eating declined among the peasants. In rural areas and among the poor everywhere, the basic foodstuffs were interminable bowls of gruel and bread made from wheat or maslin (wheat mixed with rye and barley). Peasants drank hard apple cider in the northwest, *cervoise* or beer in the northeast. Wine was grown as far north as the Paris basin—there were vineyards at Montmartre and Belleville. Inexpensive *piquette* (wine made from the second pressing of the fruit) was available in much of the country. During the Angevin period (ca. 1150 to 1450), the best wines from Gascony and Bordeaux were exported to British cellars.

For survivors of the plague and wars, diet and living conditions did improve until about the mid-sixteenth century. Eating meat, especially pork, was not uncommon among peasants, although hunting game in forests remained restricted to the aristocracy; poaching was punishable by execution. Staples varied by region and according to local taste. White wheat bread was rare, generally found in wealthy homes. For most, dark bread was made of wheat supplemented with other grains. In Brittany *blé noir* or *sarrasin* (buckwheat) mixed with water or milk was used to make gruel. In the South and on Corsica, people ate chestnuts, sometimes grinding the nuts into a flour. Nutritious oats were widely grown, although primarily to feed horses. Peas, beans, and chickpeas supplemented the grains and gave more protein. Cheese was a staple in the Auvergne. Cod fishing in North Atlantic waters provided a new, cheap staple that could be eaten during the lean days of Lent, when meat was forbidden. *Stockfisch* or salted dried cod, as well as fresh fish, made their way across the country from ships that docked at the western ports of Dieppe, Le Havre, Honfleur, and Nantes. Until 1537, the distillation of wine was the province of apothecaries, who used the resulting brandy as a medicine. Once François I granted the privilege of manufacture to vinegar makers, the market for brandies and fortified wines quickly expanded.

Around 1550, the climate changed. During the little ice age that lasted through the next three centuries, harsh winters regularly led to inadequate grain harvests, food shortages, high prices, and hunger.

Charitable institutions and paying establishments alike existed to provide venues for meals. Voluntary distribution of food was often associated with collective settings such as hospices and hospitals. The ill, elderly, and destitute received assistance in the form of meals of soup and bread. Convents, monasteries, and generous lords allocated food and wine to pilgrims, hosting them for up to three days. The duties of lords to distribute food and wine stemmed from Christian notions of hospitality and also the old feudal obligations to vassals or dependents.

Paying *hôtels* or *hôtelleries* (hostels, hostelries) maintained by municipal authorities sheltered travelers, prisoners of war, journeymen, judges, and itinerant merchants. The hostels, inns, and much later the *pensions* (boarding houses) typical in the nineteenth century served meals usually at fixed hours and almost invariably at a communal table, where the local regulars often gave travelers and newcomers a hard time. For important occasions such as weddings, elites rented out a *hôtel* and the services of a cook and his helpers, for a catered meal. Inns and the *tavernes* that served wine set up strategically near city gates, at busy intersections in town, and close to marketplaces that drew a crowd. According to region and century, one also drank wine or beer at a *cabaret* (Picardy), *estaminet* (northern France and the Burgundian territory that is today Belgium), or a *débit de vin* ("wine dispensary:" sixteenth century and later). Usually the taverns and other watering holes made some sort of food available, minimally bread and cheese or a piece of cold meat pie.

MANUSCRIPT TO COOKBOOK

The earliest French-language works on cooking reflect practice in distinguished settings. Recipes and indications for service followed the international style of the late medieval and early Renaissance courts throughout western Europe. The nobility were conspicuous consumers, interested in ostentation as well as the distribution of largesse. Nobles feasted in the great halls of their castles. Each course of a meal had several dishes, and the table was set with a *nef* or ship-shaped container to hold the salt. Honored guests sat above the salt close to the head of the table. Food was placed on sliced bread trenchers, which might rest on metal underplates. Myriad attendants performed separate offices. Carvers neatly dismembered whole roasted animals carried in on immense platters; pantners looked after the bread; sauciers attended to the garnishes. The spectacular service prevented diners from having to bring knives and slice their own portions from the roast, as in earlier times.

One of the earliest recipe manuscripts, *Le Viandier* (*The Provisioner*) attributed to Guillaume de Tirel (1315–1395), drew on the author's experience as *maistre queux du roy de France* or master cook to the king of France. Tirel was known as Taillevent. His nickname refers to wind cutting through sails and presumably evokes his swiftness and efficacy in the kitchen. Taillevent's résumé was superb: he cooked for the Valois king Philip VI and for Charles V and served as head of provisions for Charles VI. His cookbook has a coherent organization that reflects the relationship of the recipes to the part they play in a grand meal. Recipes are organized according to the type of main ingredient, the use of the dish for further cooking or service, and the cooking method: boiled meats, meat broths and stews, roasts and roast fowl, fancy *entremets* (meat or grain dishes served between the first and second courses), meatless stews and soups (for fast days), food for the sick, fish (including whale, in one version of the manuscript) and shellfish, and cold and hot sauces. This logic, in which the cookbook mirrors the meal in its organization and progress through time, is still current for many manuals. In 1450, Johann Gutenberg pioneered use of the printing press with movable type in Mainz, and printing came to France shortly thereafter (1470). The popular *Viandier* enjoyed numerous print editions through the seventeenth century.

Another early manuscript, *Le Mesnagier de Paris* (*The Parisian Household Guide*, ca. 1393), evokes a different, if also wealthy, milieu. The author was a well-heeled bourgeois who wrote the instructional booklet for his teenage bride, who had to learn to run the *ménage* (household), including supervising the kitchen. *Le Mesnagier* is thoroughly didactic. Chapters on the obligations of a virtuous wife, moral theology, and economics accompany those on meals. The author describes how to dress game taken on the hunt and indicates when the various garden vegetables should be planted seasonally. He gives menus for feast and fast days, and even tells his wife where she should go shopping for ingredients and utensils in Paris, and how much money she should spend for each item. Many of his recipes borrow directly from Taillevent's *Viandier*, although there is some adjustment in the direction of modesty. After all, the author wrote for his own *ménage*, not for service in a *château* (castle).

Late medieval recipes hold surprises for the modern French palate. Notably, sweet flavors combined with salty tastes in the same dish, as cane sugar, imported from the Middle East and Sicily, was used as a spice. Many recipes demand a heavy-handed application of spices. A typical list includes cloves, grains of paradise (Malagueta pepper), long pepper, cinnamon, ginger, and the irreplaceable black pepper. The spice mixtures reflect the Roman heritage. They also indicate the circumstances of the eaters. Expensive foreign spices were status symbols. To serve or consume them was to demonstrate wealth and prestige. Other intriguing features of medieval recipes include elaborate substitutions and gastronomic trickery, as in the recipe for "imitating a bear [or stag] steak with a piece of beef."[6]

MEDIEVAL AND RENAISSANCE STREET FOOD

Taking food and meals outside of the home had a strong association to the urban centers, where walking down the street revealed a wealth of edibles. Beginning in the twelfth century, specialists such as bakers, butchers, shoemakers, smiths, and town criers joined with colleagues to form guilds (*communautés de métier*, later called *corporations*). The collectivities regulated entry into each trade and defended practitioners' interests, giving a taste of independence to master workers if not their apprentices. The tantalizing list of food specialists for Paris in Étienne Boileau's *Livre des métiers* (*Book of Trades*) of 1268 mentions sellers of bread; of leftovers from the grand houses; of geese, pigeons, and fowl; of meat or fish pasties and cheese and egg pies; and of tripe and offal. Later in the same century, the poet Guillaume de Villeneuve's *Crieries de Paris* (*Parisian Vendors' Calls*) adds that pears, vinegared herring, onions à *longue haleine* (having a lasting effect on the breath), milk, and bowls of gruel were available. People purchased these street foods at the exterior counter of a boutique, from an ambulatory vendor with his cart, or from a merchant stationed at an *échoppe* (booth or shop). Roasted meats came from a *rôtisseur*, cooked and cured pork from a *chaircuitier saulcissier*. The *gaufrier* specialized in waffles; a similar unleavened egg and butter cake called a *fouace* was the province of the *fouacier*. The *oublie* (a waffle decorated with religious symbols) recalled the *oblation* (sacrifice; by extension the symbolic offering of bread and wine in the Catholic liturgy). Stationed at the entry to churches on feast days, the *oubloyer*'s portable oven was sometimes called a *fournaise à pardon* ("absolution furnace"). During the fourteenth and fifteenth centuries cities grew rapidly, and bureaucracy displaced tribal and familial relationships. In urban settings, industry and trade prospered, and self-sufficiency declined. Types of street food multiplied over the centuries as sellers increased in number, but one had to purchase one's repast piecemeal. In principle, each vendor had to stick to his specialty, defined by corporate rules and royal statutes revised periodically until the attempt was made to suppress the trade guilds in 1776; they were definitively dissolved in 1791.

Risks accompanied eating out, including in the street. Concerned municipal authorities did pass ordinances to regulate sales. Meat sellers, for instance, had to responsibly discard or burn any meat older than two or three days and meat that smelled off. But the customer had to be on the alert. To stretch profits, tavern keepers were known to *sophistiquer* (adulterate) their wine. An unscrupulous wine merchant might push ignoble plonk as a good vintage from one of the better wine towns, raising the price accordingly.

NEW WORLD FOODS

Cornerstones of modern cooking such as potatoes and tomatoes are relatively recent additions to the French pantry. These New World foods came to France as a result of European voyages made beginning in the late fifteenth century. By this time, Portugal had cornered the market on black pepper, and Spain wanted its own supply of this expensive commodity. Commissioned by the Spanish monarchs, Christopher Columbus first set out in 1492 to find a fast water route to "the Indies" (that is, Asia) to make it cheaper to import pepper and other spices. Neither Columbus, the Florentine Amerigo Vespucci, nor Hernando Cortès, who reached Mexico in 1519, made it to the Far East. Bumping instead into the Americas, they returned with marvelous foods: tomatoes, bell peppers, turkey (in French *dinde* abbreviates *coq d'Inde* or "Indian chicken"), and new varieties of beans. In 1537, Spanish soldiers found "floury roots" in a mountain village in Peru[7]; potatoes arrived in Europe in the 1570s. Muscovy duck, chocolate, vanilla, and pumpkin returned with European voyagers, who also encountered pineapple, papaya, guava, corn (maize), and strawberries.

Belated French voyages to the New World brought further culinary discoveries, including the Jerusalem artichoke and wild rice. The French state came late to ambitious maritime exploration. Rather, private funds sponsored the earliest trading and colonizing voyages, as well as the famous *corsaires* or pirates who raided Spanish and Portuguese ships. Samuel de Champlain finally founded a successful colony at Québec in 1608, and Henri IV began sending Jesuit missionaries to North America shortly thereafter. From Canada, Champlain returned with the *topinambour* or Jerusalem artichoke (or sunchoke), which is appreciated today. The knobby tuber has a firm texture and a sweet taste reminiscent of artichokes. As with many new foods, there was initially some confusion as to how to name it. Nicolas de Bonnefons was the valet to Louis XIV whose books *Le Jardinier françois* (*The French Gardener*, 1651) and *Les Delices de la campagne* (*The Delights of the Countryside*, 1654) laid out instructions for gardening and then cooking from one's own harvest. Bonnefons called the Jerusalem artichoke a *pomme de terre* ("earth apple"; this would become the word for potato). Another writer referred to it as a *poire de terre* ("earth pear"). *Topinamboux* is the French name of a native Brazilian tribe (the Tupi). Perhaps the name *topinambour* stuck for the Jerusalem artichoke because it so intriguingly evokes exotic origins. The voyagers to North America also found Virginia strawberries (larger than the tiny, seedy Old World *fraises des bois* or wild woodland strawberries), blueberries, cranberries, and the aquatic grass known as wild rice, which the Ojibwa taught the French to harvest from canoes and to cure.

Many of the New World foods were incorporated only gradually into the diet. Hot chili peppers in the *Capsicum* family never took hold at all; spicy flavors are still disliked today. Other foods came through Spain and went to Italy before ending up in France, where cultural obstacles prevented their quick adoption. Today, it is difficult to imagine cooking without tomatoes; however, it took two centuries before the tomato was incorporated into the diet. A member of the deadly nightshade family, it was thought poisonous. The potato, from the same family of *Solonacae*, was also viewed with suspicion. Of course, the voyagers attested to its edibility. A few others quickly recognized that the potato would be useful against grain shortages, and fields were planted in Alsace and Lorraine, in the Auvergne, and in the Lyon area. Because of the importance of bread and the periodic famines resulting from lack of grain, potato fanciers experimented with using potato flour or mashed potatoes to replace wheat in leavened loaves; however, the potato had a bad reputation. It was accused of causing leprosy and was thought of as food fit only for the poor. By the eighteenth century, the old excuse was taken up that spuds were flatulent. Finally, potatoes were distributed to members of an agricultural society, and the naturalist Auguste Parmentier (1737–1813), with the support of Marie-Antoinette and Louis XVI, promoted them tirelessly. Parmentier's great coup was to plant potatoes in a field belonging to Louis XVI that was heavily guarded during the day. When the guards retired for the evening, temptation lured the local population in to poach whatever was so very valuable in the king's fields. By the nineteenth century, people had begun to rely on potatoes as a staple.

Turkey was accepted relatively quickly. By the eighteenth century, it often replaced goose as a festive roast. Today, turkey is popular for the winter holidays, and, as a pale-fleshed meat, it often replaces veal. In the seventeenth century, southern French peasants began to grow corn to eat as *millasse* (porridge like Italian *polenta*) or as corncakes or pancakes, selling the more profitable wheat that they grew. Elsewhere corn was primarily grown as animal fodder and to enrich soil depleted from other crops. It is hardly eaten today; most people still think of corn as food for animals.

CLASSICAL COOKING

Late seventeenth-century cookbooks emphasized tastes and codified procedures that persist today. In the 1660s, the satirist Nicolas Boileau poked fun at vulgar types who scour far-off Goa for pepper and ginger and whose idea of refinement consists of too much pepper mixed up in the sauce.[8]

Spices, which had become relatively inexpensive, were out of style in aristo-cratic contexts. Instead of disguising flavors of the principal ingredients with baroque flourishes, some clarity and sense of proportion were now sought. Even humble vegetables were required to taste a bit more of themselves. Cooks working for elite diners turned to the kitchen garden for the flavoring palette. Cookbooks from this period, such as François Pierre de La Varenne's *Le Cuisinier françois* (*The French Cook,* 1651), Pierre de Lune's *Le Cuisinier* (*The Cook,* 1656), and L.S.R.'s *Art de bien traiter* (*Art of Entertaining Well,* 1674), show that cooks did use spices such as cloves. They certainly retained salt and pepper, although, often enough, only *un peu* (a little bit) in the case of pepper. A remarkable feature of these cookbooks is the use of plants to provide seasoning. Fresh herbs, onions, and garlic appear repeatedly in the recipes. Pierre de Lune explained how to use an herbal *paquet* (packet) that could be dropped into cooking liquids to give them flavor. The little bundle included thyme, chervil, and parsley and was tied up with a piece of string; the optional strip of *lard* (fat bacon) was taken out for *jours maigres* (lean days). Pierre de Lune's *paquet* is the ancestor of the modern *bouquet garni*. Increasingly, salty flavors were separated from sweet, and sweets relegated to the end of the meal. A harmonious balance of flavors and the enhancement, rather than disguise, of the main ingredients were desired.

Fresh parsley, scallions, shallots, and garlic are essential ingredients and flavorings in French cuisine. Courtesy of Hervé Depoil.

The late seventeenth-century cookbooks reflect the preference for order. The Classical-era manuals allude to the sequences of procedures that are necessary for complex cooking. The cook must keep on hand an all-purpose meat stock *pour la nourriture* ("for the alimentation") of other dishes such as sauces and to moisten meats. He must make *roux* (flour cooked in butter) as a thickener, and he must use butter and fewer breadcrumbs as *liaisons* or binders. To complete the time-consuming preparations—mashing, grating, peeling, chopping, slicing, scaling, soaking, blanching, boiling, reducing, barding, mixing, kneading, whipping, stirring, sieving, clarifying—on the large scale required to cook grand meals, an army of kitchen help must assist the head chef. These preparations had to be carried out *before* a dish could be finished. Today, chefs spend hours in the kitchen completing their *mise en place* ("putting into place" or preparation, i.e., chopping parsley, peeling vegetables, and so on) before actually beginning to cook. The Classical cookbooks laid the foundation for the lush cooking that went on in wealthy houses during the eighteenth century. The recipes and procedures also underpin *haute cuisine*, the refined, complex style of cooking that chefs practiced in restaurants and hotels in the nineteenth century. The contemporary descendent of aristocratic banquet cuisine is today's *cuisine gastronomique*, such as in the Michelin-starred restaurants.

Despite the advances toward modern taste in Classical cooking, aristocratic banquet meals retained the ostentatious *service à la française* (French-style service) typical of the Renaissance. Each course consisted of a profusion of different dishes laid out in a perfectly symmetrical geometry on the table. One was obliged to take from whatever serving plate was near at hand.

The ceremonial court meal served *à la française* reached its apogee in the dining rooms of Louis XIV (r. 1661–1715). The Sun King's reign had begun with an unfortunate slight delivered by means of dinner. With money skimmed off from the state's tax income, Nicolas Fouquet, the superintendent of finances, built himself an estate and gardens at Vaux-le-Vicomte, then began to entertain in a style that fit his grand circumstances. In the summer of 1661, he staged two full days of festivities, including a parade of costumed allegorical figures who served supper and a massive edible monument of sugar confectionary, shiny preserved fruits, and ices, to honor Louis XIV. The mastermind behind the ill-fated but gorgeous banquet at Vaux was the *maître d'hôtel* or executive chef François Vatel. The king grew disgusted at Fouquet's opulence, arranged for his minister's arrest, and was never again outdone in the area of magnificent entertaining.

Under the reign of Louis XIV, France subdued Spanish and Austrian rivals in Europe and set the standard for cultural brilliance across the Continent. Louis XIV ordered gardens and a brilliant hall of mirrors to be built at his château at Versailles. There he surrounded himself with his aristocratic entourage. The scheme was astute. The king made sure that people danced attendance upon him even when he arose from bed in the morning. For a noble, to risk an absence from a feast or the king's intimate but ceremonial morning *lever* was to incur his displeasure and risk banishment to the yawning provinces. By holding political rivals in pleasing captivity at Versailles, Louis XIV prevented interference with his own monopoly on power.

Protocol for serving and eating, like nearly every other aspect of court life, was designed to reflect and increase the greatness of the monarch. The king was the only man allowed to eat bareheaded. His food was marched in from the far-away kitchens by a long procession of guards, servants, and tasters. Although the use of the fork was firmly established by now among members of the aristocratic classes, Louis XIV was the only person at the table who did not bother with one, preferring to eat with his hands.

Unsuccessful attempts had been made to recruit Vatel into service at Versailles; however, Vatel did stage one more dinner for the king. In 1669, now working for the Prince de Condé—long a rival to the king and suspected of a conspiracy against him—at the Château de Chantilly, Vatel staged an entertainment and weekend of feasting designed to restore his master to the good graces of the king. So great was the pressure of the occasion that the ingenious Vatel panicked when the delivery of fish failed to arrive, and he committed suicide. The epistolary chronicler Madame de Sévigné was not even there, but she habitually gathered all the gossip, and her account of Vatel's death is practically the only credible information that survives. Madame de Sévigné wrote to her daughter that the fish wagons finally arrived, and the meal was a great success, at least for the Prince.

Clearly, food and table manners were weighty matters during the Classical era. The table was a stage on which dramas of power were enacted every day. This is quite clear in the sly comedies of the playwright Molière, responsible for many of the evening entertainments at Versailles, just as he had been for the play presented by Fouquet at Vaux in 1661. In *Tartuffe, ou l'Imposteur* (*Tartuffe, or The Imposter*, 1669), for instance, the dynamics of the meal reveal the moral and psychological conflicts. A wealthy, gullible bourgeois has taken a devout individual into his household, but the soulful friend turns out to be a destructive parasite and first-rate hypocrite. Tartuffe literally eats his host out of house and home, attempts to seduce his virtuous wife, and nearly swindles him of everything he owns. As gluttonous Tartuffe grows fat on bread and wine that are not his own, the mistress of the house grows sick and faint and cannot eat. The shared meal turns into a perverse, vampiric anti-communion, showing the social order gone wrong.

Cookbooks and other documents pertaining to meals reveal the strong sense of social hierarchy that prevailed at the height of the ancien régime. Visible conformity to rank and acceptable social mores, such as Tartuffe's show of devout Catholicism (shared with Louis XIV), was the order of the day. The anthology called *L'École parfaite des officiers de bouche* (*The Finishing School for Cooks*, 1662) borrowed not only recipes from cookbooks but also information from the tradition of treatises dating to the Renaissance on topics such as carving and serving. The anonymous compiler of the *École parfaite* included diagrams that show the steps for cutting up roast meats and whole cooked fish and fowl in order to serve them. The introduction and the written instructions that accompany the pictures remind the carver that he should serve the best morsels, appropriately sauced and garnished, to those with the highest social standing. The lesser pieces were doled out to the less distinguished guests.

Published at the very end of the seventeenth century, the title of Massialot's *Cuisinier roïal et bourgeois* (*Royal and Bourgeois Cook*, 1691) responded to the incipient social changes that brought cookbooks aimed for use in nonaristocratic households. During the eighteenth century, Menon's anonymously published *Cuisinière bourgeoise* (*The [Female] Bourgeois Cook*, 1746) even acknowledged, by its title, that the person cooking in any but the very wealthiest households was usually a woman. Menon's cookbook was a best-seller and the only ancien régime cookbook to be reissued immediately after the Revolution of 1789. Regional cookbooks appeared in the nineteenth century and encyclopedic yet accessible references both to grand cooking and to home cooking in the twentieth. Today, the many illustrated cookbooks that are designed to appeal to the broad swathe of the middle classes combine the visual appeal of the art or photography book and the personal tone of the memoir with the practical methods in the recipes themselves.

COFFEE, CHOCOLATE, TEA, AND SUGAR

During the seventeenth century, chocolate, coffee, tea, and sugar became fashionable among elites; a century later, they would be commonplace. Mexican chocolate (drunk as a beverage) was adopted at the Spanish court and then in the Spanish Netherlands before coming to

France, where the aristocracy considered the drink an aphrodisiac. Coffee made its way from Ethiopia and Yemen, through the Arab world to Turkey, then via the Mediterranean port cities to southern Europe, and by boat from Venice to the trading center of Marseille. Separately, in 1669, an Ottoman ambassador on diplomatic mission from Constantinople also introduced coffee to the court of Louis XIV at Versailles. Perception of coffee's effects varied, but generally it was seen as a sobering, intellectually stimulating drink. The Dutch East India Company brought Chinese tea to Europe, but the supply to France increased substantially after Henri IV chartered the French East India Company in 1604. As all three beverages were thought to be overly strong and bitter, Europeans added cane sugar to sweeten them.

In antiquity cane sugar had been a curiosity known to come from India. During the Middle Ages, cane cultivation spread with Arabian settlements to areas of the Mediterranean and North Africa, and crusaders supervised sugar plantations in Jerusalem. Sugar was so expensive that only small quantities returned to Europe. From the thirteenth century, sculptures made of spun sugar and marzipan (ground almonds mixed with sugar), decorated royal tables as symbols of wealth and power. Columbus brought cane to Santo Domingo, and from there it spread to other Caribbean islands and the South American mainland. In this era the sugar industry depended on the slave trade for labor. Portuguese and Spanish colonial plantations staffed by slaves in the Atlantic, then British and French ones in the Caribbean, sent quantities of sugar to Europe. In eighteenth-century France, in view of the competition from other colonial nations, to drink coffee imported from the Antilles and to eat sweets made with Martinique or Guadeloupe sugar was to support the economy. Throughout the nineteenth century, sugar was rare to unknown in peasant households. The taste for sugared coffee and the other beverages was initially restricted to aristocratic and bourgeois circles.

In the nineteenth century, France became a major producer of sugar, and by the twentieth century the hot drinks, especially coffee, had entirely replaced beer, wine, and soups as morning meals. When Napoleon boycotted trade with Britain in the early nineteenth century, Britain blocked French ships from landing in the western ports. France's colonial sugar could not reach the country. As early as the late sixteenth century, the botanist Olivier de Serres had remarked on the high sugar content of beets. Napoleon now called for the cultivation of sugar beets in northern France and the Belgian provinces. The banker, industrialist, and amateur botanist Benjamin Delessert developed a dependable refining process, for which Napoleon named him *chevalier de la Légion d'honneur*. France soon

had a reliable local source of sugar. During the 1860s, consumption averaged 5.3 kilograms (about 11.7 pounds) of sugar yearly. This works out
to about one teaspoonful each day. As late as the 1890s, working class
prejudice mitigated against sugar. In contrast with the nourishing, savory
staples of meat and bread, sugar was viewed as unhealthy[9]; however, sugar
manufacturers began to advertise heavily, and this attitude changed. No
longer a medical wonder, rare spice, or wondrous decoration for luxurious
tables, sugar became the common sweetener and preservative that it is
today. At present, the average person consumes nearly 33.5 kilograms (74
pounds) of sugar each year.

ENLIGHTENMENT CAFÉS

In the eighteenth century, cafés became common in Paris and modern-style
restaurants developed. In this era new customs blurred old divisions among
the social orders. Nobles engaged in trades such as mining to exploit their
land, yet retained hereditary privileges. The monarch sold administrative
offices to raise money, allowing bourgeois citizens to purchase power along
with noble titles. The rags-to-riches story in Pierre Carlet de Marivaux's
novel *Le Paysan parvenu* (*The Parvenu Peasant*, 1735) marked rungs on the
social ladder through culinary and gastronomic distinctions. At the novel's
start, the protagonist is fed by the cook in the back kitchen of the house
where he is a servant. By its end, he has married his way into a family of
fermiers généraux (tax farmers), the bourgeois fiscal administrators and money
lenders whose opulent eating habits rivaled those of the previous century's
aristocrats, and he presides over his own richly appointed table. Four-fifths of
the population still lived in villages and rural areas, but the sway of the merchant and bourgeois classes, including bankers, grew in the urban centers.

France's first successful café had been opened in the 1670s by the young
Francesco Procopio dei Coltelli, known as François Procope; the café still
operates in Paris. Following Italian practice, Procope eschewed the eastern
custom of leaving the grounds in the cup, and instead served filtered coffee,
along with ices, liqueurs, and candied fruits. Many cafés served a selection of
foods as well as coffee. They notably provided an ambiance quite different
from the boozy miasma of the tavern. Over the stimulating small bowls or
cups of coffee, people from all walks of life sat down to read the newspaper,
play chess, discuss politics, and debate the latest play. Because cafés were
open to all comers, coffee-drinking acquired its lasting association with conversation and the free exchange of information. Since then, many a café has
served at once as office, salon, dining room, and daily or nightly haven for
writers scribbling away under the gaze of the *garçon de café* (café waiter).

Little escapes the watchful eye of the
café waiter. Courtesy of Hervé Depoil.

PHILOSOPHICAL FOOD

The democratic attitude that flourished in the café guided the
Enlightenment approach to food in other spheres. The topic is treated
with interest in the great *Encyclopédie, ou Dictionnaire raisonné des Sciences,
des Arts, et des Métiers* (*Encyclopedia, or Reasoned Dictionary of the Sciences,
Arts, and Trades*, 1751–1765) that the *philosophe* Denis Diderot, the
mathematician Jean Le Rond d'Alembert, and others wrote collab-
oratively at mid-century. The editors believed that analysis and reason
should be applied in all domains. Accordingly, they solicited articles not
just on the expected topics of theology, history, and jurisprudence, but
also on pastry-making, bread-baking, butchering, and strawberries. Mate-
rialist thought even rationalized pleasure by means of the table. Although
of delicate digestion, Diderot notoriously loved to eat and drink, and he
took pleasure into account. The word *gourmandise* or gluttony had referred
since the fourteenth century to the Deadly Sin. In his article on the topic
for the *Encyclopédie*, Diderot gave the word a new, secular definition and
introduced the notion of moderation. Now *gourmandise* also meant the
deepened enjoyment that comes with understanding. Cultivated into an

intellectual as well as a sensual experience, the bodily necessity of eating could enhance, rather than simply maintain, everyday existence. Today, informed appreciation for the daily pleasures of cooking and eating is a defining aspect of the French approach to food.

Social critics associated with the later Enlightenment couched their discussions in a more polemical way. Writing during the 1780s, the reformer and journalist Louis-Sébastien Mercier recorded in the *Tableau de Paris* (*Picture of Paris*) the misery that ecclesiastical fasting require-ments inflicted on the poor. On lean days, all observant Catholics were still supposed to avoid prohibited foods or foods of unclear status, such as eggs, a staple for many who did not have the means to pay for meat. Mercier observed with chagrin that any prohibition unjustly strained the poor, whose real problem was getting enough to eat at all. Bread riots that continued through the most of the century bore out this view.

Ever the contrarian, the philosophe and novelist Jean-Jacques Rousseau, saw both urbane gastronomic pleasure and urban food shortage as two sides of the same decadent coin. In his novel *Émile* (1762), about educating children, he recommended pure, simple food as the most wholesome and also as the best for character formation. Rousseau was actually a franco-phone Swiss. He complained that, contrary to the received idea that the sophisticated French eat well, they are in fact the only people "who do not know how to eat, because so specialized an art is required to make dishes edible for them." Given the choice, he observed, children incline to vegetables along with "dairy products, pastries, [and] fruits," and they eschew meat, which makes people "cruel and ferocious."[10] Foods should be prepared with as few alterations to their original state as possible. One should not, for instance, apply heat to butter and dairy products. One should eat foods in season. In defiance of contemporary norms for those with any disposable income, Rousseau advocated that mothers, rather than hired wet-nurses, breast-feed their new babies. His ideas for a natural diet reached a wide audience. Parents sought guidance in *Émile* to raising their own children, and Rousseau's novel *Julie, ou la Nouvelle Héloïse* (*Julie, or The New Heloise*, 1761), which portrayed an ideal family and household economy, was a bestseller.[11]

MODERN RESTAURANTS

The modern restaurant experience took shape in Paris in the late eighteenth century. Beginning in the 1760s, a few guilded *traiteurs* or cook-caterers expanded business by offering meals in a different kind of setting than the rough *table d'hôte* of the innkeeper. The word *restaurant* designated a "restorative" soup or bouillon made from meat or fowl that was reduced to a rich essence. In new *maisons de santé* ("health houses") or *salles du restaurateur* ("restaurateur's rooms") the caterers aimed to appeal to clients by providing the health-giving decoctions on a flexible schedule. In addition to broths, they served items such as boiled capons, soft-boiled eggs, fruit preserves, and rice puddings. The light, salubrious preparations could also, conveniently, be kept or quickly prepared for service at a moment's notice. The new establishments listed the available dishes and their prices on a *carte* or menu; the customer chose exactly what and when he or she wanted to eat. Although they frequented a public place, diners sat at private, individual tables. Before long, the term *restaurant* meant the eating house itself. They caught on quickly, although the first trip to a restaurant could be fraught with peril. It was necessary to decipher the menu and sometimes to outsmart a sneaky *maître d'hôtel* who could run up the bill by bringing extras.[12] The famous early establishments were based in Paris. These included the *Trois Frères Provençaux* (Three Brothers from Provence), who served southern specialties such as *brandade de morue* (creamed salt cod) and *bouillabaisse* (Provençal fish soup); the *Grande Taverne de Londres* (Great London Tavern), opened in 1782 by Antoine Beauvilliers, who had cooked for the Count of Provence, the future Louis XVIII; *Véfour*, which is still open today; and *Véry*. After the revolutionary decade (1790s), some private cooks who had been employed in great houses had to start over, either within the country or elsewhere. Many opened restaurants, exporting abroad for commercial purposes not just *la cuisine française* (French cooking) but, notably, an entire French dining experience.

COMFORT, QUALITY, AND ENJOYMENT

The largely unsung hero of the modern working class and middle class table was the eclectic aristocrat turned food critic Alexandre Balthazar Laurent Grimod de la Reynière (1758–1837). After the Revolution and the chaos of the Terror in the early 1790s, legal reforms enacted under Napoleon shaped a country changed by republican ideas although still breathing ancien régime air. The new *Code Napoléon* or Civil Law Code of 1804 scripted autonomy and equality (at least, for men) before the law. It fostered meritocracy rather than entitlement based on inherited name or rank. "Quality" now came from work or performance, rather than bloodlines. Grimod, who had trained as a lawyer, had a serious interest in food and deep skepticism regarding the motives of the powerful. His satirical response was to develop a mocking *code gourmand* or food connoisseur's canon of laws for the table.[13] During the Napoleonic Empire (1804–1815), he invented (in 1804) a clever system for judging quality and "legitimating" all that was best to eat. This meant that he persuaded caterers and restaurateurs to give him samples of their wares. Food producers did so, in part for the advertising, and in part for fear of reprisal from this fearsome new species of ally-adversary, the food critic. Grimod's guides fueled the nascent gastronomic industry made up of restaurants, boutiques, eaters, and writers; all belonged to a consumer culture that was expanding in many domains. Good taste and knowledge now emerged from interactions among producers and consumers, or chefs and eaters, and writers and readers. What is remarkable is that fashion in food no longer emanated from exclusive removes associated with the centralized power (the court, through nearly the end of the preceding century), but rather from establishments open to the public (or at least, the wealthier segments) and from the response of that public.

Grimod's system had its coercive aspects; the same is true for the complex relationships that exist today among food producers, critics, and consumers. At the same time, Grimod had a strong sense of duty as a public advocate. During the national conversion to the metric system and uniform system of weights and measures, Grimod vociferously criticized unscrupulous shopkeepers and traders who took advantage of the situation to overcharge customers or short-weight meats or produce. Like many others of his time, he soon tired of Napoleon's all-conquering military sweep across Europe and worried over the hostilities with Britain. The latter interfered with the flow of goods so necessary to support fine dining. To protest the former, he championed (from his desk chair and dining table—Parisian central command for gastronomic operations) specialties of, for instance, the German states, such as the fine mineral waters, meat stews, and steamed dumplings.

Despite his own distinguished, exceedingly wealthy origins, Grimod had a modern taste for comfort and enjoyment. He disdained the old aristocratic preference for ostentation. He recommended that meals be simplified. He was an early advocate of serving in the style then called à la russe (Russian style). Instead of the old service à la française, Grimod preferred that each service or course of a meal consist of a single dish. Each preparation should come to the table completely prepared and perfectly done. This allowed the eater to fully appreciate each food at the peak of its perfection and to enjoy it hot, while resting assured that he had a similar portion to his neighbor. The service of a full meal in separate courses became standard in the most elegant and expensive contexts by the 1860s. Simplicity made the method adaptable for modest households, too. Today, the

Enjoyment is the best praise for good cooking. Courtesy of Christian Verdet/ regard public-unpact.

ceremonial yet simple structure is typical for any full meal, whether served at home or in a restaurant.

If Grimod mobilized a comprehensive revolution at the table, the more famous writer Jean Anthelme Brillat-Savarin (1755–1826) spread the word with the deliciously amusing *Physiologie du goût* (*Physiology of Taste*, 1826). Brillat was a magistrate who fled France during the Terror, ending up in New England, where he taught French and music and famously shot a wild turkey in the "virgin forests" of Connecticut before making his way back home. Food appreciation, in Brillat's view, is fundamental to the understanding of nearly everything, and nearly everything makes its way into his book. Notes on the physical faculties of taste and digestion, a history of science culminating with "the science of gastronomy" triumphant, observations not only on feasting and fasting but also on thirst, a discussion of the "Influence of Gourmandise on Marital Bliss," recommendations for fattening and slimming diets, gossipy anecdotes, jokes for enlivening a dinner party—all have their place in the *Physiologie*. Brillat's cheerful, sociable banter demystified dining rituals formerly associated with grand tables and endeared the author to generations of readers.

The chef Antonin or Marie-Antoine Carême (1783–1833), like Grimod and Brillat, participated both in the ancien and in the nouveau régimes—political, social, and dietary. He was a private chef in the old style who served some of the most prominent individuals in Europe, including Charles-Maurice de Talleyrand-Périgord (wily politician, rakish bishop, and notable gastronome who served under several administrations: the republican Directory of the late 1790s, the Napoleonic Empire, the Bourbon monarchy restored in 1815) and Baron James de Rothschild. Carême was also a self-made man and phenomenal self-promoter who achieved fame and professional success in a thoroughly modern fashion. He authored several volumes on pastry-making and cooking, including the great *oeuvre* heavily entitled *Art de la cuisine française au 19e siècle: Traité élémentaire et pratique suivi de dissertations culinaires et gastronomiques utiles au progrès de cet art* (*Art of French Cuisine in the Nineteenth Century: Basic and Practical Treatise Followed by Culinary and Gastronomic Dissertations Useful to the Progress of this Art*, 1833). The five-volume cookbook (the last two volumes were finished by his executors after his death) modernizes aristocratic *grande cuisine* for the grand bourgeois table. His cooking was famous for its variety, sense of proportion, and delicacy of flavor. Carême had nothing good to say about the use of spices, but he felt strongly that magnificence and elaborate decoration had their place on the table, and he preferred a modified version of *service à la française*. He was a great fan of the expensive truffle and other such luxuries. As a cook for fancy clients, he clearly had a professional interest in avoiding the truly modern simplicity advocated by Grimod. The employment of highly accomplished private cooks in many wealthy and upper middle class houses continued until well after the mid-twentieth century. The socialist politics of the 1980s finally made the situation somewhat embarrassing for at least some employers. By that time, few people capable of cooking on a high level cared to work as private servants, preferring jobs that better integrated them into the professional community of cooks.

NINETEENTH-CENTURY RESTAURANTS

Restaurant culture expanded rapidly during the nineteenth century. The accounts of travelers and memoirists, treatment by novelists, contemporary studies of eating out, and documents such as balance sheets and menus give a sense of why this was so. The nineteenth-century population was predominantly rural and agricultural. All the same, industrialization favored urbanization, and a steady stream of people left the country for the northern and eastern coal-mining cities and places such as Lille, Mulhouse, and Rouen, which had mechanized factories beginning in the 1830s. Restaurants, at this juncture, like the taverns and cafés that preceded them, opened primarily in cities and were a mainstay of workers.

Quality of the food, ambience, and price varied, as they do today. The multiplication of fancy restaurants during the First Empire had fostered a connoisseur culture peopled by the new food critics and *gastronomes*, as well as ostentatious consumption by high rollers of various stripes. This *grande cuisine* or *haute cuisine* culminated late in the century in the cooking and cookbooks of chef Auguste Escoffier (1846–1935) and in dining rooms within the new "palaces" or grand hotels. But an equally or perhaps even more remarkable phenomenon was the spread of decent but inexpensive restaurants that served a modest *prix fixe* (fixed price) menu aimed at a middle class clientele. Such menus listed prices for full meals in three or four courses, not for individual items, giving one a package deal. Workers favored inexpensive *bouillon* shops, where they chose from a limited range of *à la carte* (individually listed) items served in small portions; the series of beef and bouillon restaurants opened in the 1860s by the butcher Duval are an early example of a chain restaurant. Dairy restaurants were also popular among the working classes. Cheap *gargotes* catered to the impecunious, such as students and laborers. *Guinguettes* (outdoor cafés and dance-halls) opened seasonally outside city limits to avoid the municipal taxes. The *café-concerts* had music as well as coffee, alcohol, and food. *Restaurants de nuit* had dancing and usually a dubious reputation. Menus in these diverse restaurants had in common that they varied by season and offered three and sometimes four courses to compose a full meal.

Two massive studies based on interviews of workers begun in the mid-nineteenth century, Pierre-Guillaume-Frédéric Le Play's *Ouvriers Européens* (*European Workers,* 1855) and the collective work completed by his followers entitled the *Ouvriers des Deux Mondes* (*Workers from Two Worlds,* 1859–1930), show that motivations for frequenting restaurants were diverse. These ranged from periodic indulgence or overindulgence in food and wine, usually right after payday, to making oneself available for encounters that would drum up business and increase one's income. Sometimes one simply purchased at a restaurant what was needed to supplement the essentials of a meal brought from home.[14] In many cases, small, cramped city apartments without amenities for cooking made eating out a matter of necessity. New lighting technologies—stable-burning oil lamps (by the 1790s), gas lamps (1860s), and electricity (1880s)—strategically adopted by businesses increased the appeal of restaurants and lengthened opening hours.[15] The legacy of the affordable public eating culture has been quite influential. Today, motivations for eating out differ, but it is typical that throughout the country one can eat a meal of decent quality outside the home without breaking the bank.

OLD WAYS AND NEW

In the late nineteenth century, outside of the cities with their mechanized factories and restaurant culture, the picture was quite different. Two-thirds of the population lived in rural areas and villages. The lifestyle was agricultural, and farming was essentially preindustrial; it is ironic that in this era, Third Republic (1870–1940) politicians famously justified ambitious colonial expansion as a *mission civilisatrice* or mission to civilize and assist in the modernization of the occupied countries. At home, meals for most people still reflected the aim of self-sufficiency. With the exception of a few items such as salt, sugar, and coffee that had to be purchased, what was eaten came from the kitchen garden or the family farm. For farmers, still called *paysans* (peasants or country people), main meals were built around soups, which stretched ingredients as far as possible. Other staples were the garden vegetables that stored well: potatoes, carrots, cabbages, and beans. If animals were kept, butter and eggs could be sold. If a pig was killed, it was pickled or smoked, to last the whole 12-month cycle.[16] Bread came from the village baker, or might still be baked at home.

For those who lived and—for the moment, stayed—in the country, it was not so much the texture or material aspect of life but rather attitudes that underwent a certain revision. The early years of the Third Republic were characterized by a mix of nationalism and protectionism, on the one hand, and democratic ideals and liberal economic policies, on the other. The relationship among village bread baker, priest, and schoolmaster in the classic film *La Femme du boulanger* (*The Baker's Wife*, 1939) poignantly depicts the difficult changing of the conceptual guard.[17] The 1880s had brought free, compulsory primary school education for all children and the abolishment of religious education in public schools. The schoolmaster was charged to represent the Republic and universally to inculcate its values in his pupils. He supplanted the priest as an exemplary figure in villages. At the same time, at least in some rural areas, the routines of everyday life had hardly changed. In the film, when the village baker is deserted by his wayward wife, he becomes so distraught that he cannot make bread, and the village begins to worry about its stomach. Priest and schoolmaster, who conversed by peevish argument, now join forces to—of all things—ford a stream to reach the baker's wife and coax her into returning home. The priest is hampered by the voluminous skirts of his cassock and suffers being carried on the shoulders of the teacher, who wears a modern (and masculine) suit. The waters part neither for the priest nor for the teacher. The teacher seems better equipped to meet the challenges of modern life, but the priest has a practiced bedside manner. Both are instrumental in reestablishing harmony and unity in their community. Communion in the village is now secular. It takes place at the baker's and in each family's dining room, as much as in the church, with the baker's bread rather than the host distributed by the priest, and over the sociable glass of *pastis* (anise liqueur typical in the South) taken at the one village café rather than with the sip of consecrated wine. The film presents a nostalgic, idealized vision of village life, yet it is also accurate in some of the essentials. It is notable that rituals of communion—or community—persist so strongly. Participation in the collectivity of the village and shared cultural memory exert a strong force.

INDUSTRIALIZATION AND AUTHENTICITY

Industrialization brought the looming threat that the individual character of foods and food production, associated with quality and safety, could be obliterated by impersonal processes beyond the ken of consumers or of most producers. Adulteration of wine, either to doctor the flavor or to attempt to preserve it, had always been a problem, although some practices were considered acceptable. Fraud and the definition of words complicated the issue. For instance, "wine" made from raisins rather than fresh grapes technically *was* made from grapes. In the late nineteenth century, new chemical processes of synthesis forced people to imagine the weird possibility that a liquid sold as wine might not be made from grapes at all.[18] Wine, bread, and meat were the essential sources of calories for urban workers. A further strain was caused by increased demand for wine in the cities at the same time that a devastating string of contagions decimated vines in the countryside. Destructive mildews, grape phylloxera (a kind of aphid) and other plagues caused wine production to plummet in the 15 years from 1875 to 1889 to a mere quarter of earlier levels. A hygenics movement concerned with the rise in alcoholism insisted that it was the modern adulterated wines that were causing problems. The ancestral beverage of the Gauls, on the other hand, was touted as nourishing and healthy. The regulations and attitudes that emerged were part of the reaction to the complex of issues presented by industrialization, production in difficult times, and rising demand.

Laws passed in the late nineteenth century provided ever more precise descriptive definitions of wines and methods of wine production.

The Griffe Law of 1889 specified that "No one shall expedite, sell, or cause to be sold under the name of wine any product other than that deriving from the fermentation of fresh grapes." This was *le vin naturel* or "natural wine." *Vin factice*, which meant "artificial" or "elaborated" or "synthetic" wine, was not condemned, but it was now clearly to be distinguished from "natural" wine. The idea was that information would orient people to choose "natural" wine; fraud, it was assumed, would be eliminated as a consequence. When this did not happen, more interventionist statutes were passed to prevent certain types of adulteration. Notably, a new law passed in 1894 forbade *mouillage* or stretching wine with water (from *mouiller*, to wet or moisten) and *vinage* or increasing the alcohol content by adding must. *Mouillage* did not threaten the health of anybody who drank the treated wine, but the motivation for making it illegal was to promote transparency in business transactions. The longstanding law of 1905 against fraud enlarged on this idea, leading to debate among winemakers and finally to a new statute in 1907 that precisely detailed how words such as *vin* (wine) and *méthode champenoise* (Champagne-making method) should be used to correspond to specific processes of production. Later in the century, socialist and protectionist politics continued in the same direction of regulation, but for different reasons than the earlier laws inspired by liberal motives. Strict regulation of fraud and a politics of quality served the national economic interest; for the same reason, the concern for public health became another primary motive for food regulation.

TERROIR AND CONTROLLED DENOMINATION OF ORIGIN

Late nineteenth-century regionalism and the *retour à la terre* ("return to the soil" or peasantism) that flourished between the two World Wars contributed to defining the singular nature of foods through *terroir*. To be sure, neither regional specialty nor the term *terroir* was anything new. Gallo-Romans knew that their best oysters came from Brittany and Normandy and that there were no better hams than those from Bayonne. The royal tables of the absolutist era groaned under the weight of what was best from all over France. In the first decades of the nineteenth century, Grimod de la Reynière advocated gastronomic tourism, writing that one had to travel to Riom (Auvergne) to eat the best frogs legs, properly prepared by a knowledgeable local expert. In 1808, the lawyer and pharmacist Charles Louis Cadet de Gassicourt published a *carte gastronomique* (gastronomic map) keyed with small pictures to show the typical foods for each region and town. Awareness of regional particularity increased throughout the

century and was key both for rallying nationalist sentiment and stimulating the tourist industry. During the twentieth century, the effort to
decentralize culture from Paris into the provinces led to cooperation
between the state and the regions to develop local identities.

Like regional specialty, the term *terroir* is as old as the hills that it long
designated. *Terroir* is related to *terre* (earth, dirt) and *territoire* (territory,
area). Of Latin origin, the term has been used in French since the thirteenth century to mean a plot of land suitable for cultivation. In the
nineteenth century, as trains and other forms of transport made it easier
to travel and also to perceive regional variations, the term took on an
association with other characteristics perceived as local. A person's way
of speaking, if redolent of the countryside, was called the accent of his
terroir.

Today, the term *terroir* is used to evoke the connection among place,
manufacturing process, and taste that defines good-quality, artisanal wines
and foods. For wine, components of *terroir* include the climate (temperature, rainfall) of the location where the grapes are grown, sunlight, topog-
raphy (slope, altitude), and soil (its physical characteristics, chemistry,
interaction with water). *Terroir* also includes historical and cultural practices of the people involved, or the human element. One speaks of a wine
or a food, such as lamb from the *prés-salés* (salt marshes) and *garriguettes*,
the elongated strawberries originally grown in scrublands, as having the
goût du (taste of) *terroir*. This meaning of the term *terroir* informs the
familiar French metonymy for wine. Whereas American wines are identified first by the name of the grape (merlot, pinot noir) from which they
are made, French wines are identified first by the place from which they
come: a Côtes-du-Rhône, a Chablis, a Bordeaux, or the specific vineyard
within a geographical region or even a town. Additional details, such
as the *cépage* (type of vine or grape: gamay, cabernet, and so on) and
the year or vintage, are named second. A food or wine with the taste of
terroir is understood in opposition to commercial or industrial fast food
and supermarket products seen as sterile and impersonal, of unclear provenance and little savor.

The specificity that informs *terroir* also underpins the *Appellation d'origine
contrôlée* or AOC (Controlled Denomination of Origin). Regulations
for the AOC derive from classifications for Bordeaux wines instituted
in the mid-nineteenth century. During the seventeenth and eighteenth
centuries, inexpensive Spanish and Portuguese wines were cutting out
French wines from European markets. Bordeaux wines, at that point,
were not known as being unusually good or even very distinctive, as they
are today. As a way of competing, winegrowers from the Médoc region

applied themselves to strategically developing *grands crus* or distinguished Bordeaux wines that stand up to long aging and command very high prices. To improve quality, they carefully cultivated the oldest and best vines. They paid special attention to aging the reds in oak barrels. Along the way, these growers also consolidated the cultivated parcels on their estates. This reinforced the connection between the place where grapes where grown and the resulting wine. As a measure of protection for their exceptional wines, proprietors evolved special classifications that were applied beginning in 1855. The best label of *premier cru* (first growth) and even the least distinguished label of *cinquième cru* (fifth growth) vastly increased the market value of these wines. The prestigious labels were not easy to obtain. In the first year, the *premier cru* designation was awarded to wines from four estates. The fifth estate was not added until 1973.[19] The many winemakers whom the grades excluded naturally wished to obtain some sort of distinguishing label for their own bottles. The fraud laws became important for winemakers, as imitations of the distinguished bottles came on the market. More capacious legislation passed in 1935 established the *Appellation d'origine contrôlée*, which could be applied to wines from locations other than in Bordeaux. In 1990, the AOC was expanded to cover all manner of foods as well as wines. Today, the AOC certifies the place of origin, the specific type, and the mode of production of a variety of products, from the *poulet de Bresse* (Bresse

Village appellation red burgundy from the Côte de Beaune district of the Côte d'Or. Courtesy of Philippe Bornier.

chicken) and *beurre d'Isigny-Sainte-Mère* (Isigny-Sainte-Mère butter), to various fruits, and including some of the *vins de table* (table wines).

Because the designation AOC indicates a historical pedigree and also functions something like a patent for the final product, extensive research and documentation are necessary to establish the application dossier for a food. The certification of the AOC gives a concrete, practical form to the appreciation for quality and particularity. It embodies the general acknowledgment that food with the best flavor and the most appealing textures may result from carefully, even painstakingly, overseen processes of cultivation and manufacture. The AOC also functions as a protection-ist measure that is a boon to sellers and producers and to tourism.

FRANCE AND EUROPE

Because of membership in the European Union, laws pertaining to food must now be negotiated within that framework. In 1992, the European Community Council passed regulations based on the French AOC that extend to all the member states. Today the European Commission administers a set of indications based on geography and origin for food and wine in all the member states. The passage of the European legislation coincided, ironically, with the reduction of trade barriers within the member

Farmer selling artichokes, radishes, and lettuce at market shortly before the conversion in 2002 from the French franc to the Euro as the unit of currency. Courtesy of Philippe Bornier.

states of the European Union. This has led, on occasion, to conflicts of interest. Compliance with European economic policy imposes common standards on member nations. This includes a relatively liberal approach toward free trade and privatization. Despite compliance in other areas, France is notorious for refusing to abandon, or even much reduce, subsidies in place since the early 1960s for its farmers. In the spring of 2005, a popular vote defeated a referendum to approve the proposed draft of a European Constitution, for fear of the consequences that greater liberalism could have on cherished social protections and on the quality of life. At the time, the negative vote was seen as a major setback for Europe. But these stances hardly prevent ongoing engagement with European projects. Rather, they simply make clear that, at present, the primary challenge is to balance the particular concerns of France with the larger endeavors of Europe.

NOTES

1. Salvian of Marseille, *On the Governance of God* (c. 440s), from *The Writings of Salvian, the Presbyter*, translator Jeremiah F. O'Sullivan (New York: Cima Publishing Company, 1947).

2. Anthimus, *De observatione ciborum (On the Observance of Foods)*, translator and editor Mark Grant (Totnes, Devon: Prospect Books, 1996), 54.

3. *Vita Sadalbergae abbatissae Laudunensis* 20, editor Bruno Krusch, in *Monumenta Germaniae Historica: Scriptores rerum merovingicarum* 5 (Hanover: Impensis bibliopolii Hahniani, 1910), 61. Cited in *Sainted Women of the Dark Ages*, editors and translators Jo Ann McNamara and John E. Halborg with E. Gordon Whatley (Durham: Duke University Press, 1992), 189–90 and Bonnie Effros, *Creating Community with Food and Drink in Merovingian Gaul* (New York: Palgrave Macmillan, 2002), 16.

4. *Karolus Imperator Capitulare de Villis*, LXX, "Volumus quod in horto omnes herbas habeant…" (We want that all the plants be cultivated in the garden…), in *Capitulare de villis; cod. guelf. 254 Helmst. der August Bibliothek Wolfenbüttel*, 2 vols., editor Carlrichard Brühl (Stuttgart: Müller und Schindler, 1971).

5. Einhard the Frank, *Life of Charlemagne* (ca. 829–36), translator Lewis Thorpe (London: Folio Society, 1970), 64–67.

6. *Le Mesnagier de Paris* (ca. 1393), editors Georgina E. Brereton and Janet M. Ferrier, translator Karin Ueltschi (Paris: Librarie Générale Française, 1994), 636 and 674.

7. Juan de Castellanos, *Historia del Nuevo Reino de Granada* (ca. 1538, published Madrid: 1886). Cited in Redcliffe N. Salaman, *The History and Social Influence of the Potato* (Cambridge: Cambridge University Press, 1949), 36.

8. Nicolas Boileau, *Satires* (1663–1701), in *Oeuvres* vol. 1 (Paris: Garnier-Flammarion, 1969), III and VII.

9. Martin Breugel, "A Bourgeois Good? Sugar, Norms of Consumption and the Labouring Classes in Nineteenth-Century France," pp. 99–118 in *Food, Drink and Identity,* editor Peter Scholliers (Oxford: Berg, 2001).

10. Jean-Jacques Rousseau, *Emile, ou de l'éducation* (1762), Book 2 (Paris: Garnier-Flammarion, 1966), 194.

11. Robert Darnton, "Readers Respond to Rousseau: The Fabrication of Romantic Sensitivity," in *The Great Cat Massacre and Other Episodes in French Cultural History* (1984; New York: Vintage Books, 1985).

12. Rebecca Spang, *The Invention of the Restaurant* (Cambridge: Harvard University Press, 2000).

13. Grimod de la Reynière, *Almanach des gourmands,* Cinquième année (Paris: Maradan, 1807), 233.

14. Anne Lhuissier, "Eating Out during the Workday: Consumption and Working Habits among Urban Labourers in France in the Second Half of the Nineteenth Century," pp. 337–49 in Marc Jacobs and Peter Scholliers, eds., *Eating Out in Europe* (Oxford: Berg, 2003).

15. Adel P. den Hartog, "Technological Innovations and Eating Out as a Mass Phenomenon in Europe," pp. 263–80 in Jacobs and Scholliers.

16. Eugen Weber, *The Hollow Years: France in the 1930s* (New York: Norton, 1994), 37.

17. Dana Strand, "Film, Food, and 'La Francité': From *le pain quotidien* to McDo," in *French Food: On the Table, on the Page, and in French Culture,* editors Lawrence R. Schehr and Allen S. Weiss (New York: Routledge, 2001), 203–20.

18. Alessandro Stanziani, "La construction de la qualité du vin, 1880–1914," in *La qualité des produits en France (XVIIIe-XXe siècles),* editor Alessandro Stanziani (Paris: Belin, 2003), 123–50.

19. Robert C. Ulin, *Vintages and Traditions* (Washington: Smithsonian Institution, 1996), 46–50.

2

Major Foods and Ingredients

An astounding variety of foods are eaten in France. This is due to the diversity of agricultural production, to long-standing traditions of cultivation and of practices such as hunting, and, more recently, to the many imports. Americans are of course quite familiar with items such as beef, the common orchard fruits, and eponymous exports such as Champagne. Even so, different butchering practices, for instance, as well as the typical preparations give beef a special flavor in France. Horse is not treated as food in the United States. The taste for, say, grated raw celery root salad with a cream dressing—a favorite bistro lunch—may come as a a surprise. To present the major foods and ingredients, this chapter broadly follows the structure of the traditional meal in courses. Bread, wine, and meat come first, followed by vegetables, then cheese. Dessert—fruits, baked goods—and the *digestif* (after-dinner drink) appear at the end.

BREAD

For centuries, bread was a staple of the diet, as well as a powerful religious symbol. The language has numerous expressions that refer to bread. A slang word for a job is *gagne-pain*, because it is how you earn (*gagner*) the bread that keeps you alive. To "take the bread out of someone's mouth" is to rob him of his livelihood. Your *pain quotidien* (daily bread) is the food that you count on eating every day. Only a century ago, each person ate 500 grams (on the order of a half-pound) daily. Today, about three

Buying a baguette at the *boulangerie* Au
pain chô in Sainte Maxime. The dough
rising on the racks at the back of the shop
awaits baking. Courtesy of Hervé Depoil.

or four slices of bread is average. Bread—no matter how small the quantity—makes a meal complete. In cafés, bistros, and restaurants, slices of
bread are placed on the table in a basket to accompany food, as a matter
of course.

Breads are identified by name and, for country-style loaves, by weight.
Bread is rarely made at home, rather in *boulangeries* (bakery shops) or
industrial bakeries. The long (70 cm or 27.5 inches), thin, crusty white
baguette is typical of Paris, although it is eaten all over the country. At
best, the crust is crispy, and the crumb chewy and delicate. In a bakery
the *baguette* can be purchased *bien cuite* (well cooked), that is, darker and
dryer, or *pas trop cuite* (baked less), that is, taken out of the oven when
it is still pale gold, delicately crispy, and moister on the inside. A slim
relative of the baguette is the *ficelle* (string), similarly long but half the
diameter. Large round *boules* used to be a staple, and darker bread made
from unrefined wheat or rye was typical for the poor. Recent interest in
eating whole grains for health has brought dark breads back into fashion.
The *bâtard* (bastard) is a free-form loaf named for the mixed leavening
agents—both yeast and a sour-dough starter—used to make it. Rustic

pains de campagne (country breads) can be enriched with dried figs, olives, and nuts. In Paris, Metz, and other cities with Jewish communities, Jewish bakeries sell challah, the braided loaf fortified with eggs that is eaten on the Sabbath, as well as bagels covered with poppy or sesame seeds.

Most bread is sliced in the kitchen or at table, or else broken off in chunks, to eat with a meal. Bread and crumbs have numerous uses in cooking. Sprinkled on top of a dish of meat, vegetables, or potatoes that is baked in the oven, they form an attractive crust. *Panade* is a carryover from poorer days and peasant traditions, when adding bread to soup made a heartier meal. The taste for *croûtons* (toasted slices of bread) with soup remains. *Croûtons* are placed in the bottom of onion soup bowls, and they accompany fish soups.

When bread-baking practices were standardized and mechanized in the second half of the twentieth century, quality declined. Recently, some bakers have begun to reverse this trend. They use older processes, such as proofing with sourdough or wheat flour starter instead of with fast-rising yeast. They choose better ingredients, such as organic, unrefined, or stone-ground flours. The old-style processes are slower. They require more labor, skill, and attention from the baker, however, the artisanal methods result in bread that has a deeper flavor, a silkier and more elastic crumb, and better keeping qualities. The old-style breads cost more than industrially produced loaves but taste so much better that people seek them out.

WINE

Wine has been produced on French soil since antiquity. Today, France is the premier producer in the world, responsible for a fifth of global production. Wine has long been thought of as hygienic and nourishing, a safe beverage that gives life and strength. Before the modern understanding of water cleanliness and contamination, it really was often safer to drink wine, beer, and cider, effectively sterilized through the presence of alcohol. Wine was usually mixed with water. In the mid-nineteenth century, poet Charles Baudelaire evoked the infinitely variable "soul" of wine in a series of poems. The "different" wines drunk by rag-pickers, assassins, and lovers, not to mention poets[1] lead variously to drunkenness (either divine or simply boorish), spiritual transcendence, poetic inspiration, earthly contentment, and deep sleep. As recently as the late 1930s, wine consumption averaged 170 liters (45 gallons) per person yearly, about a half-liter (the better part of a pint) each day. It usually was drunk mixed with water. The high level of alcohol consumption led to high levels of liver problems and alcoholism. In certain *métiers* or trades, such as among

Historical, economic, and religious significance contribute to the importance of wine, the national beverage. Courtesy of Christian Verdet/regard public-unpact.

tannery workers, old drinking traditions have not disappeared. This causes concern for colleagues, as heavy drinking is now understood to threaten health and safety. Today, wine is drunk undiluted but in smaller quantities. The average stands at approximately 60 liters (15.75 gallons) of wine per person each year, or less than one glass each day. Although only one in four French men and women regularly drinks wine, it is essential to the culture of the table.

Alcoholic beverages generally are always accompanied by food, and wine is integrated into meals. For an everyday meal, people drink water and wine, taking them separately; diluting wine with water is now quite rare. A separate wine for each course is *de rigueur* for formal and celebration meals. Wine sets off food, and vice versa; each brings out the tastes and textures of the other to best advantage. It is one of the components that contributes to making a meal complete—structured, harmonious, and balanced—and as enjoyable as possible. The individual flavor and character of each wine derives from the grapes as well as from the production processes. Some wines are dryer, having less sugar, and others sweeter. Some are lighter and simpler in flavor, others richer and more complex. Tradition and experiment suggest rules of thumb for pairing wine and food, although combinations ultimately depend on personal preference. Dry Champagne marries well with just about anything and may be drunk throughout an entire meal. Sweet white wines such as Sauternes, any Muscat, and Monbazillac pair with *foie gras* or with a salty appetizer at the beginning of a meal. Dry white wines accompany fish or seafood to good effect. Red wines that are light in character complement chicken dishes, veal, and *charcuterie*. Full-bodied red wines from Burgundy, Bordeaux, and Languedoc set off sturdy or rich savory foods, such as red meats and cheese.

Although wine drinking overall has declined, the trend is to drink better quality wines. Standards and methods of production vastly improved throughout the twentieth century. Today, even the cheapest *vin ordinaire* (everyday wine) tends to be of decent quality. The gut-searing *piquette* of days past has practically disappeared. Since 1975, the consumption of fine wines has doubled. These are the exceptional wines that mature and develop over time (measured in years), improving over a long, although finite, period. Of course, most people simply purchase inexpensive bottles along with the rest of the groceries. Such bottles are not meant to be kept or aged after bottling. They are best drunk within at most a few months.

Cooking assigns wine a large number of tasks. Both whites and reds are used for flavoring. In larger amounts, wine is a cooking medium for meat stews and bean dishes. After a piece of meat is sautéed in a pan, wine is poured in over high heat to deglaze the pan and mix with the meat juices to form a sauce. The alcohol cooks off, leaving only the flavor (and color, if red). Poured cold over fruit or berries, wine forms a marinade. Fruit macerated or soaked in wine acquires tenderness as well as flavor.

MEAT

In today's affluent society, consumption of *la viande* (meat) is high. Concerns for health are causing perceptible shifts in this pattern, although for the moment the trend to eat significantly less meat occurs largely at the highest rungs of the economic ladder; there are few vegetarians in France. France is the foremost producer of meat in the European Union. It raises more than enough for its own population, but imports to meet the large demand for cuts such as steaks and roasts. On average, each person eats 100 kilograms (220 pounds) of meat yearly, only slightly behind Australians (110 kilograms or 242 pounds yearly) and Americans (105 kilograms or 231 pounds) as the biggest consumers of meat in the world. Meat is the centerpiece for most main meals. French cooks have the reputation of being creative and frugal, ingenious and resourceful. They have invented succulent dishes that use all parts of animals slaughtered for meat, wasting nothing, although the modern lifestyle prefers fast, simple preparations.

Beef and Veal

Most *boeuf* (beef) comes from the powerful white Charolais cows originally used as draft animals or from cows formerly bred for milk: the black-and-white Normande and the Salers from the Auvergne. French butchering practices differ from American. The cuts of meat are more numerous and smaller. Nearly all methods of cooking are used for beef: boiling, stewing, braising, frying, sautéing, grilling, roasting, and broiling. Thin steaks are accompanied by fried potatoes for *steak-frites*. Thicker steaks are eaten *bleu* ("blue," quite rare), *saignant* ("bloody," rare), or *à point* (medium rare), according to preference. Tastes do not run to well-cooked steaks. Overcooking dries out the meat, ruining the flavor as well as the texture. For *hachis parmentier* (shepherd's pie), ground beef is arranged in a baking pan between two layers of potatoes mashed with milk. The dish is baked, then served cut in squares. Beef or horse chopped up and eaten raw is *tartare*. The delicate, sweet-tasting raw meat is garnished with pungent, highly flavored condiments, including chopped onion, mustard, salt, pepper, capers, pickles, and parsley; sometimes a raw egg is broken over the *tartare*. Fattier cuts of beef are cut into small chunks or cubes, then cooked slowly to make stews. Provençal *boeuf en daube*, flavored with red wine and orange peel, and *boeuf Bourguignon*, or beef stew with Burgundy, mushrooms, bacon, and small onions, are typical regional dishes. *Pot-au-feu* combines several types of meat for a rich boiled dinner.

Veal is considered white meat, rather than red, because of its color. Cuts of veal are roasted, sautéed, grilled, or stewed.

Lamb, Horse, Venison, and Goat

Studded with garlic and perfumed with rosemary, a roasted *gigot d'agneau* (leg of lamb) is the favorite celebration or Sunday meal. Lamb gives chops, meat for stewing, and racks (with bones in) for roasting. It features in recipes adopted from the cuisines of France's former colonies, such as Moroccan *tagines*, stews cooked in an earthenware pot with a conical cover and a hole in the top like a chimney through which the steam escapes, leaving only the concentrated flavors of the dish.

Cheval (horse), much of it imported from the United States, is eaten on a smaller scale than in the past. Large quantities of horse bones at Upper Pleistocene sites at Solutré, in Burgundy, date the consumption of horse to prehistoric times. Before horses were domesticated, the preferred hunting method was to drive large numbers of them off the edge of a cliff. In the early Christian era, eating horse was frowned upon, as the practice was associated with pagan rituals. Two popes, Gregory III in 732, and

Zaccharias in 751, forbade eating horsemeat. Their interdictions affected consumption throughout Europe. By the nineteenth century, any horsemeat that was available was cheap because it was unpopular. In the 1850s, the government promoted horsemeat, on the principle that it would improve the diet of the laboring classes, and productivity would rise. In 1866, the first *boucherie chevaline*, or *boucherie hippophagique*, opened in Paris. A few of the specialized butcher shops remain. Horse enjoyed a short-lived rise in popularity after the mad cow scares of the 1990s, especially in the Paris region and in the Northeast toward Belgium. Horse is darker red than beef, lean, and flavorful. It is prepared like good-quality beef, such as chopped raw and garnished in *tartare* or cooked as steaks and cutlets. *Chevreuil* (venison) is available in markets and on restaurant menus in the form of steaks, sausages, and dried sausages. *Chèvre* (goat) is eaten on Corsica, primarily in stewed and braised dishes. *Chevreau* (kid) is eaten in the South in the early spring.

Pork and *Charcuterie*

Porc (pork) is relatively inexpensive and served in roasts, fillets, steaks, stews, chops, and ribs. In 1808, the food writer Grimod de la Reynière praised the pig as "encyclopedic" and a "generous animal."[2] He meant that nearly every part is edible, including the skin. The dictum *Tout est bon dans le cochon* (Everything from the pig is good) echoes this observation. In a historically rural country, it was a mark of prosperity to be able to keep a pig, which would be slaughtered for its meat. Today, farm-raised *sanglier* (boar, wild pig) is also cooked using similar methods as for pork. A *cochon de lait* (suckling pig) is roasted whole. *Pieds de porc* (trotters, pigs' feet) are braised, and then fried or baked, or pickled.

More than any other meat, pork takes to processing through salting, drying, smoking, and pickling. The range of *charcuterie*—cured and cooked preparations primarily from pork—testifies to the ingenuity of generations of butchers and *charcutiers*. In the past, smoking and drying preserved meat that could not be consumed right away and must be stored against hunger. Whereas the wealthy could afford freshly slaughtered meat, *charcuterie* was food for the poor. Today, the taste for *charcuterie* is general; some preparations are marked with the AOC (Controlled Denomination of Origin).

Lard, meaty fresh bacon, is indispensable. Small pieces flavor omelets, enrich soups and stews, and garnish salads, potatoes, and vegetables. *Lardons* are strips or cubes of pork back fat or lean salt pork that are seasoned, then tucked into a roast, added to stews, and pan-fried to add to salads. Richly fatty, salty, and crisp, *lardons* are served to accompany a before-dinner drink. *Saucisses* or fresh sausages require cooking before being consumed, whereas *saucisses sèches* or *saucissons secs* (dry or salami-type sausages) need only to be sliced. Dry sausages have a firm, oily texture and a sharp flavor from the salt, pepper, and other spices that flavor them, such as whole peppercorns. Whole green pistachios may add sweetness and crunch to a hunter's venison sausage. *Saucisses de Morteau*, boiling sausages, are recognized by their seal and a tiny wooden peg tied into the end of the sausage; the enormous, lumpy *Jésus de Morteau* was originally a Christmas sausage. *Merguez* are spiced beef or lamb sausages of North African origin, outstanding when cooked on a grill. *Boudin noir* (blood sausage) is coagulated beef or pig blood. It has a soft, rich, unctuous texture, and is purplish-black in color. It is double-cooked: lightly poached, then pan-fried. *Andouille* or *andouillettes* is chitterling sausage, made of pig intestines and stomach that are cleaned, marinated, smoked, soaked, and then cooked. Sliced *andouille* has a firm, chewy texture and a swirly appearance from the strips that compose it. *Rillettes*, native to Tours, is a finely textured pork sausage made from bits of the belly, shoulder, and gullet. Braised in fat, with vegetables and spices added for flavor, the meat breaks down into a smooth, pale, creamy, mass. *Rillettes* are served sliced into rounds and spread on crusty bread or toast to accompany an *apéritif* such as a glass of dry white wine. *Jambons* (hams), boiled and smoked, are a staple. French hams are less salty than American, and none have a sweet coating on the outside. Some hearty stews are based on chunks of fresh ham. Ham is eaten as an appetizer, as part of a light lunch, or sliced into an omelet or quiche. It appears in the spectacular cold preparation *jambon persillé* from Burgundy. Bits of pink ham and chopped bright green parsley are molded in clear aspic to make colorful, jewel-like slices. Dry, salty hams sliced paper-thin are eaten with figs and slices of melon, like the Italian treatment of *prosciutto*.

Offal

In defiance of mathematics, butchers call *les abats* (offal) the *cinquième quartier* (fifth quarter) of a slaughtered animal. The "noble" cuts, or steaks and roasts, derive from the two forequarters and hindquarters. *Les abats* are the rest: organ meats, glands, the feet, the head. Offal has always been the cheapest meat, although the choice pieces—calf livers, kidneys, and brains—were often reserved for feasts or celebrations. François Rabelais, the priest turned physician, professor, and scribbler, wrote an offal feast into his novel *Gargantua* (1534): *Les tripes furent copieuses, comme entendez, et tant friandes estoient que chacun en leichoit ses doigtz* ("The tripe was so copious and so luscious, that everyone licked their fingers"). There are few specialist *tripiers* these days, but butchers and supermarkets sell offal. Pale, delicate *foie de veau* (calf liver) is coated with a minimal dusting of flour, then gently sautéed in butter, or lightly stewed or braised with a sauce such as tomato and red wine. Livers are also grilled, and pork liver is used in pâté. *Rognons de veau* (calf kidneys) have the finest texture and flavor, but pork and lamb kidneys are eaten as well, sometimes as *brochettes* (grilled on skewers). Beef kidney requires braising, as it is large and firm. *Tripes* (tripe or stomach) have a honey-comblike appearance. Cooked *à la mode de Caen*, tripe acquires an apple flavor from cider or Calvados, and a tender texture from slow braising, traditionally overnight. *Gras double* is beef tripe that is cleaned, cooked, and ready to eat. The *langue* (tongue) from a cow, calf, or lamb is boiled or braised, then served with a sauce having a strong acidic component from tomatoes, lemon, vinegar, or wine. Lamb or calf *cervelles* (brains) are marinated, then fried or sautéed. *Ris de veau* (sweetbreads, i.e., the thymus gland and sometimes the pancreas), *animelles* (testicles; also called, metaphorically, *frivolités*), and *coeur de boeuf* (beef heart) are eaten. *Tête de veau* (calf's head) is carefully boned so that the features are maintained, then rolled before cooking. Beef and lamb offal further features in the East European and North African Jewish and Muslim cuisines that enrich French cooking.

Poultry and Rabbit

La volaille (poultry) is a versatile basic. France exports more *poulet* (chicken) than any other country in the world. Most birds are raised on industrial chicken farms, although domestic demand increases for organic and free-range birds. The blue-footed, white-feathered, red-crested *coq gaulois* or Gallic cock that is the symbol of France is a Bresse fowl and has the AOC; they are sold with head and feet intact. Whole chickens are roasted to a golden brown. Cut into pieces, they are fricasseed or braised. Elegant *suprême de poulet* is a chicken breast stuffed with vegetables sliced very fine, then garnished with a red wine sauce. *Poule-au-pot* ("chicken in the pot") is a favorite dish for a weekend meal. Like the beef *pot-au-feu*, it is a boiled dish that gives both soup and a main course from the meat. *Chapon* (capon), *pintade* (Guinea fowl), *canard* (duck), *oie* (goose), and *dinde* or *dindon* (turkey) are eaten. Duck is considered dark or red meat, and it is served with the breast done slightly rare and pink. Turkey and goose are fare for the Christmas season; however, turkey is in demand year round. The game birds *caille* (quail), *pigeonneau* (squab), *faisan* (pheasant), *perdrix* (partridge), *bécasse* (woodcock), and *bécassine* (snipe) are considered special treats. The small birds, which tend to dry out, are often sold already barded or wrapped with strips of bacon or salt pork that melt during cooking.

Lapin (rabbit) and *lièvre* (hare) are sold with poultry. The association derives from the practice of keeping chickens and rabbits in proximity in a *basse-cour* (farmyard). Today, rabbit and hare are farmed, but the wild animals are fair game for amateur hunters. Rabbit responds especially well to moist cooking such as a braise. *Civet de lapin* is rabbit stew flavored with red wine and thickened with the rabbit's blood or with pig blood, giving a distinctive unctuous feel on the tongue and a dark color.

Foie gras and Confit d'oie

The Egyptians, Phoenicians, and Romans ate *foie gras d'oie* or fattened goose liver[3]; French household manuals from as early as the sixteenth century give explicit instructions for fostering *grand foie* ("big liver") in geese[4] through *gavage* (force-feeding with grain). Geese lack a gag reflex, so they can swallow about a cup of grain at a time if it is gently funneled into their throats. The resulting fat is stored primarily in their livers, which enlarge and develop the characteristic silky, melting texture. The tradition was long associated with Jewish communities in Metz and Strasbourg, as kosher dietary laws permitted eating fowl. Most *foie gras* now comes from several departments in the Southwest; ducks are given the same treatment as the geese. Some fresh livers are sold raw to be cooked at home. More frequently they are cooked first, then sold jarred or canned. At this point the *foie gras* requires no further cooking. Whole lobes are considered higher quality; large sections from different livers that are lightly pressed together are less expensive; mixtures of *foie gras* and fats resemble pâtés. It is eaten hot or cold, usually as an appetizer or first course. Hot preparations of *foie gras* are in fact heated just enough to bring out the flavors and texture. Good *foie gras* is pink and firm and has a clean-looking shine. It pairs with jellies and with fortified or sweet wines. The traditional combination of *foie gras* with truffles is considered the ultimate indulgence.

Plump geese and ducks raised for *foie gras* can be cooked and then stored in their own fat, for *confit d'oie* or *confit de canard* (preserved goose or duck). The rendered fat prevents the meat from coming into contact with air, and it is used in cooking; before refrigeration, making *confit* was essential for storing the meat. Today, both the meat prepared in this fashion and the flavors of the fats are much appreciated. Goose fat lends outstanding flavor when used to pan-fry potatoes, vegetables, and omelets. Goose or duck fat flavors *cassoulet*, the hearty stew associated with the towns of Castelnaudary, Carcassonne, and Toulouse. The combination of pork rinds, duck, goose, or lamb with *haricots blancs* (navy beans) is baked in a slow oven. Traditionally, the brown crust must be punched into the pot seven or eight times during baking; the exact number is a matter of debate among cooks and members of one of the gastronomic *confréries* (brotherhoods or associations) that is devoted to *cassoulet*.

EGGS

Les oeufs (eggs) are made into innumerable dishes for lunch and dinner; they are not eaten at breakfast. Eggs appear as omelets and soufflés and in *quiche Lorraine*, short pastry filled with savory custard flavored with ham or smoked bacon, grated cheese, nutmeg, and black pepper. In the South, flat, round frittatas heavy with vegetables or potatoes are sliced into wedges like a cake for a summer meal. Eggs are scrambled, fried, poached, hard boiled, softboiled, baked, and stuffed. Hard boiled eggs are combined with vegetables and a sturdy sauce to make a main dish; poached eggs are garnished with a clear sauce such as a red wine reduction for *oeufs en meurette*, an elegant entrée. Eggs are essential in baking cakes and pastries, yolks are used in custards, and whites are beaten up into meringues. As in the United States, the term egg refers automatically to a chicken egg, although markets and farm stands sell eggs from geese, ducks, and quail.

FISH

Home cooks prepare *poisson* (fish) and *fruits de mer* (seafood) less frequently than they do meat because the cooking is perceived as difficult or delicate. In restaurants, by contrast, people order nearly as much fish as meat.[5] As in many coastal countries, industrial fishing has exhausted natural populations, and waste and toxins pollute fishing waters. The same is true for France's rivers, which have supplied very little fish since the mid-twentieth century. Farm fishing adds to the supply but stresses the environment. Cultivated fish further lack the flavor and texture of their wild counterparts. The international trade networks and the use of freezers make most kinds of fish and shellfish available year round.

Creamy fish and seafood soups including bisques are popular in the Atlantic region. *Bouillabaisse* is a Provençal specialty from the Côte d'Azur. As with any great dish that is widely loved, every *bouillabaisse* cook claims an authentic and superior recipe. Most interpretations involve a base of vegetables (onions, garlic, tomatoes) and herbs, to which stock or water is added, followed by several kinds of fish and shellfish. *Rascasse* (Mediterranean rockfish, scorpion fish) is the cornerstone. Other fish added according to preference include *loup de mer* or *bar* (sea bass), *merlan* (whiting), *Saint-Pierre* (John Dory), and spiny-scaled *grondin* (gurnard). Saffron gives color and flavor. It is common to add a few fennel seeds and a shot of anise-flavored liquor such as *pastis* or some white wine. Fish soups are accompanied by a red-brown *rouille* ("rust"), the sauce that takes its color from cayenne pepper. For *rouille*, olive oil is beaten into a mashed potato or some bread crumbs, then flavored with mashed fresh garlic, chilies or cayenne pepper, salt, and pepper; sometimes an egg yolk is added to make the sauce richer. *Rouille* is spread on toast or stirred by the spoonful directly into the soup. *Bourride*, another fish soup, lacks tomatoes but contains mussels along with white fish such as *cabillaud* (cod) and *lotte* (monkfish). *Bourride* is pale in color and enriched with cream. It is served with toast and *aïoli*, fresh mayonnaise flavored with crushed garlic. *Oursinade* is fish soup served with sea urchins and a creamy mixture of egg yolks and butter.

Fish with the best texture and flavor is not disguised in soup, but rather poached, grilled, baked, broiled, or steamed; frying and smoking feature in fish cookery, as well. *Saumon* (salmon) has been overfished from the Loire River where it was once plentiful; imported Atlantic salmon is what is usually eaten. The flatfish *turbot* (turbot) and *sole* (sole) are among the finest fish eaten. They have inspired numerous preparations, some with stuffings made of finely chopped vegetables, herbs, and shellfish. *Raie* (skate, ray) gives triangular *ailes* (wings). The silky, moist flesh has long, delicate flakes and is best treated with the utmost simplicity, unless very large. Because of its famously hideous appearance, *lotte* (monkfish) is, exceptionally, never sold whole, but always beheaded. It has flavorful, meaty flesh and no bones. It is eaten in stews, and, because of the unusual firmness of the flesh, it is the only fish that is rolled and tied into roasts. Other fish that feature in soups and sauces, as well as main dishes, are *anguille* (eel), *daurade* (bream), *carrelet* (plaice), *thon* (tuna), *brochet* (pike), *carpe* (carp), *rouget* or *barbet* (mullet), and *merlu* (hake). Finefleshed *truite* (trout) appears in classic preparations such as *au bleu*. Trout cooked *au bleu* is poached in spiced, herbed cooking liquid acidulated with vinegar. In a successful *au bleu*, the fish dramatically curls and splits. Fish cooked *à la meunière* is floured and pan fried, sprinkled with lemon juice and chopped parsley, and drizzled with browned butter. Savory mousses, dumplings, and loaf-shaped terrines are based on fish that is ground to a smooth paste then mixed with seasonings. *Quenelles* are light-textured fish dumplings that are poached and sauced. In the South, strongly flavored

Mediterranean sardines are fried or else arranged on grape leaves and vine twigs, then grilled, so that the fish absorb the flavor of the vines.

Harengs (herring) are no longer fished in French waters, but supplies are purchased from elsewhere. Herring and *maquereau* (mackerel), both oily fish, are often lightly smoked, then broiled or served as fillets with green salad. *Hareng bouffi* is in fact a whole herring, intact but still "stuffed" with spawn. This delicacy is lightly salted, then smoked. *Rollmops* or herring fillets marinated in vinegar are served cold with boiled potatoes. *Stockfisch* (dried salted cod) is soaked in water or milk to rehydrate it and reduce the salt. For *brandade de morue*, the mashed salt cod is mixed with mashed potatoes or bread crumbs, milk or cream, and salt and pepper, then baked. *Accras* (Caribbean fried codfish balls) have become a popular appetizer and are purchased freshly made from caterers.

SHELLFISH

Mollusks such as briny, silky *huîtres* (oysters) and *palourdes* (clams) are eaten raw on the half-shell and cooked, such as in creamy bisques. *Moules* (mussels) are always cooked; *moules-frites* is a favorite bistro meal, although ostensibly of Belgian origin. The *moules* are steamed open in a broth lightly flavored with tomato. This becomes the sauce; the fried potatoes are on the side. To eat *moules*, people use one of the half-shells as a spoon and scoop out the meat from the other mussels. *Coquilles Saint-Jacques* and *pétoncles* (large and small scallops) are sold with the smooth orange roe sac attached to the white cylinder of flesh. Scallops are quickly seared over high heat or baked in a sauce that is somewhat liquid. Shell fish appear in soups and sauces and in stuffings for larger fish.

The Mediterranean coast provides *oursin* (sea urchin), an echinoderm having a porcupine-like exterior but yellow-orange lobes that are buttery in texture and sweetly briny. While living on the Côte d'Azur, Pablo Picasso painted the picture *Le Gobeur d'oursins* (1946) showing a happy eater gobbling (*gober*) down this delicacy directly from the shell. Crustaceans such as *crevettes* (shrimp) from the North Atlantic, and *crevettes grises* (tiny North Sea prawns) are often paired with a creamy sauce. *Étrilles* (small crabs) lend excellent flavor to soups. *Tourteaux* (larger crabs) appear with smaller shellfish and with *homard* (lobster) on spectacular cold seafood platters. Larger than shrimp but smaller than lobster in size, *langoustines* (Dublin Bay prawns) and *langoustes* (crayfish) appear in cold and in hot preparations. The Mediterranean cephalopods are popular quickly fried and served with slices of lemon, or else slowly braised. *Calmars* or *encornets* (squid) are also stuffed. Reddish, firm-fleshed *poulpe* (octopus) is cut into pieces for cold dressed salads or braising. *Seiches* (cuttlefish) are cooked whole.

SNAILS

In France, as in other parts of Europe such as Italy, mounds dating to Roman times attest the long tradition of eating *escargots* (snails), mollusks found on land. Snails are most often prepared in the typical Burgundian fashion. They are cleaned, then replaced in the shells, which are filled up with butter mashed with chopped herbs and garlic. In the oven, the butter melts over the tiny beast, making a highly flavored sauce that can be sopped up with a piece of bread. For serving, plates with round concavities stabilize the shells, so they do not roll. Special utensils are used: a rounded tongs to hold the shell steady, and a miniature fork with sharp tines to spear the snail.

FROGS

The *grenouilles* (frogs) to which the French owe their nickname are indeed widely appreciated. Fresh water lakes were the source for frogs during the eighteenth and nineteenth centuries, when they were especially popular. Today, they are imported frozen from Turkey; *cuisses de grenouilles* (frog legs) are flown in frozen from China, which has a much older tradition of eating frog.[6] The *cuisses de grenouille* have a silky, smooth texture and a slightly fishy flavor. They are best deep-fried or pan fried. Like fish, frog legs are served with slices of lemon for garnish.

BUTTER AND OIL

It used to be possible to distinguish northerners from southerners by the way they said "yes" (*oui*). Northerners spoke the *langue d'oïl* or language of *oïl*, while southerners spoke the *langue d'oc*. North was also distinguished from south by the fat used as a cooking medium. Northerners used *graisse de boeuf* (suet, beef fat) and *saindoux* (lard, pork fat) from their animals. Southerners used *huile d'olive* (olive oil) pressed from the fruit grown in their warmer territories. Theoretically, *beurre* (butter) and other animal fats were to be avoided on fast days, although the Catholic Church granted dispensations to areas where oil was rare and expensive.[7]

The best farmhouse butter, associated with the cattle regions of Normandy and Brittany, has a deep yellow color and a richly developed flavor. It is used in cooking and is indispensable in pastry making. Butter is spread on bread for a plain *tartine* and for sandwiches with ham, hard sausage, or cheese. Butter is associated with distinguished, rich cooking, referred to as *la cuisine au beurre* (butter cuisine). By today's standards, however, yesterday's generous use of butter is considered heavy-handed and old-fashioned.

Olive oil is key to Provençal cooking, with its greater use of grains, vegetables, and fruits—France's local version of the Mediterranean diet. Fats and oils carry fatty acids essential to growth and reproduction, along with fat-soluble vitamins A and E. In liquid vegetable oils, especially olive oil, the more healthful unsaturated fats predominate over saturated fat (associated with blood cholesterol increase). Average consumption for olive oil is 1.6 kg annually and growing[8]; olive oil connoisseurship is on the rise, as well. The grades and labels for olive oil reflect the pressing (first or subsequent), degree of acidity, and quality of flavor. Olive oil varies in color from bright green to yellow and in flavor from lively, fruity, and peppery for the green oils, to very mild. France produces olive oil in the South and imports it from Spain, Italy, Greece, and Turkey.

Mild-flavored *huile de colza* (canola or rapeseed oil) and *huile de tournesol* (sunflower oil) are domestically grown and the most widely used oils for everyday cooking and for making salad dressings and mayonnaise. Rarer *huile de pépins de raisins* (grapeseed oil), *de noisettes* (hazelnut), and *de noix* (walnut) feature in salads and dressings that show off their outstanding taste, and the nut oils are used in baking. Imported *huile d'arachide* (peanut oil) is neutral in flavor and has a high smoking point, so it is used for deep-frying and pan-frying over high heat. *Huile de palme* or *de coprah* (palm oil) and *huile de soja* (soy oil) are used in industrial contexts such as making packaged cookies and biscuits.

MILK, CREAM, FRESH CHEESE, AND YOGURT

Lait (milk) and *laitages* (dairy products) have always been much cheaper than meat, while providing protein and, in the case of cheese, preserving milk over time. Most milk sold is from cows; most goat and sheep milk goes into cheese. Fresh milk in France is pasteurized (heat treated at 75–85 degrees C for 15–30 seconds) or sterilized at even higher temperatures. Milk that is flash-treated at 145 degrees C for UHT (*ultra-haute température* or ultra-high temperature) sterilization can then be stored at room temperature in sealed tetrapacks until opened. Milk is drunk plain primarily by infants and children. Hot milk is essential to the breakfast drinks: *café au lait* (coffee with milk) and hot chocolate, also chicory, and chicory coffee. In cooking, milk is added to soups, *purées* of vegetables and potatoes, and sauces.

Cream is beaten into *crème Chantilly* (whipped cream) and added to soups, sauces, and baked *gratins* to give them smoothness and body. *Crème fraîche* is slightly fermented, akin to sour cream. It has numerous uses in cooking. A dollop garnishes desserts made with slightly acidic cooked fruits and cakes that are on the dry side. *Fromage blanc* is not technically cheese, but simply milk that has been curdled; the curds are beaten to create a smooth texture. *Fromage blanc* is eaten as a sweet or a savory. Garnished with chopped chives, salt, and pepper, it is the cheese course or the basis of a light lunch. Sprinkled with sugar and served with fruit, it is dessert.

Yaourt or *yogourt* (yogurt) originated near the Black Sea and the Caucasus, eventually spreading through the Middle East and central Europe. Yogurt has been widely eaten in France only since the 1960s. Most yogurt is industrial, bought plain or sweetened in individually sized containers. It is eaten at breakfast, for a snack, or to replace the cheese course.

Cheese

Fromage (cheese), like wine and bread, is synonymous with France. Some types, such as hard Cantal and blue-veined Roquefort, made of sheep's milk, were already attested in Roman Gaul. Cheese was vital to store milk. Today, the appreciation of cheese is so highly developed that cheese is eaten as a course all its own in a full meal. It is the last savory course, before the fruit or dessert. To conclude a formal or festive meal, a plate of two or three or more cheeses is passed around. Each person takes a small slice or triangle of the cheeses, to be eaten with bread and wine. Factory produced cheeses are available in supermarkets. Artisanal and farm-house products are usually bought in specialty shops and market cheese stands. Aged cheeses develop heady odors. People like to joke that the higher a cheese smells, the better it tastes. This is often true, and some of the worst olfactory offenders are quite mild in flavor.

Most names for cheese refer to the place of origin, although other descriptors are used. Any goat milk cheese, whether very young and moist, or aged, crumbly, and firm, is a *chèvre*. Goat cheese in a small round disk is called Cabécou. The flat-topped pyramid with a flower of blue mold on the outside is Pouligny-Saint-Pierre. The tiny round Crottin de Chavignol is named after the Loire village, but *crottin* (a horse or sheep dropping) is an earthy, humorous reference to its shape.

Master cheese maker and *affineur* (specialist in aging cheese) Hervé Mons with goat milk cheeses, goats, and colleagues in Saint-Haon-le-Châtel. Courtesy of Christian Verdet/regard public-unpact.

Semisoft cow milk cheeses with white mold rinds are *fromages à croûte fleurie*. These include Brie de Meaux, its more recently invented relative Camembert, the square Carré de l'Est, and Saint-Marcellin, which becomes practically liquid when ripe and is eaten with a spoon. Mild, creamy Savarin, named for the food-writer and gastronome Jean Anthelme Brillat-Savarin, is 75 percent fat. Red mold cheeses with washed rinds include Époisses, Pont-l'Évêque, and Munster, which people eat with a sprinkling of caraway seeds. For the softer cheeses, the rind is eaten, but it must be trimmed off the firm cheeses. Pressed cheeses for slicing include sweet-pungent Morbier, which has a blue-gray layer of wood ash across the middle, Tomme de Savoie, and Cantal, which can be eaten quite dry. Blue mold or blue veined cheeses include the Bleus d'Auvergne, Bleu des Causses, and Roquefort. The family of hard cheeses that includes Gruyère de Comté and Emmental are aged from curds that have gone through an additional cooking process to make them firmer and dryer. Grated hard cheese is sprinkled on dishes that are browned in the oven, such as potatoes *au gratin* and the onion soup famously served at Les

Halles marketplace in Paris. Grated cheese flavors the light, savory puffs called *gougères* often served as an appetizer.

Burgundian Baked Cheese Puffs (Gougères)

- 1 cup water
- 1/2 cup (1 stick) unsalted butter
- pinch salt
- 1 cup sifted all-purpose flour
- 4 large eggs
- 2/3 cup plus an additional 1/3 cup grated Gruyère cheese

Preheat the oven to 425° F.

To make the *pâte à choux* (puff paste), place the water, butter, and salt in a saucepan, and bring to the boiling point. When the butter has melted completely, remove the pan from the heat.

Add the flour, and stir it into the liquid, using a wooden spoon. Return the pan to low heat, and continue to cook until the batter thickens, leaves the side of the pan, and coheres into a ball. Remove the pan once again from the heat.

Beat in the eggs, one at a time, making sure each egg is absorbed before adding the next one. Mix in the 2/3 cup of grated cheese.

Use a pastry bag to squeeze the batter into rings, or else use two tablespoons to drop the batter like cookies onto ungreased cookie sheets. Sprinkle the additional 1/3 cup of grated cheese on the puffs.

Place the sheets in the oven and bake for 30 minutes, until the *gougères* are golden brown and puffy. Serve warm or prick the bottoms with a skewer or sharp-pointed knife to allow the steam to escape and cool on a wire rack.

HERBS, SPICES, AND CONDIMENTS FOR SAVORY COOKING

Most any home cook draws judiciously on a selection of mild *épices* (spices) and *herbes* (herbs) to vary the texture, flavor, and color of foods. The term spice usually refers to dried bark, buds, roots, and berries. Spices are often–although not always–of exotic provenance. An herb is usually a leaf. Many herbs are native to Europe if not to French territory. The traditional and regional dishes are richly flavored, thanks in part to the addition of herbs and spices, but they are not spicy.

As in many cuisines, *sel* (salt) and *poivre* (pepper) are the most basic spices in French cooking. Along with proverbs about bread and wine, proverbs about salt abound in France as elsewhere. Since about 700 B.C.E., salt has been harvested from Breton *palus* or *paludes* (marshes, salt flats). Atlantic salt is harvested from the Île de Ré and the Guérande peninsula, and Mediterranean salt comes from Aigues-Mortes. Historically, salt was vital to preserve meat, and it is used this way in *charcuterie*. Common refined *fleur de sel* (kitchen salt) is what most people keep on hand for cooking and for table use. Coarser sea salts still gray from the presence of marine minerals or flecked with seaweed add a decorative touch along with their special flavors to finished dishes, especially any made with fish.

In the Southwest, sweet summer fruits such as figs and pears are cooked with pepper, whose heat sets off the fruit. Whole black peppercorns stud dried sausages, or a sausage may be coated with a crunchy hot layer of cracked peppercorns. Removing the external coating of black peppercorns leaves white pepper. This is used in light-colored dishes such as mashed potatoes and cream sauces. White pepper is more common in the kitchen than on the eating table. Green peppercorns are picked before they are ripe, then pickled in brine to avoid discoloration. They balance rich elements such as butter or cream to make sauces for meats.

Most *vinaigre* (vinegar; from *vin aigre*, sour wine) is made from wine that is fermented so that the alcohol converts to acetic acid. Cider vinegar, made by the same process, is also used. Vinegar is a key condiment and cooking ingredient. It goes into sauces including *vinaigrette* (oil and vinegar dressing), pickles, and marinades. It serves as a cooking medium and to deglaze the pan for meat and fish sauces.

Moutarde (mustard), like vinegar, is ubiquitous in the kitchen and on the table. The seeds are crushed or ground, then blended with spices and vinegar to form a pungent mixture. Smooth Dijon mustard is made from milder yellow seeds. Rustic, grainy, old-style mustard has in it brownish bits of hull as well as crushed seed, and it is made from hotter red-brown seeds. Mustard is a condiment for boiled meats, sausages, cold cuts, and omelets. It flavors sauces, salad dressings, and glazes and dressings for oven-bound dishes such as rabbit or chicken. Dishes labeled *à la diable* (deviled) are seasoned with mustard.

Quatre épices (four spices) is a standard combination of white pepper, cinnamon or dried ground ginger, nutmeg, and cloves that flavors pâtés and meat dishes. *Muscat* (nutmeg) and *macis* (mace) are added to cooked vegetables and sweet egg dishes such as custards. *Clou de girofle* (clove) spices winter fruit compotes. Bright red threads of *safran* (saffron), the dried stigmas and styles (female organs) from the *Crocus sativus*, is sprinkled into fish soups and added to baked goods. It imparts a yellow-orange color and a clean, warm flavor. Saffron adds color to egg glazes for pastry and to butter used in fish and chicken dishes.

Carvi (caraway seed), associated with German and Scandinavian cooking, is used in pickling and is served with Munster cheese. *Anis* (anise seed), native to southern Europe, is the principal flavoring for *pastis* and is used in fish dishes and southern pastries. *Coriandre* (coriander seed) is paired with meat, and *genièvre* (juniper berry) flavors game and pork.

Standard combinations of herbs flavor many dishes. *Fines herbes,* composed of fresh minced *persille* (parsley), *cerfeuil* (chervil), *estragon* (tarragon), and *ciboulette* (chives), go into omelets, salad dressings, and herbed mayonnaise. *Bouquet garni* includes sprigs of parsley, *thym* (thyme), *laurier* (bay leaf), and sometimes *sarriette* (savory) and *romarin* (rosemary). The herbs are tied together, then dropped into broths, sauces, poaching liquids, and pots of vegetables to lend flavor in cooking. *Herbes de Provence* is a mixture of dried herbs that may include rosemary, *basilique* (basil), thyme, savory, tarragon, *marjolaine* (marjoram), and *lavande* (lavender). It flavors roasts and chops as well as chicken destined for baking, and it is added to southern sauces with a tomato base. By itself, parsley is essential in cooking and as a raw garnish. Curly-leaf parsley appears in the North; the flat-leaf variety is typical in the South. *Persillade* is finely chopped parsley and either shallots or garlic added to a hot dish just before the cooking is done. *Sauge* (sage) flavors pork and game. Basil is the primary flavor, along with crushed garlic, salt, and olive oil, in *pistou* (pesto) for stirring into vegetable and bean soups. Tarragon flavors lamb and chicken and goes into sauces, and thyme is used in fish dishes. A *feuille de laurier* (bay leaf) is added to marinades and to pots of beans and lentils.

ONIONS, GARLIC, SHALLOTS, AND LEEKS

The *Allium* genus is all-important for French cooking. Chopped sautéed *oignons* (onions) combine with carrot and celery as the basis for many dishes, and they are the principal ingredient in *soupe à l'ognion* (onion soup). Cooking onions very slowly until they are sweet, soft, and caramelized makes *confit* or savory jam that accompanies meat dishes; flavored with mashed, salted anchovies, it tops Provençal *pissaladière* (onion pizza). Minced *échalottes* (shallots) add zest to green salads. *Ail* (garlic) is roasted, and whole unpeeled *gousses* (garlic cloves) accompany chicken roasting in the oven. Along with tomatoes and olive oil, garlic is ubiquitous in the cooking of the South. *Poireaux* (leeks) flavor soups and sometimes appear in a *bouquet garni* used for soup. *Vichyssoise* is leek and potato soup; this and a salad of braised leeks with vinaigrette dressing are

Braised leeks accompany poached fish. Courtesy of
Philippe Bornier.

the most common preparations. *Ciboulette* (chive) is used both raw and
cooked, as an herb.

GRAINS, PASTA, RICE, AND POTATOES

Of Italian origin, *pâtes* (pasta) seem to have been made in France by
northern Jews as early as the eleventh century and in Provence within the
next 200 years. The exception is Alsatian *nouilles* (egg noodles), an innovation from the Rhineland. Later, pasta were made using hard or durum
wheat flour in Paris, Clermont-Ferrand, and Marseille.[9] Today, most *pâtes*
eaten in France are made within the country, but the shapes borrow from
the Italian traditions. Pasta and noodles are most often boiled and eaten
as a side dish for meats.

Couscous, eaten in the former colonies of Tunisia, Morocco, and Algeria, has become a typical dish. Semolina flour (from hard wheat) and
water make a paste that traditionally was rubbed between the hands into
tiny balls. *Couscous* steams in the fragrant vapors coming up off a stew
whose ingredients vary: lamb, fish, seafood, greens, and vegetables are
all common components. A typical Moroccan couscous combines lamb,
pumpkin, carrots, turnips, onions, and chickpeas; the stew is then served
with the steamed pasta. Spicy Tunisian harissa (a paste of red pepper,
crushed garlic, coriander, cumin, and olive oil), more or less diluted with
hot water or broth, is added at table as a sauce. Sweet couscous prepared

with nuts, raisins, and flavorings such as rosewater is a festive dessert. The word *couscous* refers both to the pasta and to the finished dish. Many people have a *couscoussier* or couscous steamer in their home kitchens. Dried industrial *couscous* is available, and people do steam it alone (without making the stew) to eat as they would pasta of Italian origin.

Cracked wheat, or bulgur, is made into *tabbouleh,* the Lebanese salad with olive oil, lemon juice, chopped parsley, cucumber, tomato, scallions, and spices.

Riz (rice) was cultivated in the wet Camargue region from the seventeenth century through the mid-twentieth century. Rice consumption has more than tripled since the 1970s, and now nearly all is imported. Long-grained rice is used in cold salads and in side dishes for meat. Short-grained or Arborio rices are made into desserts such as *gâteau de riz* (rice cake) and puddings.

Orge (barley), used in making ale and then beer, is now little used in cooking, although cream of barley, a powder ground from the grain, thickens soups and boiled dishes. *Seigle* (rye) is used in bread-making and in a few sweet baked goods, such as spice breads. New World *maïs* (corn) has been adopted in a very limited fashion, as corn is still thought of primarily as animal fodder. Corn is eaten as flakes in cereal, and canned corn added to cold salads. More interestingly, Nice, formerly part of the Italian Piedmont, borrows the Italian tradition of making *polente* (polenta) out of cornmeal, and related preparations appear in Basque cooking. *Épeautre* (spelt) goes into Provençal soups, and it has come back into fashion among bakers of organic and whole-grain breads. *Blé noir* or *sarrasin* (buckwheat), cultivated in Brittany, is the key ingredient for the dark *crêpes* associated with that region.

Breton Buckwheat Crêpes (Galettes bretonnes or galettes de sarrasin)

- 1/2 cup buckwheat flour
- 1 cup all-purpose flour
- pinch salt
- 4 large eggs
- 1 1/4 cups apple cider
- 1 1/4 cups milk
- 1/4 cup water
- 1/4 cup unsalted butter, melted

Mix or pulse to blend together in a blender or food processor the flours and salt. Add eggs, cider, milk, water, and melted butter to make a thin batter. Let the batter stand for one hour, covered, or refrigerate overnight.

Briefly blend or mix the batter once more. Heat a crêpe pan or large flat saucepan until very hot. Brush lightly with butter, then pour in batter to thinly coat the pan (about 1/3 cup of batter for a 12-inch pan). Swirl the pan to spread the batter over the bottom of the pan and up its sides (if using a crêpe pan). Cook about a minute, until the crêpe is brown on the bottom and at the edges and set firm in the middle. Turn the crêpe out flat onto a plate or board. Fold it in quarters or turn in the edges to make a square. Serve hot, with a filling or plain.

Makes about 15 crêpes.

When exotic New World *pommes de terre* ("earth apples," i.e., potatoes) were first introduced, they were viewed with great suspicion. Now it is difficult to imagine French cooking without them. No matter what the preparation, the peel is not eaten, but always removed before cooking or just before serving. Boiled or steamed potatoes are eaten in salads or tossed with butter. *Pommes frites* (French fries or fried potatoes) are popular. Potatoes are sliced and baked, pan-fried, sautéed, and added to stews and soups. *Purée de pommes de terre* (mashed potatoes) is served as a side dish

Peeling potatoes for cooking. Most potatoes presently cultivated and eaten in France are the BF 15, Bintje, and Ratte varieties. Courtesy of Hervé Depoil.

and may be further elaborated into fried *croquettes* (puffs). Potatoes are a mainstay of student cafeterias and other industrial restaurants, where they are usually bought frozen and already peeled, sliced, prepared for cooking, or dried in powder for *purée*.

PULSES

In the past, *légumes à gousses* (pulses) were staples. Pulses are the edible seeds of pod-bearing plants cultivated for food. Eaten in combination with grain, peas and beans provide complete proteins that contribute to a healthy diet with little meat or none at all. *Pois chiches* (chickpeas) and *fèves* (fava beans) were particularly important in the southern regions. Today, pulses usually accompany meat or fish as a separate course or side dish. Dried green beans called *haricots verts* and *chevriers* go with lamb, whose flavorful juices they absorb. *Haricots blancs*, *cocos*, and *lingots* (dried white beans) combine with meat in rich stews such as *garbure* and *cassoulet* and marry well with cream and tomatoes. Chickpeas go into *couscous* and salads. Tiny, firm, green Puys lentils are used in salads and served with salmon; larger, flatter, pale green and yellow varieties go into soups and *purées*. Lentils and split peas are often combined with pork, sausages, or bacon for flavor.

Fresh green and white beans at the Place des Halles market in Dijon. Courtesy of Philippe Bornier.

VEGETABLES

The term *légume* (vegetable) as used in everyday speech covers several botanical groups: roots, leaves, rhizomes, flowers, and even fruits such as the *tomate* (tomato). Vegetables are eaten in savory preparations as side dishes and as individual courses of a main meal, and they are prominent in soups and stews. The French are masters of the salad, which may be a plain tossed lettuce mixture, cooked pulses such as lentils tossed with *vinaigrette* and some sliced onion, or a *salade composée* "composed" from whatever is at hand and attractively arranged on a flat plate. The composed salads often include cooked vegetables and pieces of cheese or meat, as well.

Among the root vegetables, *carottes* (carrots) are eaten cooked, rather than raw, except when grated and dressed as part of a platter of *crudités* (composed salad of raw vegetables—a colorful mosaic). Grated *betteraves* (beets) also appear served in discrete, individually dressed mounds on the plate of *crudités*. Steamed, mashed, or puréed, carrots form a vegetable course. They feature in sturdy winter soups and stews to which *navets* (turnips) are usually added, as well. Salsify or oyster plant (*salsifis*) is cooked with butter, cream, or meat juice from whatever it will accompany. The bulbous, hairy, forbidding-looking *céleri-rave* (celery root or celeriac) is appreciated for its warm celery flavor and versatility. Once it is scrubbed under running water, the outer rind is trimmed; and the vegetable is then cut into chunks, braised in milk, and made into a purée or soup. Raw celery root is grated, dressed with mustard *vinaigrette* or with cream, and served with slices of salty dry ham. Small red and white *radis* (radishes) are dipped in salt and eaten raw along with bread and butter. They also appear in some cooked dishes, such as braised with lettuce and peas. The giant, tempestuous *raifort* (horseradish) is grated and tempered with *crème fraîche* or unsweetened whipped cream as a garnish for smoked fish. Horseradish also garnishes boiled meat dishes like *pot-au-feu*.

Chou (white cabbage) is eaten salted or pickled as *choucroute* (sauerkraut), associated with Alsatian cooking. Curly-leafed *chou de Savoie* or *chou frisé* (Savoy cabbage) is stuffed, added to soups and stews, and braised. Greens such as sour *oseille* (sorrel) and spicy dark green *cresson* (watercress) add color and flavor to soups and sauces. Narrowly sliced into a *chiffonnade* (ribbons), sorrel lends its lemony tang to eggs and fish. *Épinards* (spinach) are usually served cooked, although very small, tender, young leaves appear in salads, sometimes garnished with morsels of hot *lard*. Provence's characteristic vegetable is chard, which is often cooked with olive oil, pine nuts, and raisins as in other areas of the Mediterranean. In the sweet version of *tourte aux blettes* (chard tart), from

Nice, eggs, grated apple, powdered sugar, and a dash of Parmesan cheese make a custard that balances the flavor and texture of the vegetable. France is the biggest producer in the world of compact, pale yellow *endives* (Belgian endive). Raw endive leaves add a silky crunch to salad. Most often the whole vegetable is steamed or blanched and served hot under a *béchamel* sauce with ham.

Green salads are served after the main dish in a full meal, when their cool crunch refreshes the palate; composed salads appear now on restaurant menus as first courses or on full-sized plates as a main dish. Fresh *laitues* (lettuces) mean green salad to most people. A head of lettuce is often referred to simply as *une salade* (a salad). For plain green salad, Bibb-type lettuce, Romaine, or green leaf lettuce is tossed with oil-and-vinegar dressing that may be emulsified with mustard or flavored with a sliver of garlic or a spoonful of minced shallot. Other popular salad greens include *scarole, escarole,* or *cornette* (chicory or curly endive), *mâche* (corn salad or lamb's lettuce), and peppery *roquette* (rocket or arugula). A few classic preparations call for cooked or braised lettuce, as in combination with peas.

Haricots verts (fresh green beans, string beans, or French beans) are a favorite vegetable across the country. They are boiled in salted water, then served with butter alongside roasted or grilled meat. They combine with other vegetables in composed salads and appear in soups and purées. *Petits-pois* (fresh green peas) came into fashion in the seventeenth century and have remained popular ever since. Classic simple preparations flavor the peas with a small quantity of sugar, then add mint and butter or lettuce and cream. Tiny *artichauts* (artichokes) are eaten raw with salt; larger ones are cooked whole then served with a *vinaigrette* or melted butter and lemon as a sauce for dipping the leaves. The sweet hearts are braised in water, lemon juice, and olive oil, or in a *blanc* or white cooking liquid consisting of boiling water and a bit of flour. *Céleri* (celery) is blanched, braised, and served with tomato sauce or meat marrow, alongside boiled meats. Stalky *cardes* (cardoons) are cooked like artichoke hearts, then dressed with a rich sauce such as *hollandaise* (based on butter and egg yolks) or served *à la bagna cauda,* with the Provençal dressing of olive oil, lemon, minced garlic, and anchovy. Classical cooking gives methods for cooking *concombre* (cucumber); however, it is most often eaten raw, seeded, and sliced. It is dressed with olive oil and lemon in a *salade grècque* (Greek salad) with tomatoes or else sauced with cream and chives or mint. Fleshy *fenouil* (fennel bulb) is sliced raw to eat with lemon or with a full-fledged dressing for a salad. It is also braised or blanched to be eaten cooked, and it is an ingredient in some tomato sauces. Fennel stalks and leaves are

Everyday vegetables in inviting profusion: lettuce, carrots, cucumbers, and cauliflower at market. Courtesy of Philippe Bornier.

placed under fish that is grilling to give it flavor. White *asperge* (asparagus), grown under mounds to avoid exposure to light, is preferred over green. The vegetable is thick, sometimes woody toward the bottom, and usually requires peeling, but it has a mild flavor. Asparagus are steamed or boiled, often served with a creamy or eggy sauce such as *hollandaise,* or with vinaigrette dressing.

Cooked *chou-fleur* (cauliflower) appears boiled or steamed in composed salads; the florettes are fried; most often it is par-boiled then baked *au gratin* with milk or cream and grated cheese. *Chou-fleur d'Italie* or *broccoli* (broccoli) made its way to France from Italy and is still somewhat less common than cauliflower. It is usually converted to *purée* or made into a cream soup.

The *aubergine* (eggplant), *poivron* (bell pepper), *tomate* (tomato), and *courgette* (zucchini) are workhorses in the French kitchen. None are native, but all flourish in the warm, dry Mediterranean climate of the South. Indian eggplant was introduced to Spain during the Middle Ages by the Moors and from there made its way to Italy and France. Peppers and tomatoes are New World plants that were brought back to Europe in the late Renaissance. Zucchini traveled from Italy into France. All four are eaten stuffed with meat, rice, or breadcrumbs. Eggplant is roasted then diced into cold salads. Zucchini puréed with cream and butter is a side dish that is much appreciated in the summer. Tomato halves sprinkled with herbs and bread crumbs and then baked to concentrate the flavors accompany meat. Strips of roasted, peeled peppers are made into cold salads. The quartet of vegetables is particularly associated with southern cooking, as in the summer stew *ratatouille*.

Summer Vegetable Stew (Ratatouille)

- 7 tablespoons olive oil
- 1 pound zucchini and/or yellow crookneck squash, sliced into rounds
- 2 green or red peppers, seeded, membranes removed, and sliced
- 1 eggplant (about 1 pound), cut into 1-inch cubes
- 2 pounds tomatoes, halved and seeded
- 1 1/2 cups chopped onion
- 2 tablespoons chopped garlic
- 6 sprigs thyme, leaves stripped from the stems
- 6 tablespoons chopped parsley
- 8 tablespoons chopped basil
- salt
- ground black pepper

Heat 2 tablespoons of the olive oil in a large skillet over moderate heat. Sauté the zucchini about 6 minutes until lightly browned. Using a slotted spoon, transfer to a large bowl.

Add 1 tablespoon of oil, then sauté the sliced peppers for 5 minutes, and transfer to the bowl.

Add 3 tablespoons of oil to heat in the skillet, then put in the eggplant. Stir to prevent the eggplant from sticking to the pan. Cook until the eggplant is soft, light-colored, and smooth in texture (about 8 or 9 minutes). Add to the bowl with the other vegetables.

Pour the last tablespoon of olive oil into the pan, and sauté the onion and garlic about 3 minutes, watching carefully to prevent them from browning much. Add the tomatoes, thyme and half the parsley. Simmer for 10 minutes. Return all the vegetables in the bowl back into the pan with the tomatoes, stir gently to mix, and cook for 10 more minutes. The vegetables should be cooked through and tender, but not mushy.

Take the pan off the heat. Stir in the rest of the parsley and the basil. Season with salt and pepper.

Serve hot, cold, or at room temperature.

Citrouille or *potiron* (pumpkin) is made into soups, sautéed in butter, baked in the oven, and used in *couscous*. Occasionally it is co-opted for service in egg desserts such as pumpkin *flan* or pumpkin *crème brûlée*.

MUSHROOMS

The fungi known as *champignons* (mushrooms) grow naturally in wooded areas or meadows. In the past, they were also cultivated in caves and abandoned underground stone quarries. France is now the world's third-largest producer of cultivated mushrooms, of the type called *champignons de Paris* or *champignons blonds* for their pale, creamy color. Mushrooms are sautéed, fried, braised, baked, grilled, and put into soups. At best, they have a rich, dark, mineral flavor and a natural sweetness. Other varieties are gathered wild. Netted black *morilles* (morels) and dense, long-stemmed, golden *chanterelles* or *girolles* (chanterelles) do appear in markets, and they are often cooked in combination with cream and chicken. Mushrooming is popular in the countryside, but mushrooms must be gathered under the supervision of an experienced person who can distinguish edible ones from poisonous varieties that look similar.

Truffles

All but impossible to cultivate, *truffes* (truffles) grow wild in forested areas, usually underneath oak trees from which they derive carbonic nutrients and to which they give back mineral salts and other elements. Truffles are so highly prized that they are called *diamants noirs* (black diamonds). Although they look like dark chunks of coal or earth, they are quite expensive and fetch high prices on the market. Truffles are especially associated with the Périgord, where the best ones grow. Truffle hunters develop an eye for locating patches in forested areas and are notoriously secretive about this information. Truffles are so hard to spot that people train pigs and dogs to sniff them out, although the four-legged assistants must be prevented from eating their finds. Generous quantities of truffles feature in the old aristocratic cuisine and in contemporary elite restaurant cooking. Eggs delicately scrambled over very low heat with black truffle is a typical treatment. Chicken roasted with slices of black truffle tucked under the skin is called *demi-deuil* (half-mourning) because of the dark appearance the truffles give the bird. For modest budgets, shavings of black truffle are added to excellent effect to omelets, pâtés, and cream sauces for pasta. Bits of truffle steeped in high-quality oils impart their perfume to salads.

FRUITS

Fresh fruits are eaten out of hand for a snack and as a sweet course at the end of a meal. They are cooked into *compotes* and used to stuff pastries and fill tarts. In the industrial context they are squeezed for juice and puréed or reduced to syrups used to sweeten and flavor yogurt, ice cream, and candy. *Pommes* (apples) are the most popular fruit and account for approximately one-quarter of all fruit eaten. Sweet apples such as the Golden Delicious are eaten out of hand, but most apples are transformed by cooking into pastries and desserts. *Tarte Tatin* or upside-down apple tart appears on restaurant dessert menus and is baked at home to end a festive dinner. Apples are sliced into large pieces or quartered, caramelized by sautéing in sugar and butter, then arranged in a pan with a single layer of short crust on top. After baking, the tart is turned upside-down to reveal the caramelized apples. The trick is to eat the dessert straight out of the oven, otherwise the crust becomes soggy underneath the apples. Hard, sour *coings* (quinces), available in the fall, are cooked into *compote*, preserves, jellies, and *pâte de coing* (quince paste), which is enjoyed as a Christmas sweet. *Poires* (pears) are eaten raw, poached, or baked in wine, and on flat cakes. *Rhubarbe* (rhubarb), a member of the knotgrass family, is treated like the firm fruits. Its long, red, fleshy, astringent stems are sliced, cooked in syrup, and made into tarts and pastries.

Soft-fleshed, pitted drupes such as *nectarines* (nectarines) and meltingly sweet *brugnons* (white nectarines), *pêches* (peaches), *abricots* (apricots), or *cerises* (cherries) are placed whole in bowls on the table after a meal in summer for dessert. Cooked, these fruits stuff pastries and top cakes; flavor yogurt, ices, and ice creams; and form sauces that accompany pork or game. *Prunes* (plums) came west to France with Crusaders returning from Syria. *Prunes d'Ente* and fat, purple-black *pruneaux d'Agen* (prunes) are a specialty of the Lot-et-Garonne region in the Southwest. The berries—*fraises* (strawberries), *framboises* (raspberries), *myrtilles* (blueberries)—are eaten fresh served in small bowls, and people take up sprays of delicate, jewel-like *groseilles* (red currants) with the fingers, then pull the fruit right off the stem with their teeth. These *fruits rouges* ("red fruits" or berries) also garnish tarts and cakes. *Raisins* (grapes) are a late summer dessert. In recent years the New Zealand kiwi has become extremely popular and is now widely cultivated in France. Other *fruits exotiques* ("exotic" or tropical fruits) imported for sale in markets include mangoes and star-fruit. Green and black *figues* (figs) and *grenades* (pomegranates) with their ruby flesh have been cultivated for centuries in Provence. They are eaten raw in the late summer when they ripen, and figs also appear in jams. Imported *bananes* are widely available in shops and nearly always eaten raw. The most popular melons are the small green-skinned varieties known as Chantal, Cavaillon, and Charentais. Their juicy orange flesh is intensely sweet and flavorful; they are usually served halved, to be eaten with a spoon for a summer *entrée*. *Pastèque* (watermelon) is popular during the summer in the South. *Avocats* (avocadoes) are technically fruits; however, they are used in salads and soups, frequently in combination with shrimp and crabs. *Oranges* (oranges) are the most common of the thick-skinned citrus fruits. *Citrons* (lemons) are used in both savory and sweet preparations; in cooking they have a special affinity for fish, chicken, and veal. *Pamplemousses* (grapefruit) are usually pressed into juice; they are sometimes served peeled and sliced as a light first course. *Citrons verts* (limes) are used in mixing drinks, and *cédrats* (citrons) are candied for use in baking and confectionary.

JAMS, JELLIES, AND COMPOTES

La confiture, say the French, *est comme l'intelligence: moins on en a, plus on l'étale* (Jam is like intelligence: the less you have, the more you spread it around). Before modern refrigeration and freezing, making preserves ensured that one could eat fruits in some form during the cold winter months. Containers of jewel-like preserves were often exchanged as gifts. Most jam is industrial, but during the summer people macerate fruit in sugar overnight, then boil it down the next morning. Jam is ubiquitous on breakfast tables: strawberry, raspberry, apricot, and plum are popular flavors to spread on bread for a *tartine*. Preserves have many uses in baking; *abricoter* ("to apricot") means to glaze a cake or tart with a coating of boiled, strained apricot preserves. The lovely sheen on strawberry tarts and other pastries in bakery windows is usually due to an apricot glaze. A *gelée* (jelly) is a fine-textured, clear preserve from which all berry seeds or chunks of fruit have been strained off; jellies are also made from decoctions of lavender or from wine. Rowanberry and elderberry jellies and gooseberry jam are served with game to temper the headier flavors of the meat. Sweet-acid currant jelly is a traditional accompaniment to hot preparations of *foie gras*. *Compote* is a simple dessert of fruits stewed in syrup or wine. It is prepared from fresh or dried fruits, or both, such as apples, quinces, prunes, figs, and raisins.

NUTS

Dried Isère *noix* (walnuts; the word also refers to nuts in general) are used in baking and confectionary and in savory cooking to garnish salads and hot dishes. They pair with poultry and meat, with salads, and with blue cheeses, and they are served as dessert (instead of fruits) during the winter months. Sweet *amandes* (almonds) are in fact pit fruits related to peaches; in cooking they are often paired with trout. *Noisettes* (hazelnuts or filberts) garnish meat concoctions such as pâtés and are added to hard sausages. *Châtaignes* (chestnuts) are ground into flour that is used to make bread and cakes. Whole chestnuts go into stuffing for turkey and combine with cabbbage to make hearty winter braised dishes. Candied in sugar syrup, they are called *marrons glacés* and are used in sweet preparations such as chestnut cream. Tiny green *pistaches* (pistachios) are used like hazelnuts, with meats and in confectionary. Salted and left in their shells, they accompany an *apéritif*. *Pignons* (pine nuts) are lightly toasted in a pan, then strewn on salads and used as garnishes. Although most nuts are eaten dried, fresh hazelnuts and almonds appear seasonally in markets. When fresh, the pithy, still-green shells are carved open with a sharp knife. Fresh nutmeats are pale white, with a crisp texture, a milky moistness, and a sweet flavor.

SUGAR, HONEY, CHOCOLATE, AND SWEETS

Sucre (sugar) was long a luxury consumed by the affluent and considered a spice rather than a cooking staple or a food. Today, France leads the European Union in the production of sugar from sugar beets; worldwide it is second. As in the United States, sugar is widely used in the food industry as an additive to fruit juices, preserves, biscuits, pastries, breakfast cereals, and yogurt.

Despite the prevalence of industrial candies, the tradition of artisanal confectionary is quite strong in France. Few confectioners today make the elaborate sugar sculptures that featured on aristocratic tables in the past. Contemporary *bonbons*, if more modest, are nonetheless exquisite, and small, decorative boxes of hand-made candies such as chewy *nougats* (made with egg white) or nut *pralines* (in a crunchy sugar coating) are often given as gifts. Hard sugar candy is shaped in molds or else blown like glass from heavy syrup, perhaps into naturalistic forms such as roses and leaves; working with sugar is an art in itself. *Berlingots* and *bêtises de Cambrai* are both bonbons with a glasslike appearance typical for flavored, colored, hard sugar candies. The *petits-fours* or very small cakes known as *calissons d'Aix* are made of sweetened melon paste and egg white. The paste is glossed with hard white sugar icing, then carved into the typical almond shape.

Sugar is essential to *chocolatiers* or chocolate makers. Chocolate is widely consumed in France, although in smaller quantities than in other European countries. Most chocolate is eaten in the form of the industrial milk chocolate bars available in every supermarket and grocery store.

In recent years, it has become fashionable for cafés to serve a small square of chocolate with their coffees, the result of promotional efforts on the part of chocolate manufacturers. As in the United States, connoisseurs seek out dark chocolate with a significant cocoa content (at least 50 percent), viewed as more natural, better tasting, and of higher quality than the overly sweetened and less saturated mixtures. Artisanal chocolate makers produce bonbons stuffed with fruits or creams, flavored with liquors or spices, mixed with nuts. *Chocolats* come in imaginative shapes, according to the inspiration of the confectioner; a Lyon specialty is the cocoa-dusted *hérisson* or hedgehog, so-called for its spiky appearance. After a festive meal, a box of elegant chocolates may be passed around the table as a last morsel to follow coffee.

Miel (honey) has been a familiar if not widely used sweetener since Celtic and Roman times. During the late Middle Ages, fermented honey drinks were made in Lorraine, Metz, and the Vosges, and bees were also important as a source of wax to make the votive candles lit in churches. At breakfast honey is eaten like jam—spread on buttered bread or spooned over plain yogurt for flavor and sweetness. Honey from meadow flowers and crop fields is the most common. Lavender honey, orange flower honey, pine honey, and thyme honey are harvested in the South and have delicate, distinctive flavors. Honey gives *pain d'épices* (spice cake) from Dijon its characteristic flavor and dark color, and it is a traditional ingredient in ginger cakes. Apiculture or the cultivation of bees for honey is a common hobby that recalls the rural agricultural life of the recent past. Residents of rural areas and also many suburban dwellers keep a hive in the garden and collect their own honey.

PASTRIES AND DESSERTS

One of the many seductions of France is the large range of imaginative desserts and *pâtisseries* (pastries). These range from simple, homemade preparations, to complex confections made only by *pâtissiers,* the pastry professionals. *Viennoiseries* or fine pastries such as *chaussons de pomme* or baked apple turnovers, *brioche,* raisin-filled spirals, and flaky, buttery *croissants* are eaten at breakfast along with a bowl of coffee or hot chocolate. *Pains au chocolat,* which are croissants filled with chocolate, are a favorite with children. For a special occasion such as a weekend dinner or a birthday celebration, home cooks craft a simple chocolate or pound cake, a basic layer cake with fruits, desserts such as *oeufs à la neige* or *île flottante* (eggs in snow or floating island: egg whites poached in milk and served on *crème anglaise* or thin custard, the whole garnished with caramel), *mousse au chocolat* (chocolate mousse), *sabayon* (zabaglione, a frothy egg cream whisked over a double boiler and flavored with sweet wine such as Muscat), or a fruit tart. For an elaborate dinner, a cake or tart will be bought from a *pâtissier*. Professionally made tarts lined with pastry cream or almond cream and topped with fruits are perennial favorites, but far more elaborate classic confections are widely available in the pastry shops. Small puff pastry balls filled with cream, arranged in a circle, and garnished with flavored whipped cream or custard sauce make a *Saint-Honoré*. A *Paris-Brest*, recognizable from the powdered sugar and almonds that decorate the top, layers puff pastry with almond and hazelnut cream. The family of frothy cakes that includes the *Roussillon* and the *Framboisine* are made from layers of *gelées*, thinly sliced fruit, and nut creams on a light sponge cake, which soaks up the flavors and colors of the spreads. These cakes are finished with a fruit glaze or jelly to give the outside a transparently colorful liquid sheen. To make an *Opéra*, invented in 1954 in Paris in honor of the Palais Garnier opera house, a thin biscuit is soaked in coffee syrup; butter cream and chocolate cream are spread on alternate layers, and the whole is iced with chocolate.

ICE CREAM AND SORBET

Ices and ice creams can be traced to ancient China and were eaten at the court of Alexander the Great and by the Emperor Nero during the first century. During the seventeenth century, ices made their way to France via Italy. French *glace* ("ice," i.e., ice cream) differs from American ice cream, being closer to an Italian gelato. It contains little cream, is not terribly sweet, and is slightly granular in texture. Vanilla and chocolate are favorite flavors, and raspberry, strawberry, hazelnut, and pistachio are common; mango and passion fruit, which is sweet-sour, are summer flavors. In the South, flavors are based on local fruits, herbs, or produce, such as lavender, rosemary, and honey. During the summer, people buy cones at street stands and ice cream shops, and restaurants feature *coupes de glace* and *bombes* on the menu for dessert. A *coupe* is an oversized concoction garnished with fruits, fruit *purée* as sauce, nuts, and a crisp cookie. Served in a large, bowl-shaped glass *coupe* (goblet), it is usually meant to be shared by two people. A *bombe* is ice cream molded into a round shape, then similarly garnished with sauces and fruits. *Sorbets* and *granités* or true ices made without any cream, milk, or eggs are appreciated as light, cooling, and refreshing desserts. In formal settings, a tiny quantity of sorbet is served between courses of a meal, to refresh the palate.

HERBS AND FLOWERS USED AS SWEET FLAVORINGS

Some herb, spice, and flower flavors are primarily associated with sweet dishes. *Vanille* (vanilla) is a staple of bakers, *violette* (violet) flavors candy and black tea, and whole violet flowers candied in sugar garnish cakes and pastries. The use of *eau de fleur d'oranger* (orange flower water) and *eau de rose* (rose water) in pastry-making in the South reflects a Middle Eastern influence that came via Spain with the Moors. Until the mid-twentieth century, the perfume industry centered in Grasse also supplied cooks; today, most blossoms used in perfumes and flavorings are imported from India and Asia. Orange flower is the distinctive flavor in the sweet version of the yeasted pastries called *fougaces*. Mint is used primarily for *tisane* and as a flavor for syrups drunk over ice. Green sweet-sour angelica stems, taken in the past as medicine, are candied by repeated dipping into sugar syrup and then carved into attractive shapes.

COFFEE, TEA, TISANES, AND HOT CHOCOLATE

Nearly everybody drinks *café* (coffee). France is the third largest purchaser of coffee beans in the world, after the United States and Germany. *Café au lait*, hot milk with strong coffee, is drunk at breakfast. Throughout the day and after lunch and dinner, people drink small cups of black coffee, similar to Italian espresso, in demitasse cups. This is simply called *un café* (a coffee) or a *petit noir*. Dark roasted Robusta or Arabica beans are used, and the coffee is brewed with relatively little water. The result is a strong, rich-tasting beverage. Coffee drunk at mid-morning or in the late afternoon is a pick-me-up; sipped after the varied flavors of a meal, coffee refreshes the palette. *Chocolat* or hot chocolate is a popular beverage among children. It is drunk at breakfast from the same kind of bowls that adults use for *café au lait*. Children may also be given bowls of *chicorée* (chicory), which used to be drunk as an inexpensive, domestically produced substitute for coffee. Chicory is a green related to endive; its roasted, ground roots are sold in powders or granules that resemble instant coffee and may be dissolved in hot milk, less frequently hot water. Chicory is naturally nutty and sweet in flavor and lacks the bitterness and caffeine of coffee.

In the past, brewed black and green teas were associated with elegant, light afternoon refreshment. In recent years, tea has gained popularity as a breakfast drink. This is due in part to health concerns. A cup of tea contains far less caffeine than a cup of coffee, and tea may offer other health benefits, as well; connoisseurs appreciate the delicate variety of flavors.

A *tisane* or infusion is a made from a dried flower or herb such as *verveine* (verbena), *guimauve* (mallow), or *menthe* (mint) steeped in hot water. Infusions are taken before bed or as an after-dinner hot drink instead of coffee. They are given to the sick, and the various decoctions are appreciated for their medicinal properties.

WATER

Spring waters are heavily marketed, giving the false impression (shared by many of the French) that tap water is never drunk. In fact, tap water is the most commonly drunk liquid in France[10] and may safely be consumed throughout the country. Some small towns, particularly in the South, still have public fountains that antedate the installation in homes of filtered running water.[11] General preference runs to drinking water that is cool or room temperature, not cold or iced. During meals, a pitcher or carafe of tap water or a bottle of spring water is placed on the table, so that glasses may conveniently be refilled. Liter-sized bottles of water are available at grocery stores and corner stores. Still waters from springs at Evian, Contrex, Volvic, and Vatel are popular. The flavors of spring waters vary according to their mineral content (or the lack thereof) indicated on the bottle label. Waters with high mineral contents are appreciated for their healthful properties, such as calcium for bone health. Fluorine, potassium, and sodium are other common mineral elements in spring waters. Natural or added carbonation is responsible for the bubbles in sparkling mineral waters, such as Badoit and Perrier.

SODA AND SYRUPS

Soda is everywhere available, although it is not consumed on the same scale as in the United States. Coke, Fanta, and other imported beverages are easy to find, along with a few French sodas. The most distinctive is Orangina, easily spotted in its squat, orange-shaped bottle.

More typical than soda are *sirops* (syrups). A small quantity of thick, sweet, heavily concentrated syrup with a distinctive fruit or herbal flavor is mixed with water to make a refreshing drink. Beloved by children and popular with people of all ages during the summer, *une menthe à l'eau*— green mint syrup and water—is cooling in hot weather. *Orgeat* is barley syrup, although sometimes it is based on almonds, despite its name. *Grenadine* (pomegranate) and *cassis* (black currant) are well-loved flavors. Sodas and syrups are not drunk with meals, but as a refreshing beverage for the late afternoon, and they are often ordered in cafés.

BEER AND CIDER

Cervoise (ale) antedates wine in France and can be traced back to the Gauls. Ale is malt, or toasted, germinated barley that has been fermented with yeast and water. By the end of the eighth century, people had begun to add medicinal hop blossoms to ale, making true *bière* (beer). The hops give the characteristic bitter flavor and act as a natural preservative. For centuries, beer was an important source of food calories for northern Europeans. Today, a handful of industrial breweries in Alsace, such as Kronenbourg and Météor, produce most of the French beers, and beer consumption is heaviest in this region and along the Belgian border. In cooking, beer is an ingredient in the beef stew *carbonade* and in some fish stews. A *panaché* is a summer drink made of beer mixed with lemonade. For a bubbly red *Monaco*, a shot of grenadine syrup is added.

Cidre (cider) in France is what Americans call hard cider, the bubbly fermented apple juice that is mildly alcoholic (4.5 percent alcohol by volume). Since the sixteenth century, when new varieties of apples and cultivation techniques were brought from Spain, apples and cider have been typical of Normandy, Brittany, and the Maine. Cider is consumed on a much smaller scale than wine or beer. Most is drunk near where it is made, in the countryside of the Northwest; there it rivals wine in importance.

BRANDIES AND LIQUEURS

Eaux-de-vie (fortified alcohols or distilled liqueurs) are drunk as *apéritifs* and *digestifs* (before- and after-dinner drinks) and have many uses in cooking. They flavor sauces, stewed dishes, and desserts and are flambéed for a dramatic presentation. Liqueurs have been manufactured in France since the distilling process was brought back from the Middle East during the Crusades. Most distilled liqueurs were originally concocted as medicines.

By far the most popular liqueur is anise-flavored *pastis*. Pastis, Pernod and other anise liqueurs became popular in the nineteenth century, when they were marketed as a substitute for *absinthe* (absinthe), also flavored with anise and fennel. *La fée verte* (the green fairy) was so called for the milky green color it assumes when mixed with water, not to mention for its magical transformative powers. Absinthe is quite bitter and has to be sweetened with a cube of sugar. The problem was that it contained wormwood (*Artemesia absinthium*), an ancient tonic that is also potentially toxic. Excessive consumption and bad quality mixtures produced unfortunate effects, and the government banned the sale of absinthe in 1915. Conveniently, *pastis* and other anise mixtures were available. Unlike its lethal ancestor, *pastis* is regarded as having a beneficial effect on health, notably by soothing the stomach and intestines. It is drunk mixed with chilled water. A clear light brown by itself, *pastis* turns a light milky yellow when mixed with water. *Pastis*-and-water is the basis for a handful of simple, popular cocktails. Mixed with mint syrup, the green drink that results is a *perroquet* (parrot). Adding grenadine makes a pink-red *tomate* or "tomato." The addition of barley syrup gives a *Mauresque* or Morisco. In the Midi, *l'heure du pastis*—time for a sociable pastis—is practically any hour of the day: before lunch, in the late afternoon, before dinner.

Most liquors draw their distinctive flavor from an herb, root, or fruit. The bitter flavor of Suze, originally from French-speaking Switzerland, comes from gentian roots that have soaked in eau-de-vie. Suze is drunk over ice and mixed with sparkling water from a tall, narrow, straight-sided glass. Gin is based on rye, barley, and oats, but owes its flavor to a strong infusion of juniper berries. Vermouth is based on grapes, but flavored with herbs and spices; *un Martini* in France is a before-dinner glass of herb-flavored vermouth, not the American mixed drink. Among after-dinner drinks, classic Cognac is the most famous grape brandy. Calvados or apple brandy is beloved in the apple-growing regions of Normandy. A shot of Calvados is sometimes drunk between courses during a meal, to promote digestion and help eaters make their way through a particularly rich repast. The theory goes that the small glass of apple brandy, known in this circumstance as a *trou normand*, opens up a "hole" (*trou*) so that you can eat more. Most of the herbal liqueurs have monastic origins, as the monks concocted them for use as medicines. Bright yellow or green Chartreuse was developed by a Carthusian sect, for instance. Orange-flavored Cointreau and Grand-Marnier were invented in the mid–nineteenth century, however, by commercial distillers. In the countryside, where gardens with fruit trees are common, people still concoct their own brandies by soaking fruits such as pears or plums in a neutrally flavored alcohol; it is a mark of respect and a gesture of friendship to offer a guest a glass of house-made brandy.

NOTES

1. "L'Âme du vin," "Le vin des chiffoniers," "Le vin de l'assassin," "Le vin du solitaire," and "Le vin des amants," *Les Fleurs du mal* (1857), in Charles Baudelaire, *Oeuvres complètes* (Paris: Robert Laffont, 1980), 76–81.

2. Grimod de la Reynière, *Le Manuel des Amphitryons* (Paris: Cappelle et Renand, 1808), 14.

3. Silvano Serventi, *Le Livre du foie gras* (Paris: Flammarion, 2002), 16.

4. Charles Estienne, *L'agriculture et la maison rustique*, French translation by Jean Liébault (Paris: Chez Jaques Du-Puys, 1570).

5. Michel Maincent, *Technologie culinaire*, preface by Pierre Troisgros (Paris: BPI, 1999), 281.

6. Edward H. Schafer, "T'ang," in *Food in Chinese Culture: Anthropological and Historical Perspectives*, editor K. C. Chang (New Haven: Yale University Press, 1977), 131.

7. Jean-Louis Flandrin, "Et le beurre conquit la France," *L'Histoire* 85 (1986): 109, 111.

8. "L'huile d'olive, un 'or jaune,'" *Le Monde* (May 24, 2006).

9. Silvano Serventi and Françoise Sabban, *Pasta,* trans. Antony Shugaar (New York: Columbia University Press, 2002), xiv, 47, 179.

10. Gilbert Garrier, *Histoire sociale et culturelle du vin* (Paris: Larousse-Bordas, 1995; 1998).

11. Didier Nourrisson, *Le Buveur du XIXe siècle* (Paris: Albin Michel, 1990), 18.

3

Cooking

Elements that shape cooking practices include available ingredients, kitchen technologies, and of course the cook. The transition from a largely agricultural way of life to a fully modern urban and suburban one was completed in the last century. From the kitchen garden, home cooks have moved into the small shop and the supermarket, not to mention the oversized *hypermarché*. Efficient stoves and the taste for lighter foods, as well as time pressure and busy schedules have contributed to the rise of fast-cooked foods as rivals to old-style, economical *plats mijotés* (slow-cooked dishes). The roles of professional cooks are diverse. In elite restaurants, executive chefs are astute managers as well as gastronomic high priests and food designers. In fast-food eateries, cooking has become an assembly process where employees carry out simplified, highly rationalized preparations.

SUPERMARKETS

As in other urban consumer societies, the French acquire nearly all provisions in stores, and most food shopping is done at commercial chain *supermarchés* (supermarkets), defined as having 1,000 to 2,500 square meters (about 1,308 to 3,270 square yards) of selling space. This is a recent innovation. At the end of the Second World War, most food shops were specialized and expensive. Price-fixing was common, as conservative shopkeepers sought to shield themselves from competition; before the war, they had fought tooth and nail to curb the growth of cooperative *magasins à succursales* (chain stores).[1] In this atmosphere, a store that stocked a wide variety of competitively priced comestibles was revolutionary if not actually heretical. It was in these circumstances that the first of the modern domestic commercial chains got its start. In 1949, fresh from a decade of schooling in Jesuit seminaries, the young Édouard Leclerc began buying large quantities of groceries directly from factories and producers, then reselling them at a full 25 percent below the shop prices. This practice made a hit among his neighbors in Landerneau (Brittany) as they shopped for dinner. His outraged colleagues, the small shopkeepers, turned belligerent. Leclerc had to write to the federal government to defend himself, and the *Ministère des Finances* (Ministry of Finance) took the opportunity to affirm the illegality of price-fixing. As Leclerc grew his first store and then opened other outlets, he had to do battle with urban department stores such as Monoprix and Prisunic, whose discounts hardly differed from small shop prices. By the 1960s, self-service supermarkets had become prevalent and Leclerc's practices the norm.[2] As in the United States, *supermarchés* stock perishables as well as items designed for long storage such as dried pasta, canned goods, and milk or juice in sealed tretrapacks or bricks that can be stored at room temperature until they are opened. The fancier stores have specialty counters such as for fresh fish, bread, and wine.

Today, some associate the large chains, like fast-food restaurants, with an impersonal, sterile or Americanized way of life. In most towns where an Auchan or other big store opens, small shops close. Nonetheless, ever on the lookout for bargains and a favorable *rapport qualité-prix* (quality-price ratio), the French more than any other European population frequent not just *supermarchés* but also *hypermarchés* or *grande surfaces* (superstores), defined as having selling space greater than 2,500 square meters (about 3,270 square yards), and *discounters* (discount stores). In the interest of maintaining commercial diversity and protecting the small shops, legal limits have been imposed, however, such as the ban on building an *hypermarché* within city limits in Paris.

A recent trend for commercial supermarkets and the food industry is to marry the appeal of fresh items with the convenience of food that is prepared, packaged, and ready to eat. Fresh potatoes that are peeled, cooked, then sealed in plastic can be added directly to a dinner dish as it heats up. Sealed containers of fresh fruit salad kept under refrigeration are meant to be sold and eaten within a few days. A chain of supermarkets that is unique to France sells only *surgelés* (frozen foods). In addition to packages of flash-frozen vegetables or fruits and containers of ice creams and sorbets, these stores sell items such as appetizers that can be quickly prepared by heating in the oven and tart shells to be filled with fruits for dessert or with a savory filling to make a hot lunch.

SPECIALTY SHOPS

Small specialty stores such as the *fromagerie* (cheese shop), *charcuterie* (shop for cured meats, especially hams, sausages, and other pork products), *boulangerie* (bread shop), and *pâtisserie* (pastry shop) recall older shopping traditions. In city neighborhoods, rows of different kinds of food shops cluster together. In villages and small towns, the shops are usually located in the town center. As relatively few households had ovens until the mid-twentieth century, the *boulangerie* has long been an institution even in villages, bread being practically a synonym for life itself. The specialty shops recall that through the eighteenth century, royal statutes and guilds or cor-porations structured the manufacturing and retail sectors of the economy. Guild rules limited what a merchant could sell, but also gave the merchant an effective monopoly in that particular line of business. The old rules are

Sausages, hams, terrines, and pâtés at the *boucher-charcutier* Lavigne in Montceau-les-Mines. Courtesy of Janine Depoil.

no longer in place, but boutiques cultivate the aura as well as the practice of specialization, a strategy opposite that of the generalist supermarket.

For the shopper filling a basket with provisions, the small shops now offer access to products perceived as high quality and of reliable provenance. Most small shops are not self-service. Food items are displayed behind glass or on shelves behind a counter. Interaction between the customer and the shopkeeper is required for the purchase to be transacted. Shopkeepers slice ham to order, recommend cheeses to be eaten the same day or two days later, and bag produce, although fruits and vegetables are displayed in open bins. It is considered rude to walk in to a small specialty food store simply to look around. Those who regularly frequent such stores often refer not to the shop itself, but to the person who runs it. One may make a trip *chez mon poissonnier* ("to my fish seller's"), who, it is understood, may be relied on for his expert knowledge in the matter of fish. Similarly, one refers to the good vegetables *chez mon marchand de légumes* ("at my grocer's"), or praise a bottle discovered through *mon caviste* ("my wine seller"). In affluent areas, specialty shops run by *traiteurs* or caterers, as well as upscale supermarkets, sell prepared dishes that are ready to eat. At this end of the economic spectrum, connoisseurs with the means for leisure spending further extend their shopping circuits to venues formerly frequented largely by food professionals. Private attendance at annual or seasonal food and wine expositions and trade shows increases yearly.[3] The picture is quite different for less affluent areas, especially outside of the densely populated cities and in small towns. Here specialty shops struggle to survive or have disappeared entirely, replaced by supermarkets that sell products more cheaply.

STORE AND SHOP HOURS

Until as recently as the 1980s, shop hours followed those of the business day. By earlier norms, in the bourgeois classes the woman of the house remained at home and could shop and cook, or supervise the shopping and cooking, during the day. As middle- and upper-class women entered the workforce and the professions in larger numbers, this schedule became inconvenient and impractical. Now most supermarkets and small shops keep evening hours, remaining open until 7 or 8 P.M. *Supérettes* (convenience stores with selling space measuring 120 to 400 square meters, or about 157 to 523 square yards) and corner stores may remain open later still, until 11 P.M. or midnight. Pharmacies alternate night shifts against medical emergencies, but other stores do not stay open round the clock. Food shopping is part of the business of the day.

MARKETS

The daily, weekly, or weekend outdoor *marchés* (markets) in cities and towns can be traced through medieval trade and monastic fairs and to the marketplaces established in Gaul by the Romans. During the late nineteenth century, the novelist Émile Zola "scientifically" described the sprawling Parisian market located for centuries at Les Halles. In *Le Ventre de Paris* (*The Belly of Paris*, 1873), the market is the rapacious gullet and grumbling gut of the city, swallowing up the lives of the individuals whose work there keeps the rest of the capital alive. Zola documents in fascinating detail the nocturnal march that country dwellers made to arrive in the city by early morning, driving cattle before them or carrying heavy baskets of provisions to sell; rivalries among merchants who compete for customers; the fresh perfume from the flower stands; the rank stench that pervaded the fish and the meat sections by the day's end in summer—the first modern refrigeration technology was still in its infancy and it was not yet widely available. In the 1960s, the market relocated to Rungis, south of Paris, to expand while easing urban traffic congestion. Today, Rungis is a wholesale market open to professionals and retailers such as restaurant chefs and grocers. An ultra-modern supply chain provisions the market. Truckloads of domestic produce arrive every morning, and imports are flown in daily from Israel, Turkey, Benin, Morocco, China, and other locations.

The heart and soul of food shopping dwell in the smaller retail markets. Ironically, in some instances, the produce, meats, and cheeses for sale at outdoor markets are identical to those in the supermarkets.[4] Yet the notion that markets offer the best local items directly from a farmer or producer is not always wrong. At a good market, a special rich odor hangs in the air. Fruits are at the peak of ripeness. Meats have been hung to develop their flavor and tenderness. Cheeses have been fully aged under proper conditions of temperature and humidity. *La cuisine du marché* (market cooking) implies taking inspiration from seasonal ingredients. French cooking in general and *la cuisine du marché* in particular seek to bring out or improve the inherent features of good ingredients. Beyond access to fresh foods, outdoor marketing offers possibilities for socializing and a picturesque experience. The stroll through the outdoor market is an end in itself, and the market is a place to see and be seen. As much as the opportunity to buy edibles and ingredients, it is these elements of market culture that draw crowds.

COOKING AT HOME

Cooking at home, like housework and childcare, was long the province of women. The education of women including higher education, the entry of women into the professions, and contemporary notions of gender equality have brought men, as well, into the home kitchen as cooks and nurturers for their families and households. Particularly in younger couples, the tasks—or pleasures—of cooking and food shopping are likely to be shared; however, nostalgia centered around food and *cuisine de ménage* or *cuisine familiale* (home cooking) tends to have an association with women. When people reminisce, they recall "my mother's" version of a dish as the very best. The phrase *la cuisine grand-mère* (grandmother's cooking) describes dishes that are thought to be old-fashioned and soul-satisfying, familiar, and comforting, such as the simple home dessert *compote de pommes*.

Stewed Apples (Compote de pommes)
- 6 large apples, preferably a firm cooking variety such as Granny Smith
- 2 tablespoons freshly squeezed lemon juice
- 1/2 cup water
- 2 cups water, apple cider, hard apple cider, or white wine
- 1/2 to 3/4 cup sugar
- pinch salt
- 1 2-inch piece of a vanilla bean or 1 teaspoon vanilla extract
- 2 2-inch cinnamon sticks
- 2 whole cloves
- nutmeg

Mix the lemon juice and 1/2 cup water in a bowl. Peel, core, and quarter the apples, dipping each section briefly into the lemon mixture to prevent discoloring.

In a saucepan, combine 2 cups water (or cider or wine), sugar, salt, vanilla bean (if using), cinnamon sticks, and cloves. Bring the syrup to the boil, then reduce the heat and simmer slowly for 10 minutes. Add the apples, cover the pot, and gently simmer for about 5 minutes, until the apples are cooked but still intact. You may need to baste and turn the apples once or twice to make sure they are coated with syrup.

Take the pot off the heat. If no vanilla bean was used, add vanilla extract. Allow the apples to cool in their syrup.

Grate a dash of nutmeg over each serving. If desired, serve the apples with cream or a scoop of ice cream.

Regardless of professional accomplishments that women realize outside the home, participation in the family meal still often relies on the performance of roles that remain defined by gender. In addition to preparing meals, female family members are likely to stack up used plates and carry them away from the table, bring in fresh plates for the next course, and carry in food from the kitchen. Men uncork wine bottles, refill water and wine glasses, and carve roasts.

Until quite recently, recipes were transmitted within families primarily as cooking techniques. A written recipe often consisted of only a few words jotted on a scrap of paper or in a family book as an *aide-mémoire* (prod to the memory). A family's entire kitchen library consisted of one or two basic printed cookbooks, used primarily as references for proportions or methods. The continuity and sense of tradition that marked these practices corresponded to repetition, coming from the kitchen. Today, despite the prevalence of eating out, cooking remains a central feature of home life. Basic kitchen equipment and a dining table with chairs are among the very first items that a young person or couple setting up house will buy. Home cooking today, however, is more varied and experimental. The repetitions imposed by time, tradition, budget, personal taste, and technical competence are balanced by any number of outside influences, from televised cooking shows to the wide variety of domestic and imported foods in stores.

FAST COOKING AND SHORTCUTS

In home kitchens, the economical, slow-simmered soups or stews of past centuries have largely been replaced by quick dishes. Cooking technology, affluence, and time pressures factor into this trend. Searing or sautéing, baking for items that do not require long exposure to heat, steaming (for vegetables), and pressure cooking are the preferred methods. Supermarkets sell items suited to the fast cooking methods, such as fish in fillets, meats in fillets and chops, and produce that can be eaten raw in salads. Ready-made, prepared, and semi-prepared elements further facilitate the task of cooking and serving meals at home. Bread is almost never made at home, although it is a part of nearly every meal. Breakfast pastries such as *brioche* and *croissant* are purchased from the *boulanger* or *pâtissier*. For a holiday or birthday celebration, a cake may be bought from a *pâtissier*. Other staples of the kitchen and table purchased ready-made include jams, yogurt, cheese, *charcuterie,* and the mustard that is ubiquitous in *vinaigrette* dressing for salads and as a condiment for meats. Home cooks take advantage of fresh preparations from specialty shops, such as a butcher's mixture of fresh, loose raw sausage meat or ground pork with spices or herbs. At home, one simply spoons the flavored meat into hollowed-out tomatoes or zucchini, then gives the stuffed vegetables a quick turn on the stove in an inch of liquid or pops them into the oven. Minimal fuss yields a fresh, home-cooked main dish. Similarly, simple preparation but lively flavor describe this typical recipe for baked fish with a tomato sauce, an easy *plat* (main course) for a summer lunch or dinner.

Baked Cod with Tomatoes (Cabillaud à la portugaise)

- 2 pounds fresh cod fillets
- salt
- pepper
- 1/3 cup olive oil
- 1/3 cup chopped onion
- 4 medium tomatoes
- 3 cloves garlic, crushed
- 1/2 cup dry white wine
- 1/2 teaspoon sugar
- 6 sprigs parsley, chopped

Preheat the oven to 350° F.

Coat the fish thoroughly with 3 tablespoons of the olive oil, then sprinkle on both sides with salt and pepper, and lay out flat in a baking dish.

Drop the tomatoes in boiling water for 20 seconds to facilitate peeling, then peel, seed, and dice them.

Stir the onion, tomato, garlic, and remaining olive oil together in a saucepan over medium heat for about 5 minutes, until the onion and tomato soften and the sauce thickens. Pour in the wine, add the sugar, then taste and season with salt and pepper.

Pour the tomato sauce over the fish. Bake 25 minutes. Before serving, sprinkle the whole fish or each serving with chopped parsley.

TOOLS IN THE HOME KITCHEN

The efficient, rationalized kitchen that is typical became so only during the last half-century. As in any western kitchen, the central features are running water, which became standard in France in the 1950s, and a modern stove. The stove has evolved in a particularly dramatic fashion. In rustic dwellings having no separate room for cooking, one cooked over a brazier or else in pots suspended above an open fire that vented through the roof. Situating the fire on a hearth against an exterior wall and venting through a chimney imposed a sense of containment. By the seventeenth century, fires in chimneys in the great houses conveniently supported spit roasting, and brick- or tile-covered *fourneaux* ("furnaces") slow simmering and stewing in pots on the stovetop. By the end of the eighteenth century, cast iron and other metal stoves became available. In addition to the top range, metal stoves came to include multiple ovens with individual access doors. This modification facilitated baking and the simultaneous preparation of multiple dishes. The 1850s saw the invention of the gas stove, which became widely available in the 1930s. The gas stove avoided the burden of stocking wood or charcoal, allowed easy control over the cooking flame, and released fewer particulate pollutants. Electric stoves with burner disks or coils that come to temperature became common in the 1960s. Today, both gas and variations on the electrical stove—efficient for slow cooking—are prevalent in home kitchens. The *four* (oven), often separate from the stovetop, is usually electric. Recent innovations such as smooth ceramic stovetops and *plaques à induction* (magnetic induction cooktops) that do not retain heat when no cooking is in process double as countertops. The multipurpose surfaces are appreciated in city apartments, where space comes at a premium. Their engineering and design reflect contemporary interest in safety, aesthetics, and energy conservation, as well as in cooking as such. Accomplished amateur cooks prize restaurant-grade appliances such as oversize gas stoves that throw powerful flames.

Today, even a simple or modest kitchen has connections for the full range of *appareils électroménagers* (appliances) now considered basic and essential. A *réfrigérateur* or *frigo* (refrigerator) has been standard since the late 1960s, although wealthy families purchased *Frigidaires*, made by General Motors, as early as the late 1920s. *Congélateurs* (freezers) are less common; suburban dwellers with spacious houses may have a larger refrigerator with a substantial freezer section and keep a separate deep freezer in a basement or garage. Dishwashers and range vents above the stove are prevalent. *Fours à micro-ondes* (microwaves), an offshoot of radar technology developed in the United States during the Second World War, have been popular since the 1970s. Beyond the major appliances, common gadgets in home kitchens include coffee makers, food processors, beaters, hand-held plunge *mixeurs* (blenders) that convert vegetables into soup, and, recently, self-contained electrical steamers for vegetables.

Ustensiles or *petits outils* (utensils), *la batterie de cuisine* (pots and pans), and *la vaisselle* (dishes) complete the equipment in the home kitchen.

Despite the capacities of electrical food processors, a variety of *couteaux* (knives), a *couteau économe* (peeler), and surfaces for chopping, cutting, and paring are essentials. Many people use the *mandoline*, a firmly anchored, angled surface holding multiple blades, over which one slides vegetables, fruits, or cheese that must be scored, julienned, sliced, or grated. In the South, some cooks insist that the only way to make good *pistou* (pesto for stirring into vegetable soup) is by hand using a *mortier et pilon* (mortar and pestle). The whirling blades of a food processor or blender produce an unattractive mixture that is too uniform in texture. By contrast, crushing together garlic cloves and salt, basil leaves and olive oil, gives the desired consistency and subtly blends the strong perfumes. For centuries wooden and metal spoons have served to stir, mix, toss, and beat ingredients in mixing bowls or in pots or pans. Newer utensils made of hard plastic and, recently, silicone supplement the wooden spoons. With its extraordinary flexibility, durability, heat resistance, and impermeability to stains and odors, silicone is becoming ubiquitous in the kitchen for flexible kneading and baking surfaces, cake molds, and trivets, in addition to utensils. A *fouet* (whisk), *spatule* (spatula), *raclette* (scraper), *passoire* (colander), and *râpe* (grater) complete the basic kitchen tool kit.

Home cooks use porcelain and stoneware dishes to bake *gratins, tartes,* and other preparations destined for the oven. Sturdy enameled cast iron pots for simmering soups and stews over a steady heat and for baking in the oven are appreciated. These implements are designed to last for decades, although it is often weekend cooks and connoisseurs who take the time to use them. *Poêles* and *sauteuses* (pots and pans) are used for boiling, poaching, frying, sautéing, braising, and searing. Early experiments with pressure cooking date to the seventeenth century. However, the *marmite à pression* or *autocuiseur* (pressure cooker) became popular only after the Second World War, when the *Cocotte-Minute* was marketed for fast cooking and energy efficiency. The *cocotte* is still appreciated for these qualities, and it is a feature of many kitchens.

Since the importation of porcelain from China and the efforts of Louis XIV to promote luxury industries, including commissioning the Sèvres manufacture, France has been known for elegant china. Equally typical rustic glazed terra cotta is found in the South; the various regions are known for their local styles, such as decorative Quimper ware from Brittany. Sets of plates usually include the typical hemispherical breakfast bowls for *café au lait* in addition to flat dinner plates, smaller plates for *amuse-bouches* (appetizers), dessert plates, shallow soup plates with a wide diameter and deep flat rim, and after-dinner coffee cups. In sets of silverware or stainless steel flatware, forks are designed to be attractive from the back, as the tines of the fork face down on a set table.

PROFESSIONAL COOKS

Professional or career chefs, whether *chefs de cuisine* (executive chefs) or *cuisiniers* (line cooks), have with few exceptions been men. Paid cooks have long toiled in the worst of conditions, winning little recognition and minimal remuneration for long hours in dangerously hot, smoky kitchens. The grand cooking that evolved in aristocratic houses and that under-pins elite cooking in today's fine restaurants was carried out by individu-als regarded as little more than servants. Boys and young men learned the cooking trade through apprenticeship, and one had to work one's way up from the very bottom. The lowliest apprentice scoured pots and washed dishes before being promoted to chopping vegetables, preparing sauces, and cooking. Few chefs achieved independence or autonomy with the rise of the restaurant in the eighteenth century. Restaurants and job opportunities multiplied during the nineteenth century, but most cooks worked under a *maître d'hôtel* who managed the establishment or else they reported to the *propriétaire* or *restaurateur* (owner) himself.

Nonetheless, nineteenth-century chefs made significant efforts to im-prove their working lives. In the 1840s, cooks united to form mutual aid societies. The first cooking school was established in 1881. By the century's end, the new institutions were issuing diplomas for students finishing their three-year programs, thus professionalizing the work of cooking. The cooking schools initially struggled, and restaurateurs op-posed them. For restaurant owners, it was cheaper to exploit the old sys-tem of apprenticeship than to hire relatively demanding cooking school graduates. Despite many obstacles, the culinary profession began to come into its own. Trade and professional journals emerged that were written by and for the chefs. Cooking exhibitions and competitions that showed off cooks' talents multiplied. Today, chefs train both in cooking schools and through modern apprenticeships. The *BEP* or *Brevet d'études pro-fessionelles* and the *CAP* or *Certificat d'aptitude professionelle* for cooking are the vocational diplomas for two-year programs taken at the end of high school. They replace the *baccalauréat* (high school diploma) earned at the end of (in American terms) thirteenth grade. A *BTS* or *Brevet de technicien supérieur* is a more advanced two- or three-year technical course, for instance in foodservice, that follows the *baccalauréat*. Opinion is divided as to whether a lengthy apprenticeship and a series of *stages* (shorter periods of training) under reputable chefs in good restaurants or a diploma from a respected hotel or culinary school offers the better entrée to a career.

Inherent difficulties in the profession have not changed much over the centuries. Being a cook requires long hours of manual labor, with few days off each year. The media favor a glamorous vision of the elite culinary world. To work as a chef is punishing, however, and it is difficult to fill jobs for cooks in casual restaurants and other everyday commercial contexts. One expert calculates a deficit of cooks in the tens of thousands.[5] Cooking and hotel schools, along with their students and graduates, have a relatively low status within the *Éducation nationale* (national education system), which privileges the liberal professions and professional courses. Because cooking school curricula are practical, graduates and most chefs are qualified as service workers and earn an hourly wage or contract fees. By contrast, professionals or *salariés* such as teachers and office workers earn a yearly salary and benefits.[6] A talented baker or other food producer who wins one of the widely recognized competitions is named *Meilleur Ouvrier de France* (Best Worker in France) in his category, such as *pâtissier* or *boulanger*. The award is quite prestigious. Winners proudly post it in their shop windows. Yet despite the respect for craft and appreciation for quality, the term *ouvrier* reminds the winner that he is a laborer as well as an artisan. It is significant that at present, many bistros and restaurants serving traditional, local, or regional foods are operated by immigrant families, who assume the rigors of restaurant work as a way to establish themselves within the country. Most restaurant cooks do not own the establishments in which they work,[7] and most paid cooks do not work in commercial restaurants at all. Rather, the majority find employment in school, prison, business, and hospital cafeterias, in military mess halls, and in retirement homes.[8] There is a perception that the opportunity for creative cooking is limited in these contexts, where the use of semi-prepared products often moves the food toward an industrial model. At the same time, relative to typical commercial restaurant work, such situations bring higher salaries, a more predictable workload, more reasonable hours, and the use of relatively modern kitchens.

STAR CHEFS

In the last few decades, some chefs have redefined their roles within commercial restaurants and a few achieved spectacular public success. After the Second World War, a handful of enterprising chefs took the step of buying their own *restaurants gastronomiques* (high-end restaurants). In addition to cooking, they now managed and became principal financial stakeholders. In 1951, a group of owner-manager chefs formed the *Association des Maîtres*

Chef Michel Troisgros (second from left) of the three-star restaurant Troisgros in Roanne at work with his staff. Courtesy of Christian Verdet/regard public-unpact.

cuisiniers de France. The *Association* aimed to promote high-quality restaurants and the autonomous *chef de cuisine*. In 1953, the first televised cooking show brought elegant cuisine and an accomplished, independent chef as star performer, into homes across the country.

Today, the roles played by a select group of elite chefs extend far beyond activity in a single restaurant kitchen to affect a much wider market. Since the 1970s, Michelin-starred chefs such as Joël Robuchon, Michel Troisgros, Michel Guérard, Alain Senderens, and Paul Bocuse have cultivated ties with the *industrie agroalimentaire* (agricultural-alimentary industry). Acting as a consultant and advisor, the chef assists a company to improve quality in mass-produced items, such as packaged meals for airlines or for retail in commercial supermarket chains. To this *cuisine sous contrat* (cooking on contract), the chef may also lend the cachet of his name for marketing. In return, the company underwrites the chef's restaurant, for the finest of the fine restaurants are so expensive to run that they are rarely profitable. Companies in the agro-alimentary industry and chefs themselves further cultivate links to private and government-supported research laboratories such as *INRA*, the *Institut National de la Recherche Agronomique* (National Institute for Agronomic Research). For chefs, contracts with agro-alimentary companies may be coercive or beneficial. In either case, the purview of the star chef extends beyond the restaurant kitchen and dining room to overlapping spheres of industry, finance, and government.

WOMEN CHEFS

There have been a few notable exceptions to the gender divide in professional cooking. Until as recently as the mid-twentieth century, many middle class and smaller bourgeois households employed a *cuisinière* (female cook) who worked under the direct supervision of the mistress of the house. There is also the small group of remarkable chef-proprietors known since the end of the eighteenth century as *mères* (mothers). The history of the *cuisinières* has yet to be elaborated beyond anecdote. A few of the *mères*, however, became quite well known, in part because of their influence on successful male chefs. The *mères* are associated especially with the Lyon area. Some of their restaurants began as tiny establishments that served home-style dishes to feed the *canuts* (silk-workers) who populated the city. The *mères* came to prominence starting at the end of the nineteenth century and, helped by restaurant reviewers and food writers, early in the twentieth. In contrast with the elaborate preparations and expensive exotic ingredients used in elite restaurants, their cooking relied essentially on local

Chef Monique Salera cooking in her restaurant La Dame d'Aquitaine in Dijon. Courtesy of Philippe Bornier.

ingredients and relatively simple methods. Dishes associated with their restaurants include roasted chicken, chicken poached with morels or truffles,
omelets, eel stew, savory onion tarts, pike *quenelles* (poached fine-textured
fish dumplings) with crayfish sauce, *tablier de sapeur* (tripe that is marinated,
coated with breadcrumbs, fried, then served with fresh chervil sauce), and
cervelle de canuts ("silk-weavers brains"—fresh cheese seasoned with chives,
garlic, horseradish, along with salt, pepper, and red wine vinegar). These
chefs were as often as not simply called *La Mère ...* (Mother So-and-So) by
their clients and, eventually, in the press, rather than by their first and last
names. Several won and many kept for years one or more Michelin stars,
the most widely recognized indicator of quality for a restaurant.

Today, a few talented female chefs in prominent restaurants challenge
the strong masculine association to good restaurant food, not to mention
grande cuisine or *haute cuisine*. Their success flies in the face of traditions of
food writing, restaurant reviewing, and professional cooking culture that
have been actively hostile to seeing women work in professional kitchens. Gastronomy—the knowledgeable appreciation of food—has tended
to view women, along with food items, as consumables, rather than as
capable connoisseurs. The exclusive *Club des Cent* (Hundred Club),
founded in 1912 as a private automobile club whose members sought
out restaurants for touring destinations, is to this day open only to men.
Hostility to the entry of women into the world of professional cooks has
long emanated from the ranks of male cooks who feared competition. A
congress of (male) cooks from throughout France and Algeria that met
in Paris in 1893 declared its opposition to the entry of women as apprentices in the great restaurant and hotel kitchens. The group did support
teaching women from the popular classes the art of home cooking as part
of a more general *enseignement ménager* (course in domestic economy).[9]
In this era a mandate recommended cooking instruction in the public
schools, but this also aimed to train women for their roles as mothers
and nurturers within the family. In the twentieth century, the great chef,
bon-vivant, and early promoter of *nouvelle cuisine* Paul Bocuse is said to
have scoffed at the capacity of female cooks for refined, innovative, or
grand cuisine.[10] Today, cooking school students and apprentices working
in restaurants note the macho culture and inhospitable climate prevalent
in many professional kitchens.[11]

PROFESSIONAL COOKING

Venues for professional cooking vary from local bistros and cafés
to the grand *restaurants gastronomiques*; styles of restaurant cooking

range from traditional and regional to the *cuisines exotiques* ("exotic" cuisines) borrowed from around the world. The workspace may be a tiny room that differs little from a home kitchen, a cavernous chamber appointed with industrial strength appliances and staffed by a numerous *brigade* (contingent of kitchen staff) in a large hotel, or something in between.

Influential transformations occurred in high-end restaurant cooking during the middle and late twentieth century. The style of cooking that underpins today's school curricula and that takes place in fine-dining restaurants emerged from the aristocratic traditions of the great houses and from court cuisine as well as from their continuations by private cooks in bourgeois houses of the eighteenth, nineteenth, and early twentieth centuries. The peak of success for grand cooking came at the turn of the twentieth century and is best reflected in the *Guide culinaire* (1903) of Auguste Escoffier. Escoffier's volume is a grammar of *cuisine classique* (classical cooking). He defines its basic elements and rules for combining them, codifying, and rationalizing grand cooking into a clear system. A given cut of meat, for instance, may be cooked in different ways, served with a variety of sauces, and accompanied by a selection of fillings or garnishes that lend flavor. Each combination pulled from the matrix is a specific dish with its own name, yet clearly related to other dishes with which it may be paired or contrasted to compose a full meal. The menus available on a daily basis in wealthy houses and in grand restaurants were for banquets. A proper meal in the grand style consisted of *potage* or soup, a hot appetizer or *hors-d'oeuvre* followed by a *relevé* that was seasoned to provide flavor contrast; a variety of *entrées* or first courses; a roast; a salad; an *entremets* ("between dishes," i.e., between roast and cheese) that often consisted of *foie gras*; cheese; an ice (sometimes served as an *entremets*); dessert; and coffee. Rules for menu composition imposed balance and variety. Cold and hot dishes must alternate. Repetition must be avoided from garnish to vegetable to side dish. Fish and meat must not be combined in the same dish: they belonged in separate courses. Sweet, soft dishes such as a creamy dessert must be accompanied by a dry biscuit for contrast. Dishes often featured touches such as layers of stuffings and decorative pastry shells. These elements were assembled before the cooking, and they added interest to the final presentation. Until as late as the 1970s, dishes were served *en salle* (in the dining room). Staff performed numerous tasks, in some cases to finish the cooking. The *découpage* (carving) was carried out in the dining room, desserts such as *crêpes Suzette* were flambéed tableside, and waiters served from full-sized platters that they carried around the table.

As chefs asserted their autonomy, transformations traceable to about mid-century pushed food and service in the direction of contemporary practice. Ultimately the meal was simplified to today's standard of three courses: *entrée* (first course), *plat*, and dessert. Unconventional combinations appeared. Chefs brought together items formerly separated into different courses and began to use ingredients formerly excluded from elegant cooking. Chicken and shrimp *brochettes* (grilled on skewers) were an innovation, as was green salad topped with slices of *foie gras*, *magret de canard* (breast of duck), or *gésier* (gizzard) *confit*. *Foie gras* moved from the end of the meal to the start as a first course or *entrée*. Chefs rejected as heavy and antiquated the overuse of preparations such as the *roux* (flour cooked in butter, to which liquid is added), a thickening liaison used as a sauce base. They now preferred fruit and vegetable purées and reductions, and they sought to make food taste as fresh as possible. As chefs traveled abroad and as immigrants from the former colonies introduced new foods and ingredients, "exotics" from kiwis to couscous further inflected French cooking. Beginning in the 1950s, chefs initiated a kind of control and direct contact with individual diners by plating food in the kitchen. Service was now *à l'assiette* (by individual plate); the grand serving platters disappeared. In 1973, the food critics and guidebook authors Henri Gault and Christian Millau called the new style *nouvelle cuisine* (new cuisine) and became its outspoken champions. Today, elements of *nouvelle cuisine* such as the emphasis on fresh ingredients and clear flavors are part of the culinary lexicon of nearly every discerning chef.

A fish preparation from the Troisgros kitchen shows the influence of *nouvelle cuisine*. Courtesy of Christian Verdet/regard public-unpact.

Post-modern food from the Troisgros kitchen:
pasta with a mushroom, truffle, and cream sauce
deconstructed into its component parts. Courtesy of Christian Verdet/regard public-unpact.

Several distinct trends are at work in contemporary restaurant cooking.
Varieties of *cuisine du terroir* focus on native ingredients and dishes. These
menus may be authentic, nostalgic, or deliberately conservative. In some
cases, they attach to a political ideology that seeks to resist or attenuate
outside influences and to affirm a local or regional identity. In the 1990s,
a group of chefs published a manifesto protesting the encroachment of
globalizing influences and praising all things native and local. *Cuisine de
tradition*, a kind of comfort food, offers familiar, even homely dishes to eaters whose nostalgia for home cooking finds no answer in a fast-paced lifestyle or perhaps in living alone. Relatively simple establishments serving
well-prepared, everyday fare provide a steady continuo beneath the elaborate melodies of fashion and fad. Outspoken fusion cuisine, characterized
by bold, striking mixtures of foreign and local ingredients and methods,
occupies a relatively small space in France. Within the last five years, a
nouvelle vague (new wave) of young cooks with outstanding credentials
from apprenticeships in top kitchens has moved beyond the domain of
Michelin-starred restaurants, with their old hierarchies and structures, as
a matter of principle. Instead, the proponents of *la jeune cuisine* (young
cuisine) take a personal, quirky approach to highly refined cooking that
is also creative, even ludic. For convenience, economy, or to compensate
for insufficient staff, casual restaurant kitchens exploit industrial innovations: pre-prepared vegetables, dehydrated *fonds de sauce* (sauce bases),
precooked items. Chefs in a variety of contexts adopt new materials and
industrial techniques, such as cooking *sous vide* ("in a vacuum"). A piece
of food enclosed in a sealed bag or container is cooked at a relatively low

temperature, with little added liquid, and according to precise timing. In principle, the results are predictable, standards of quality can be guaranteed, and the chef is spared worry.

COOKING AND THE MEDIA

French food has long been known for its special *éclat* (sparkle and glamour). Since the seventeenth century it has enjoyed tremendous prestige. Today, the prevalent associations are quality, variety, and coherence, along with conviviality, ritual, and shared enjoyment. Through the eighteenth century, fashion in food emanated from grand houses and the royal court. Since the early nineteenth century, the reputation and prominence of French cuisine within the country and beyond is due not only to the excellence and variety of the food but also to the elaboration of discourses about that food.[12] To be sure, paeans to the pleasures of the table are ancient. Since antiquity, histories, agricultural and medical treatises, and poems have treated aspects of food culture as a primary subject or ancillary topic, leitmotif, or obsessive theme. More recently, such works as domestic tracts and novels have done the same. The first decade of the nineteenth century, however, saw important innovations in food writing, notably the first modern-style narrative food guide and food periodical. As political and social structures evolved (highlighted by the Revolution of 1789), restaurants multiplied, and a new food publishing industry gained impressive momentum. Contained within the yearly publication entitled the *Almanach des Gourmands* (*Gourmands' Almanac*, 1803–1812), the first narrative food guide judged Parisian restaurants for quality, as well as giving their addresses. The guide author, Grimod de la Reynière, reported on restaurants and food items ostensibly as he experienced them. His judgments also affected the subsequent activities of chefs and caterers concerned to receive favorable reviews. Here, the activities of producers (cooks, food sellers) and consumers (eaters, readers, writers) exerted a mutual influence. Each reinforced the importance, legitimacy, and stakes for the other. Durable print extended the life and reach of ephemeral edibles.

Over two centuries, the players in the various culinary and gastronomic spheres have multiplied, and the scope of their activities has increased. As in the United States, chefs and food producers interact intensively with writers, publicists, and consumers. This back-and-forth democratizes food cultures and also serves to legislate and regulate standards of taste and quality. Geography or budget may prevent one from visiting an outstanding restaurant in a neighboring province. But other pleasure, interest, and knowledge derive from reading a newspaper review of the restaurant, watching a televised interview with the chef, purchasing the chef's cook-book, and perhaps making some of his recipes at home.

As in the United States, the media extension of food in France is now vast. It includes food shows on television, food-related Web sites and databases, and periodicals devoted to food and cooking. An ever-larger number of cookbooks are available in bookstores. There is a marked increase in the recent publication of cookbooks for "exotic" cuisines (of Thailand, Morocco, or Japan) or focusing on clearly foreign foodstuffs (from Anglo muffins or scones to Chinese wok dishes). The mediatization of cuisine encourages participation, teaching viewers and readers how to cook and about food, and stimulates the imagination, providing a space for fantasy in which the dining table is a vanishing point in the far dis-tance. The phenomenon indexes the social prestige of food connoisseur-ship in an affluent society.

The interactions of food producers and consumers further shape and regulate—prescribe and proscribe—standards of quality and concepts of good taste. From day to day, it is the home cooks and restaurant chefs who serve up continuity and creativity on the plate. Yet the response of writers and critics influences cooks, too. A newspaper column influences home cooks seeking ideas for dinner. A strong review sends customers flocking in droves to a restaurant. A critical piece banishes the chef to culinary and economic purgatory. The power of critics is so strong that a few chefs at the most elevated end of the cooking spectrum have rebelled. Some have stated their lack of interest in the distinction of a Michelin star and chosen to prepare food that expresses a personal preference or philosophy. They refuse, in other words, to conform. These chefs have taken them-selves out of the running for prestigious honors, in order to cook by their own lights. They ignore as interference the mediating roles of critic and reporter to please themselves and their clients directly.

NOTES

1. Gilles Normand, *Histoire des maisons à succursales en France* (Paris: Union des entreprises modernes, 1936).

2. John Ardagh, *France in the 1980s* (New York: Penguin, 1983; 1982), 396–405.

3. Marion Demossier, "Consuming Wine in France: The 'Wandering' Drinker and the *Vin-anomie*," in *Drinking Cultures: Alcohol and Identity*, editor Thomas M. Wilson (Oxford: Berg, 2005), 139.

4. Michèle de la Pradelle, *Market Day in Provence*, trans. Amy Jacobs (Chicago: The University of Chicago Press, 2006).

5. Alain Drouard, *Histoire des cuisiniers en France XIXe-XXe siècle* (Paris: CNRS, 2004), 133.

6. Drouard, 131 and *passim* in Julia Csergo and Christophe Marion, eds., *Histoire de l'alimentation: Quels enjeux pour la formation?* (Dijon: Educagri, 2004).

7. Drouard, 20.

8. Sylvie-Anne Mériot, *Nostalgic Cooks: Another French Paradox,* trans. Trevor Cox and Chanelle Paul (Boston: Brill, 2006).

9. Drouard, 54.

10. La Reynière [Robert Courtine], "Ces dames au 'piano,'" *Le Monde* (May 21, 1977).

11. Patrick Rambourg, "Guerre des sexes au fourneau!," *L'Histoire* 273 (February 2003): 25–26.

12. Priscilla Parkhurst Ferguson, "A Cultural Field in the Making: Gastronomy in 19th-Century France," *American Journal of Sociology* 104, no. 3 (November 1998): 597–641 and *Accounting for Taste: The Triumph of French Cuisine* (Chicago: The University of Chicago Press, 2004).

4

Typical Meals

Three meals each day is typical in France. The *petit déjeuner* (break-fast), taken in the morning before school or work, is insubstantial. At noon, the *déjeuner* (lunch), long the main meal for many people, may still be substantial and served in three courses (*entrée, plat,* and *fromage* or *dessert*) or may consist of a sandwich eaten on the run. The *dîner,* at about 8 P.M., is now an important meal. Because both men and women work outside the home, dinner is often the only weekday meal for which the whole family can gather together at table. The evening meal is looked forward to as a respite from the day's work, as a time to see family members, and as an opportunity to enjoy the sensual pleasures of food and drink. The structure of the French meal, with its unfolding sequence of courses, is especially conducive to relaxed enjoyment at table. As the service of dishes progresses, the familiar structure frames conversation and reinforces the separation of mealtime from the hustle and bustle of the day.

MEAL TIMES

Today's standard three meals evolved over centuries. Through the late nineteenth century, eating schedules varied greatly according to profession, region, and income. Seasonal changes and religious observance also played a role. From one to four meals daily was common, although for different groups of people.[1] Elites might eat twice daily, for example, and manual laborers up to four times each day, but this was not consistent. The names used today for the three meals recall how practices have changed over time.[2] As recently as the late eighteenth century, the first meal, then called the *déjeuner* ("to break the fast"), usually consisted of soup, most likely made of vegetables and grains, and bread; this meal could also include meat and wine, if they were available. For those in modest circumstances, the *déjeuner* might be practically the only nourishment throughout the day. A smaller meal (*le souper*), again soup or light stew, might be added in the early evening. For agricultural workers who stayed in the fields all day long and for those who worked far from home, supper was the most substantial meal. Today, the population of villagers and rural dwellers is small, but in the countryside the word *souper* is still used to mean the evening meal. For those who ate all four meals, there was the *déjeuner*, the mid-day *dîner* (or *collation*), the light *goûter* or snack, and then finally the *souper*.

As industrial jobs increased in number and urban populations became larger, the morning *déjeuner* and mid-day *dîner* each migrated later in the day. The professional classes preferred to eat a large *déjeuner* at noon or one o'clock, that is, after accomplishing the morning's work. By the early nineteenth century, the mid-day meal was sometimes called a *déjeuner à la fourchette* (fork luncheon). The name suggests that the presence for a *déjeuner* of items other than liquid soup, wine, or coffee was still somewhat remarkable. The *déjeuner à la fourchette*, which included meat and required the use of a fork and knife, was often a working meal in the sense of today's business lunches. Because the first substantial meal was now relatively late, a second, smaller *déjeuner* was added to tide over appetites until mid-day. By the 1890s, this early meal was called *le petit* (small) *déjeuner*. Despite the importance of the mid-day meal, the custom of privileging the evening *dîner* gained in the nineteenth century, as larger numbers of people cultivated the leisurely enjoyment of carefully prepared, possibly quite elaborate and luxurious meals in a sociable setting.

After the Second World War, technological modernization and the massive exodus from villages and rural areas to cities transformed society. The demographic and industrial shift resulted in the shared work schedule that now prevails. Affluence also made significant social reforms possible, including the month of paid vacation given to salaried workers since 1965 (converted to five weeks in 1981) and the 35-hour workweek instituted in the late 1990s. Today, the sense of leisure, material comfort, and convivial enjoyment that accompanies the working-class, middle-class and modern bourgeois family dinner makes an equally important contribution to quality of life. School and most work schedules are designed to allow breaks for meals. Some shops and offices close at mid-day, to reopen in the afternoon at 1:30 or 2:00 P.M.; others do not keep late evening hours, so that staff have evenings free. Because most people throughout the country take meals at about the same time, there is a strong shared feeling of the rhythm of the day. As a culture, the French place a high value on sociability and community. Eating is considered a convivial activity *par excellence*. Many think that to eat "all alone" (*manger tout seul*) is sad, that food tastes better when it is shared. The community aspect of meals strengthens social ties and even the sense of equality, making the meal an expression of shared values.

As in many countries, the family meal is at times a locus of tension. Factors such as the fast pace of modern life, larger numbers of people living alone, and the replacement or disappearance of the nuclear family as the defining social unit, make the family meal seem for some irrelevant, outmoded, or simply impossible to achieve. Especially in the younger generation, freedom from the ritual of the family meal may be experienced as an opportunity to develop a more individual lifestyle, although others worry about a decline of traditional ways and deterioration of the social fabric. Nonetheless, the family meal or a full meal with friends or colleagues is a central feature of daily life.

STRUCTURE OF A MAIN MEAL

The dishes that make up a main meal appear in a succession of separate courses. An *entrée* or first course might consist of soup, a plate of *crudités* (raw vegetables) served with a *vinaigrette* dressing, or a cooked salad. This is followed by a *plat principal* or main dish. A main dish usually contains meat, poultry, or fish; it may consist of eggs, such as an omelet. Afterward comes a green tossed salad and a cheese course, with perhaps a fruit or sweet to finish. Bread is placed on the table throughout the meal, and people take a slice or break off a piece of a loaf as desired. Although the practice is frowned on in polite (such as bourgeois) circles, small pieces of bread are used to sop up sauces and salad dressings. This is a convenient way to clean the plate between courses if the plates are not changed, as well as to enjoy every last drop of the sauce. Portions are small, so the appetite is not overwhelmed by the succession of different edibles.

The French palate prefers rich and deep flavors over sharp or spicy ones, and balance and harmony are sought when planning a meal. Edibles seek complements, so that both ingredients end up tasting even better, and a finished dish, be it ever so simple, becomes more than the sum of its parts. For a summer seasonal *entrée*, crisp, peppery, fresh radishes are balanced

with creamy dairy butter spread on fresh bread and finished with a sprinkling of salt. A rich, dense slice of *foie gras* cries out for a spoonful of sweet-
tart currant or gooseberry preserve. For a main dish, the clean acidity of
tomato and the aroma of anise seed complement the sweet marine flavors
in a fish soup. Durable combinations of flavors and textures are sought. A
hot main dish may be followed by a crisp, cool salad. Another important
feature of French meals is the distinction between savory and sweet. It
is unusual to mix salty and sweet flavors within a single dish. Sweets are
saved for the end of a meal.

Structuring the main meal in courses is both a typical practice and
also an ideal for eating well. The expectations for a proper meal color
perceptions of other forms of eating, which are thought of as substitutions or deviations. Such factors as cost, lack of time, and interest in eating lighter, smaller meals for health reasons mitigate against preparing
and eating the full succession of courses. When eating at home, many
people, especially women concerned with weight gain, replace the cheese
course with a light alternative such as yogurt. Although such substitutions
are common, there is a self-consciousness about making them, as one is
refusing what is traditional and expected. Eating a sandwich for a quick
lunch would not be called taking a meal, much less a proper meal, but
simply referred to as eating, and likely described as eating *sur le pouce* (in a
hurry). If a meal is abbreviated on a busy weeknight—say, pared down to a
hearty composed salad as a main dish, followed by cheese, the whole thing
accompanied by bread—the foods are nonetheless organized within the
traditional structure, which is still present in miniature. Similarly, restaurants serving a foreign cuisine (Vietnamese, Chinese, Thai, Moroccan,
and so on) adapt their menus to follow French custom. Whether or not
the practice coincides with eating custom in the country of origin of the
food itself, menus will group dishes into *entrées*, *plats*, and *desserts* and vary
the portions accordingly.

BREAKFAST

The *petit déjeuner* is light and simple. For the morning meal adults drink
café au lait, heated milk poured with strong hot coffee into a hemispherical
bowl. Any one of several methods is used for brewing the coffee fresh: the
paper filter method in an electric coffee maker or stove-top glass cone, a
French press that allows ground coffee to release its fragrance into freshly
boiled water before a dense hard filter is lowered in to separate out the
grounds, or a stove-top Moka device that forces water up through ground
coffee by steam pressure. People sometimes add a pinch of salt, a dash of

cinnamon, or a spoon of cocoa powder to the ground coffee to vary or balance the flavor. Restaurant-style machines for making coffee by steam pressure are available for use at home, and these are well liked by connoisseurs. Alternatively, instant coffee such as Nescafé is dissolved by stirring into hot milk. It is the hot milk in the *café au lait* or *café crème* that is considered the nourishing part of the breakfast; the small amount of food eaten for breakfast accompanies the *café au lait*. A piece of bread, such as a section of baguette spread with butter, jam, honey, or Nutella to make a *tartine*, is eaten along with the coffee. Dunking the bread or pastry into the coffee is a beloved practice. The depth and large diameter of the *café au lait* bowl are accommodating for this purpose. For weekend breakfasts or a special treat, pastry such as *croissants* or *brioche* (from yeasted dough enriched with butter) replaces plain bread. Those who seek to avoid caffeine stir powdered roasted chicory root, with its pleasing dark brown color and nutty flavor, into their morning hot milk. Children drink hot chocolate. In recent years tea has become more popular, although it is not considered a sustaining beverage. Processed cereals such as corn flakes or puffed rice eaten with cold milk are now popular enough that grocery stores stock them, including many of the American brands. The health-conscious add a glass of fruit juice or a serving of yogurt to their breakfast. In cities, a few restaurants serve brunch, but *le brunch* is considered an exotic meal, quite out of the ordinary. On late weekend mornings, people do not eat a large breakfast, but simply drink coffee or nothing at all and eat a regular lunch.

MORNING SNACK

Children begin the school day at 8:30 A.M., and at about 10:30 A.M. break for *la collation du matin*, the morning snack. The snack is brought from home, or it may be provided by the parents of each child for the whole class on a rotating schedule. An effort is made to provide foods that are considered healthful and appropriate for the late morning: bread and cheese, a small sandwich made of buttered bread with a slice of ham, fruit yogurt, or a piece of fruit such as an apple.

COFFEE BREAKS

Working people and students take a break (*une pause*) in the morning or afternoon to drink small cups of strong coffee. After the breakfast *café au lait*, any coffee drunk at other times of day is taken without milk. *Un café*, also called *un petit café* or *un petit noir*, is served in a *demi-tasse* ("half-cup," i.e., a very small cup). It is taken plain or with sugar, accord-ing to taste. The few sips of strong coffee are considered outside the range of foods and meals. The small coffees are not seen as nourishing, as food is, but rather as revivifying. In cafés, a coffee can be drunk standing up at a counter, if one is in a hurry, or at a more leisurely pace sitting at a table. In a café, or if the coffee is being made at home with a restaurant-style machine, it is common to specify a preference for coffee that is *serré* (dense), that is, stronger and smaller, with less water used relative to the amount of ground coffee, or *allongé* ("stretched out"), made with more water. At many businesses and high schools, and at airports and highway rest stops, cups of coffee can be purchased from vending machines that grind the beans and brew a fresh cup.

LUNCH

Lunch is between noon and about 2 P.M., with schools scheduling a full two hours for the mid-day meal and pause and many businesses allowing a similar break. The break is long enough to allow for a relaxed meal and for socializing with colleagues, friends, or family, so that a bit of leisure is built into the work day. Since the break is substantial, the work day and school day extend relatively late into the afternoon.

Lunch at School

Primary schools schedule the lunch break from about 11:30 A.M. to 1:30 P.M., or until 2:00 P.M. if the day ends at 5 P.M. to accommodate parents' work schedules; of course, there is some variation in these times across the country. By law emanating from the Ministry of Education, schools are required to provide lunch for children whose parents both work or whose parents are unemployed but seeking work. Both parents must provide proof of their employment status, so that their child quali-fies to eat lunch at school. About 66 percent of primary school children take lunch at school. Schools, like businesses, have a *cantine* or cafeteria that provides a full, hot meal, either prepared on the premises if there is a full kitchen facility, or hired by the school from a catering company. Starting in the early 1970s, public schools were required to provide half of the day's nutritional requirements through the school lunch. This ruling was based on the assumption that children ate the main meal at home in the evening, however, and the school lunch was often extremely simple, such as a cold plate of sandwiches or *charcuterie*. Recent demographic and nutritional information has led to changed recommendations. As of the year 2000, school lunches must provide 40 percent of daily nutritional needs; it is assumed that the rest comes from breakfast (20 percent), a snack (10 percent), and dinner (30 percent).[3]

In theory the school meal serves more than simply the nutritional needs of children and adolescents. Since the early 1980s, official statements from the Ministry of Education have noted the importance of meals for education. At table, children develop social and communication skills. In learning to eat balanced meals, they learn principles for maintaining good health and understanding food safety. In learning how to eat "well," how to eat a "proper" meal, they learn to understand and appreciate food. Thus school meals are legislated as sites for taste education, which in turn assists in the development of a national identity and to maintain the culture.

School lunches vary in character and quality, according to organization at the local level. In primary schools and nursery schools, the municipal jurisdiction or city oversees lunch preparations. The *département* or prefecture is in charge of organizing meals for secondary schools, and the regional authority takes on responsibility for high school meals. Generally, however, following the current norm, school lunch consists of an *entrée* of a salad or vegetable, a meat or fish dish accompanied by cooked vegetables, a dessert, and bread. The school lunch is a topic of ongoing debate. At issue today are interest in organizing *cantines* to include local and regional foods; to what degree schools should cater to students unable to eat the standard fare because of religious background; and the need to balance nutritional concerns with commercial pressures. A prevalent worry is how to promote milk and water over soft drinks and to ensure that children consume adequate fresh fruits and vegetables and avoid too much fat and sugar.

Culinary Heritage in Schools

If ideological concerns shape the school lunch, the annual *Semaine du goût* or Week of Taste held every October since 1991 represents another means of promoting culinary and gastronomic education in schools. Professional chefs leave their restaurants to teach lessons about food, cooking, and eating in public secondary schools. The educational effort extends even to the adult population, perceived as insufficiently knowledgeable in the culinary heritage of their own country. During the *Semaine du goût*, restaurants offer traditional meals at reduced prices.[4] The establishment of the Week of Taste owes much to the corporate interests that, along with the government, underwrite the effort. It also betrays concerns about the demise of national cultural identity in the era of Europeanization and

Butchers wearing the asymmetrical aprons of their trade distribute samples of roast beef during a school taste class. Students are wearing the protective clean-room garments that butchers put on when they break down carcasses. Courtesy of Christian Verdet/regard public-unpact.

globalization. Yet the *Semaine du goût* also manifests a democratic, universalistic idea. The cultivation of taste and the pleasure of eating well, like reading and mathematics, are a matter of education and should be accessible to all.

Lunch at Work

Many businesses offer some sort of meal subsidy to employees as a benefit. Businesses of substantial enough size and nearly every large corporation have an in-house *restaurant de l'entreprise* (company restaurant), commonly called the *cantine* (canteen), where employees eat lunch. The *cantine* is generally set up cafeteria-style. One selects the components of a full meal, placing the dishes on a tray: bread, a hot main dish, salads, cooked vegetables, yogurt, cheese, fruit, water and coffee, wine and beer. Lunch in a company *cantine* is relatively inexpensive, as companies subsidize meals there. An employee may pay in the neighborhood of 3 to 5 Euros for a full meal in the *cantine*, where the same meal would cost two to three times this price in a restaurant. Another way that businesses subsidize their employees' meals is through the *ticket-restaurant.* Employees purchase coupons from their companies at a discount, paying about 3 Euros for a coupon worth 5, for example. The voucher is used like a traveler's check in restaurants, at a *traiteur* or caterer's to buy prepared food to take out, or to purchase food from the *charcutier* and in other food shops. If no *cantine* is available, people bring lunch from home, return home, or take lunch in a restaurant.

AFTERNOON SNACK

Every day children look forward to the *goûter* or afternoon snack that marks their return home from school. Schools and the *garderie* (child care) usually let out at 4:30 P.M., or in some areas as late as 5:00 or 6:00 P.M., timed to coincide with the end of the parents' workday. The snack is partially a matter of practical necessity, as children find the wait from lunch until dinner too long to tolerate comfortably. It is also a way for parents to welcome their children home after school, reestablish contact after the separation of the afternoon or entire day, and conversationally catch up on the day's news. The *goûter* is similar to the morning *collation*, but is more likely to consist of something sweet: bread and a piece of chocolate or some Nutella; *pain perdu* (French toast, or "lost" stale bread that is brought back to life by soaking in eggs and milk, then sautéing in butter); a *tartine* spread with jam or honey; a crushed soft fresh fruit such as an apricot or peach sprinkled with a bit of sugar and eaten on a piece of toast; a piece of freshly baked pastry; a piece of fruit that can be eaten out of hand; and a glass of fruit juice or milk. To tempt the youthful sweet tooth there are any number of *produits industriels* (packaged or processed products), from *biscuits* (plain butter cookies or the same thing covered with chocolate) and *gâteaux* (individual portions of sponge cake with chocolate) to *Kinder* (the brand name and generic moniker of chocolate covered wafers, nuts, or raisins).

High-school students and adults may take a coffee or a cup of tea in the late afternoon, and perhaps an apple, a yogurt, a *tartine*, or a pastry.

Snacking versus Eating Well

Beyond the *collation* and *goûter* given to children, snacking in general is frowned on for adults, as one of several ways of eating poorly. To eat well (*bien manger, manger correctement*) or to eat "normally" (*manger normalement*) means sticking to the three main meals, eating a variety of foods thought to be reasonably healthful, and eating in moderation. Eating when one is not hungry is seen as excessive. At table people may sociably announce as they help themselves to an extra serving of a well-liked dish, that they are eating *par gourmandise*, some combination of greed and pleasure, as if to excuse themselves even as they draw attention to the indulgence as exceptional. The word is significant. Since the late eighteenth century, *gourmand*, like the later word *gastronome*, has meant a knowledgeable eater. Yet the term derives from *gourmandise* or gluttony, one of the Seven Deadly Sins of the Catholic tradition. Eating outside the setting of the large regular meals of lunch and dinner, or snacking, is seen as unnecessary, even antisocial. Nonetheless, in recent years, as eating patterns change to accommodate long commutes and intensively scheduled work days, the practice of snacking has increased, but the onus connected with it has not diminished.

WEEKDAY DINNER

Busy schedules during the week contribute to the preference for dishes that are relatively quick and simple to prepare and to some abbreviation of the full sequence of courses. At home, the preference is for fast cooking methods, such as sautéing, searing, broiling, and grilling, and for food-stuffs that respond well to these methods, such as steaks and chops, as well as fillets of firm-fleshed fish, such as salmon and tuna. A typical weekday dinner might begin with a salad of grated carrots dressed with mustard vinaigrette; progress to a portion of sautéed *onglet* (similar to hangar steak) garnished with butter, salt, and pepper and served with some *purée* (mash) of broccoli or potatoes; and finish with a green salad and a piece of cheese. Bread is eaten throughout the meal to accompany each course.

Apéritif

Drinking an *apéritif* or cocktail before a full meal, whether lunch or (more commonly) dinner, is enjoyed as an overture to conversation, as well as for whetting the appetite. On busy weekdays, the *apéritif* or *apéro* often falls by the wayside, but for more leisurely meals on weekends or holidays, it is a welcome opening act to a full meal. In summer, a kir or sweet white wine such as Muscat or Monbazillac may be served chilled; pastis, whiskey, and mixed drinks are all standard *apéritifs* for adults. Children drink a *sirop* such as mint or barley syrup poured over ice and mixed with water. Some sort of food accompanies the *apéritif*. Favorite appetizers include toasts or thin slices of bread with *rillettes* or rounds of sliced hard sausage, baked savory biscuits, a small piece of *pissaladière* (Provençal pizza topped with caramelized onions), and *gougères* (baked cheese puffs). Many families keep crunchy or salty foods on hand as appetizers to lay out in small bowls: olives, peanuts or cashews, chips, small salted crackers. It is also common to go out for a predinner drink with friends or family before moving on to dinner at a restaurant or returning home to eat. The invitation to *prendre un verre* or *prendre un pot* (go out for a drink) is social and understood to mean a drink taken together before dinner.

WEEKEND MEALS: SATURDAY DINNER AND SUNDAY LUNCH

On the weekend there is more time to create elaborate meals and use slower cooking methods and to linger over the meal with family and friends. Many city dwellers will leave town for the day if not the whole weekend, to stay at a second residence or to visit extended family. With a weekend party of family or friends, there are more hands to help out, and a great deal of socializing takes place as everyone moves about the kitchen. Saturday evening is often reserved for socializing with friends, and Sunday lunch is traditionally a meal taken with family. Both are likely to be cooked and eaten at a leisurely pace and in a festive atmosphere.

Weekend meals usually consist of the full range of courses and include a before-dinner drink. Historically, fish was eaten on Friday evenings for religious reasons, but this custom is hardly observed anymore. Some of the more elaborate dishes make large quantities of food that require a greater number of eaters to consume them. A roast leg of lamb studded with slivers of garlic and rubbed with rosemary branches and served with baked white *haricot* beans, or a chicken roasted on a bed of sliced onions and carrots, are typical centerpieces for weekend meals. *Blanquette de veau* or *d'agneau* (white veal or lamb stew) is a dish that people make at home in the spring and for Easter Sunday. The dish has many variations, including browning the meat before adding the liquid, despite the name *blanquette*.[5]

Veal Stew (Blanquette de veau)
- 2 pounds shoulder of veal
- 1 large onion
- 5 sprigs parsley
- 10 peppercorns (whole)
- 1/2 teaspoon salt
- 5 cloves garlic
- 4 cups water
- 12 pearl onions, peeled
- 5 carrots, peeled and sliced into rounds

- 2 teaspoons lemon juice
- 2 large egg yolks
- 1/2 cup heavy cream
- 1/2 pound mushrooms, cleaned and sliced, then sautéed in butter

Cut the veal into 2-inch pieces. Place the veal, onion, parsley, peppercorns, salt, and water in a saucepan. The water should just cover the other ingredients. Bring to a boil, then reduce heat and simmer gently for 60 minutes.

Add the pearl onions and carrots, and simmer 15 minutes more. Test to make sure the veal is tender. Use a slotted spoon to transfer the meat, carrots, and pearl onions to a serving dish.

Strain the broth, then simmer until it reduces by about one-third. Stir in the lemon juice. Reduce the heat under the broth so it nearly stops simmering.

Beat the eggs yolks and cream together. Stir a ladle of broth into the egg yolks and cream to temper the mixture, then pour it into the reduced broth, continuing to stir over very gentle heat until the sauce thickens. It should not boil.

Taste for seasoning, then pour the sauce over the meat. Arrange the cooked mushrooms on top as a garnish.

Enjoy the stew hot with rice or boiled potatoes.

In the summer, outdoor barbecues are popular for weekend gatherings, for a main course consisting of grilled meats such as spicy *merguez*, chicken, and steaks. A weekend meal often ends with a bought pastry such as a cake or fruit tart from a *pâtissier*, which adds to the sense of occasion.

Other traditional preparations having any number of regional variations include *daube* (beef stew), a slow-simmered *poule-au-pot* (stuffed chicken stewed with vegetables), and *pot-au-feu* (mixed boiled meats). *Pot-au-feu* ("pot on the fire") derives its flavor from the combination of three or more whole cuts of meat that are cooked together with a few vegetables and herbs. A very large pot or multiple pots are required to hold the ingredients, which usually include a combination of fattier and leaner meats, such as flank, sirloin, and tailbones (oxtail) or a marrow bone. Regional variations add other meats than beef, such as ham, veal, bacon, pork sausage, preserved duck (*confit de carnard*), or lamb. Vegetables added to the pot include carrots, celery, potatoes, turnips, onions, garlic, and leeks. Parsley or the selection of herbs called *bouquet garni* is added as well. The flavorful broth is served as a first course. Afterward, the meats are sliced and arranged on platters, and served moistened with a bit of the cooking broth. The tender, mild, richly succulent meat is balanced with pungent, salty, or sour condiments: mustard, grated horseradish, *cornichons* (small sharp pickles), capers, coarse sea salt. Inevitably *pot-au-feu* gives leftovers that can be reheated for another meal or transformed into other dishes, such as a cold salad or a baked meat tourte.

ENTERTAINING AT HOME: MEALS FOR GUESTS

When close friends are invited to share the regular family meal, there may be little extra ceremony; this is a treasured sign of intimacy. In other cases, all stops are pulled for guests invited into the home. The extra effort is made out of respect for the guest but also to do honor to the hosts. The full sequence of courses will be carefully prepared and attention given to buy the best ingredients, cheeses, and so on that the hosts can afford. Wine is considered an essential component of a good meal, and it is certainly a symbol for the successful middle-class lifestyle. Although water is the most common beverage at the dinner table, a bottle or bottles of wine, as well as other alcohols, will be selected in anticipation of having guests. The same principle of balance that guides the choices of foods in a meal also applies to selecting pairings of wine and food. After the meal, coffee may be offered, and small glasses of after-dinner liqueurs.

LATE SUPPERS

After going out to the movies or the theatre, or after a day of skiing during a winter vacation, people may make a very late meal at home or eat in one of the relatively few restaurants that keep late hours. A late *souper* or supper may consist of nearly anything: a dish of pasta or a composed salad made at home; the specialty of a favorite late-night bistro, be it oysters on the half-shell, pigs' feet boiled then roasted to a golden brown in the oven, or a cold plate of local charcuterie. A hot soup such as onion is appreciated as a restorative at any hour of the night after going out.

Simple Onion Soup (Soupe à l'oignon)
- 3 tablespoons unsalted butter
- 6 cups coarsely chopped onion
- 3 1/2 cups water or broth
- 1/2 cup white wine
- salt
- pepper

- 6 slices of day-old bread, preferably a dense-crumbed, crusty variety
- 1/4 cup olive oil
- 3 cups Gruyère cheese, grated

In a saucepan, melt the butter over low heat. Add the onions, cover, and cook for about 45 minutes, stirring occasionally. Toward the end of cooking they should form a soft mass and be uniformly brown in color. Add the water or broth and the wine. Raise the heat to medium to bring the mixture to a simmer. Uncover the pot, and simmer gently for 45 minutes. Season to taste with salt and pepper.

For the croutons, preheat the oven to 350° F. Brush the bread slices with olive oil, place on a baking sheet, and bake about 10 minutes, until golden.

To serve the soup, place a crouton in the bottom of each soup bowl. Ladle on the onion broth, and sprinkle on the grated cheese to garnish.

Or, if you prefer, ladle the soup into individual ramekins or a tureen that can go in the oven. Bake 20 minutes at 450° F to melt and brown the cheese. Serve bubbling hot.

NOTES

1. Jean-Louis Flandrin, "Les heures des repas en France avant le XIXe siècle," pp. 197–225 in Maurice Aymard, Claude Grignon, and Françoise Sabban, eds., *Le Temps de manger: Alimentation, emploi du temps et rythmes sociaux* (Paris: Editions de la Maison des sciences de l'homme and INRA, 1993).

2. Claude Grignon, "La règle, la mode et le travail: La genèse social du modèle des repas français contemporain," pp. 275–323 in Aymard, Grignon, and Sabban.

3. Isabelle Téchoueyres, "Eating at School in France: An Anthropological Analysis of the Dynamics and Issues Involved in Implementing Public Policy," pp. 373–87 in Marc Jacobs and Peter Scholliers, eds., *Eating Out in Europe* (Oxford: Berg, 2003).

4. Adam Sage, "French turn up noses at their own food," *The Times* of London (October 14, 2000); "La Semaine du goût," *Le Monde* (October 20, 1994); Jean Claude Ribaut, "Parlons goût" and "À palais ouverts," *Le Monde* (October 15, 1994); and Michele Aulagnon and Vincent Charbonnier, "La quatrième édition de la semaine du goût," *Le Monde* (October 23, 1993).

5. Jean-Louis Flandrin, *La blanquette de veau: Histoire d'un plat bourgeois*, preface by Patrick Rambourg (Paris: Jean-Paul Rocher, 2002).

5

Eating Out

Eating at home is the norm for most people on most days, yet traditions of eating out go back centuries, and the practice is typical. The French do not eat outside of the home as frequently as residents of some nations with a comparable standard of living, such as the United Kingdom. Nonetheless, the trend to take meals outside of the home increases perceptibly in France, if not as quickly as in some affluent nations. Between 1970 and 1990, household spending on eating out increased .25 percent, and expenditure for food to be eaten at home fell by a full 7 percent. An estimate from 2004 calculated 9 billion meals out taken annually. Of these people ate 3.7 billion meals in cafeterias and other collective settings and 4.6 billion in commercial restaurants, from fine *restaurants gastronomiques* to fast-food restaurants and chains. At present, the average is 120 meals outside of the home yearly, or one meal out every three days.[1] In the past, especially in urban areas, the lack of space and tools for cooking, the wish for social interaction, and the need for a public location to transact business motivated people to eat outside of the home. The current practice of taking meals in commercial restaurants is the result of affluence and the incursion of work into mealtime. Restaurant offerings are varied. Traditional or regional bills of fare, cuisines from other nations and cultures, novelty establishments where the interest lies as much with atmosphere as with food, and fast food and chains contribute to the restaurant scene.

STREET FOODS

Although it is not necessary for most people today to eat in the street, urban areas, in particular, never lack for food to tempt those on foot. In the summer, *boulangeries* open up their storefronts to display squares of pizza and triangles of quiche. Pizza can also be purchased from stationary trucks. Crêpes with a choice of fillings—sugar, Nutella, *crème de marrons* (chestnut cream), *purée de pommes* (thick, jam-like apple sauce)—can be purchased in the street. During the summer, ice cream stores open windows that face onto the street so that one can line up for a cone. In parks, cold stands or trucks for ice cream are popular among children. Regions have their own specialties that vendors sell at stands, out of trucks, or from narrow windows and counters that open up directly onto the street. Niçois *socca* is the delicate-textured, nutty-flavored savory pancake made of chickpea flour that is served up blistering hot directly from a round griddle. In the cities of the South, the favorite sandwich is *pan bagnat*, baguette filled with tuna, black olives, tomato wedges, and slices of hard boiled egg, the whole richly

The sign for Jean-Pierre Coumont's ice-cream and sorbet in Saint Tropez (Var) indicates that they are hand-made by the sellers using pure fruits and no food colorings. Courtesy of Janine Depoil.

laced with olive oil; as one eats, one peels away the waxed paper wrapping that contains the juices. During the cold months in the North, vendors sell hot roasted or boiled chestnuts and paper cones of freshly toasted peanuts made crunchy with delicately caramelized sugar.

CAFÉS

As variations on earlier establishments, cafés and restaurants emerged during the early modern era. Today there is little that is more typical than to sit in a café to talk with friends, read the paper, or simply watch people and the world go by. Cafés may have an elegant, chic, grungy, or studious atmosphere; often they are simple and unpretentious. They all serve coffee and some choice of soft drinks, syrups, and fruit juices. The latter may be freshly squeezed from citrus fruits such as oranges or lemons. More commonly, one chooses a bottled juice; apricot, apple, and tomato are usually on hand. Many cafés serve wine, beer, alcohols, and some choice of food, whether small savory dishes or a selection of pastries. Cafés open early in the morning serve *tartines* (buttered bread, usually baguette) and pastries such as *croissants* along with *café crème*, hot coffee mixed with heated milk. A more old-fashioned sort of café may have a football table for *baby-foot*, a lane for bowling running the length of the café, or a regular Sunday afternoon bingo game that neighborhood residents attend. The fusty, or comfortable, atmosphere in some cafés is typically enhanced by clouds of cigarette smoke. Smoking in public places has been illegal since 1992, and restaurants and cafés are obliged to provide space for *non-fumeurs*. In practice, however, nonsmokers are often seated right next to *fumeurs* (smokers), the barrier dividing the two being quite imaginary and certainly ineffective. The interdiction is seen by many as an infringement on personal freedom. The habit of smoking sociably while drinking and even eating dies hard, although levels of smoking are on the decline.[2] In recent years, the opening of Starbucks cafés has added a new variety of chain, along with the possibility of taking away oversized paper cups of the American-style coffee made to any number of untraditional specifications: decaffeinated, flavored, mixed with soy, whole, or skim milk.

RESTAURANTS, BISTROS, AND BRASSERIES

Types of restaurants that emerged in the last quarter of the nineteenth century shape today's culture of eating out. The term *bistro* (or *bistrot*) is thought to have appeared in the 1880s. Its etymology is unclear. It may derive from the injunction to hurry (*bystra*) up the food that Russians in Paris spoke to waiters. The term *bistouille* used in the North to mean a hearty mixture of brandy and hot coffee is a more likely source. Historically, bistros have been restaurants that serve alcohols and a relatively small selection of foods for one-course meals. There is a strong association to this term with a warm, comfortable, unpretentious atmosphere, although a recent trend that blurs this characteristic is for very chic restaurants to call themselves bistros. Bistros and restaurants have their own specialties or regional inflections, but standard popular items include such classics as oysters on the half-shell; *steak-frites*, or seared steak served with French fried potatoes on the side; *moules marinières* (mussels cooked in the shell in a light broth flavored with white wine); omelets; roast chicken; braised chicken or *pintade* (Guinea fowl) with tarragon sauce; steak *tartare*; sole *meunière*; *purée de pommes de terre* (mashed potatoes); *tarte Tatin* (cara-melized upside-down apple tart); *poire à la belle Hélène* or a poached pear served with vanilla ice cream and decorated with chocolate sauce. Since the late nineteenth century many Parisian bistros and cafés have been run by *bougnats* (from *charbonnier*, coal burner or porter; *charbougna* in the Auvergnat patois). These natives of the Auvergne initially came to Paris to sell coal mined in their region. Some began selling wine, then ended up running restaurants (including the famous Brasserie Lipp and the Café de Flore) and forming a tightly supportive community of regional expa-triates based in the capital. The term bistro is now used throughout the country for a restaurant. The typical Parisian establishment also has its counterparts in the homey local places for other cities or regions, such as the *bouchon* in Lyon and *winstub* in the Alsace region.

Brasser means to brew beer, and a *brasserie* was a brewery where one went primarily to drink beer. *Brasseries* appeared during the Second Empire, increasing in number after the Franco-Prussian war of 1870 and the development of the train line linking Strasbourg to Paris. Today, few *brasseries* brew their own beer. Rather, a contemporary *brasserie* is a café or a restaurant that serves drinks, especially *bière à la pression* (draft beer, beer on tap) and sometimes hard cider, along with a limited menu. Because of the focus on drinking, *brasseries* tend to stay open later than restaurants. Many have a distinctly Germanic or Flemish flair. A *brasserie alsacienne* serving food will offer Alsatian specialties such as cooked sausages, *choucroute* (sauerkraut), *flammekeuche* (a thin crust like that of a pizza topped with caramelized onion and bits of bacon), and *baeckeoffe* (a stew with thinly sliced peeled potatoes and a mixture of beef, pork, and lamb). Brasseries that offer literally hundreds of different bottled and draft beers are sometimes referred to as *bars belges* (Belgian bars).

The rise of trains and then automobiles encouraged travel, the growth of tourism, and more variations on the restaurant theme. *Buffets de la gare* and *cafés de la gare* became fixtures in train stations. Restaurants serving regional specialties and located far from the capital came into fashion. During the *belle époque* and by the start of the twentieth century, high-end restaurants appeared in the grand hotels. The turn of the century witnessed the spectacular collaborations between chef Auguste Escoffier and the enterprising Swiss hotelier César Ritz. Paris still had the lion's share of elegant dining spots. The new modes of transportation, however, made fashionable other locations such as Cannes, where Napoleon III and the Empress Eugénie regularly wintered, Nice, and Biarritz. Today, good restaurants and the finest *restaurants gastronomiques* or *restaurants gourmands* are to be found all over the country, in the countryside and in smaller towns as well as in the cities.

MESS HALLS AND CAFETERIAS

For many, the daily experience of eating outside the home has taken place in a collective setting such as an army mess hall or a cafeteria in school or at work. During the Middle Ages, crusaders were quartered in the towns on their routes. The diet varied with geography and the circumstances of the hosts who "offered" them bed and board, in fact a compulsory gesture. The late sixteenth century saw the organization of internal units whose task was specifically to provision troops, while sutlers tagged along behind to sell foodstuffs directly to soldiers. During the lengthy Wars of Religion in the sixteenth century, in the north and west of France, soldiers ate meat, wine, and bread, substituting fish (including *stockfisch*), eggs, and dairy products on lean days. *Vivandiers*, or specialized army cooks, appeared in the eighteenth century. Where waging war had long been the prerogative of the aristocracy, common soldiers in addition to mercenaries became more numerous in the eighteenth and nineteenth centuries. Most soldiers subsisted primarily on soup and had to share mess kits. Eventually, military doctors intervened, adding *ratatouilles* (which in this context signified meat stews or *ragoûts*, not vegetable stew) a couple of times each week. The pressing need to provision troops constantly on the move under Napoleon was answered by Nicolas Appert's development of sterile jarring techniques, later perfected with cans. In the notoriously abysmal conditions of the First World War, both private and military cooks and suppliers carried bread, beans, rice, and soup through the labyrinth of trenches directly to the front line. Canned and jarred goods had met with a largely negative reaction throughout the nineteenth century.[3] Now the appearance of a jar of jam or a can of sardines boosted the morale of the beleaguered troops. Officers fared better than their troops; as a young man Auguste Escoffier began his career in the field, cooking up miracles for French officers participating in the Franco-Prussian conflict of 1870.

Eating out as a student has ever been a conundrum: one is poor and always hungry. For centuries, educational institutions were run by the Church, with much attention paid to fast days including the long month of Lent and every Friday. In some medieval *collèges*, students were deprived of the morning meal; in contrast with the physically extenuating activities of the laborer, the student's life was sedentary.[4] Most often school meals were vegetable soups, such as cabbage, and bread. During the sixteenth century, the *collèges* instituted tables for 16 or 25 students in a *salle commune*. One was not to cultivate the art of conversation, however, but rather to keep silent throughout the meal while listening to a theological reading. As a result of the imposed silence and the exigencies of keeping one's thoughts to sacred themes, conviviality, not to mention intellectual exchange, presumably was martyred at the table. Communication was reduced to a sign language specific to the table, for instance to request the bread.[5] Through the end of the nineteenth century, food in schools varied greatly, as there was little in the way of dietary standards or accountability. Even in a wealthy school, the bursar might divert meal allowances to other purposes, to the detriment of the pupils' palettes and stomachs. Through the early years of the Third Republic (1870–1940), the best-fed pupils were often those who could afford to bring a *gamelle* (metal lunch-pail) from home. This could be placed on the stove for a few minutes at mid-day, so that the student ate a home-cooked hot meal, whether of gruel, soup, or stew.

It is easy to overlook the central role that *cantines*—cafeterias in collective settings—have played in daily life for the last century. This is due to the prestige of fine dining and commercial restaurants, on the one hand, and the ideal of the family meal at home, on the other. People often have the mistaken impression that taking a meal in a cafeteria is somehow an exceptional practice. The French, however, rely more on cafeterias than any other nation in Europe. Today, about 56 percent of meals taken outside the home are taken in an institutional cafeteria, with 40 percent of those meals at businesses, 34 percent at schools, and 26 percent at hospitals and services related to hospitals.[6]

The development of cafeterias owes to notions of equality traceable to the Revolution of 1789 and to the sense of secular social mission and conception of the public good that was cultivated during the Third and Fourth Republics. The reformist, progressive principles took their effects in both schools and business settings. In 1881, the Ferry Law mandated that a public school education be made available to all children. As a practical proviso, the government encouraged schools to provide warm meals to needy students during the cold months of the school year. The cafeteria, then, was conceived as social intervention on a national scale. The public schools are administered by municipalities. With the allocation of school budgets for cafeterias came strong associations with local politics. Schools had to balance issues of cost and efficiency with the wish to highlight typical regional dishes and the need to serve balanced and nutritious meals. As cafeterias became common, the practice of bringing food to school from home declined. Today, most students take the mid-day meal at school; however, a student must demonstrate the need for a school lunch with formal attestations that his or her parents work or are seeking work and are thus unavailable at mid-day to provide lunch at home.

The cafeterias that now serve lunch in nearly every sizeable business grew out of the development of labor unions and codes of workers' rights. Cooperative food stores for workers appeared in the late 1830s, and workers' cooperative restaurants organized by trade date to 1848.[7] Not until 1913, however, did a law decree that companies having at least 25 employees who wished to eat at work must provide an eating area. Thereafter an emendation required that this location be outfitted for reheating food. If fewer than 25 employees wished to eat at work, there must at least be a designated space for doing so. After the Second World War and the associated problems of malnutrition, it became a matter of necessity for students and workers to eat lunch at school or work. Cafeterias took on a new importance in reestablishing the nation's health and by extension its economic vitality.

Measuring in terms of the percentage of total meals taken in cafeterias, their use peaked in the late 1970s and has been declining, albeit slowly. Beginning in 1967, companies that did not run cafeterias began to offer meal vouchers for use in commercial restaurants, as an alternative benefit. Since the 1980s, liberal or capitalist economic practices have replaced some socialist and protectionist ones, such that companies may view maintaining cafeterias as an unnecessary expense. The Aubry Law of 1998 reduced the workweek to a maximum of 35 hours for private companies having more than 20 employees. This automatically excluded at least one cafeteria meal from many schedules. Cafeterias originated to provide a benefit to workers. As nonprofits, cafeterias are subject to lower levels of the TVA or *taxe à la valeur ajoutée* (VAT or value added tax) than applies to restaurants, and this savings is passed on to workers. Ironically, their presence on a company campus or in an office is sometimes now felt as a constraint, for eating in the cafeteria keeps employees in the workplace and discourages lingering over lunch in a leisurely manner. The year of army service used to be obligatory for young men finishing their secondary education, but mandatory conscription ended in 1997, resulting in less use of military cafeterias. In response, the large companies are evolving by catering for sports matches and tournaments, for festivals or holidays having parades and other outdoor events, and also by providing branded items for companies.

EATING OUT AND THE CULINARY HERITAGE

Interest in food as connected with particularities of place took on an especially clear definition in the twentieth century, with important consequences for eating out. Published travel accounts had been popular since the eighteenth century, and guidebooks such as the *Guide Joanne* circulated widely in the nineteenth century. In 1900, the tire company Michelin, based in Clermont-Ferrand, established a new *Guide pour les chauffeurs et les vélocipédistes* (*Guide for Drivers and Cyclists*) to promote the automobile tourism that would increase their profits. Following seventeenth- and eighteenth-century almanacs that listed boutiques and then restaurants, and the first descriptive restaurant guide published in the early nineteenth century, the *Guide Michelin* soon came to mention food and wine specialties for each region. In 1926, a rating system for restaurants was introduced, in the form of a star to indicate a good table. The further distinctions of two and three stars appeared in the early 1930s. The Michelin stars are still the most widely recognized, if now also deeply controversial, of laurels for restaurants. The rankings of the *Guide Michelin* (today called the *Guide Rouge*) are defined relative to the road. A single star indicates *une très bonne table*, a "very good" table in the elite category. Two stars go to a restaurant that *vaut le détour* (is "worth the detour") off of the main highway. The coveted third star indicates a menu of such quality that the restaurant is a worthy travel destination all by itself.

Gastronomic tourism was now established as a serious undertaking, and there was much to know about the culinary subcultures within the country. Concurrent to the establishment of the Michelin rating system, the novelist Marcel Rouff and journalist and food writer Curnonsky (Maurice Edmond Sailland) assembled the *Tour de France Gastronomique* published in 24 volumes between 1921 and 1928. The title echoes that of the *Tour de France* bicycle race established in the late nineteenth century, and the comprehensive scope is suggestive. A few years later and with a different collaborator (Augustin Croze), Curnonsky published another work on the same topic entitled the *Trésor gastronomique de la France* (1933). Again, the title is telling. *Trésor* means an investment, capital, or principle worth preserving (here, the gastronomic "treasury"); an undiscovered or unexpected windfall (as in hidden treasure); and a place where riches are kept. One should, in short, note the fascination and bankability of the varied food and food customs of the entire country.

During the second half of the twentieth century, food and food mores increasingly became the focus of legislation that sought to institutionalize cultural practice. In the 1950s, as part of the economic and cultural rebuilding that followed the Second World War, Charles de Gaulle appointed the novelist and diplomat André Malraux to head a new *Ministère des affaires culturelles* (Ministry of Cultural Affairs). His charge was to promote the *héritage* or *patrimoine culturel* (national cultural heritage), as well as the sense of history. The idea was to expose as many individuals as possible to the riches of French culture and to ensure the creation of artistic and intellectual works that would continue to enrich it. To avoid the usual Parisian bias, the Malraux Law of 1962 was further designed to encourage cultural activity across the nation. Underpinning the ministry and legislation was the deep respect for the past, a strong sense of *appréciation* or understanding combined with enjoyment, and the conviction that government intervention is necessary to foster and protect culture. These attitudes would soon be specifically extended to food culture, as in the *Plat du terroir* (*Terroir* Dishes) initiative begun in 1985. The charter for this undertaking noted the "incomparable" richness of France's culinary cultures. The document proclaimed the goal to acquaint not only visitors and foreigners but also French citizens themselves—who may be ignorant of their own culture—with aspects of the *patrimoine* and specifically with "the varied palette of our tables."[8] During the next decade, an initiative sponsored jointly by the state and various corporations began bringing chefs into schools for the annual fall *Semaine du goût* (Week of Taste) that gives children a practical course under professional supervision in eating traditional foods. The state commissioned the publication of the *Inventaire culinaire du patrimoine de la France* (1992–1996), a set of 22 volumes that take "culinary inventory" of the country by region. Since 1993, printed roadmaps and posted signs on highways throughout the country indicate national *Sites remarquables du goût* (Taste Sites Worthy of Note) as attractions for travelers and tourists, whether French or foreign nationals.

The state, then, invests in the institutionalization of the culinary heritage and in the promotion of quality, and it may be said to pursue a gastronomic and culinary policy. It does so through specific legislation that complements regulation against fraud, laws to protect health and safety, and policies of agricultural protectionism, today the source of ongoing tension within the country and, notoriously, with other nations in the European Union and beyond. The notions of regional cuisine and local specialty, of *terroir*, and of the *patrimoine culinaire* derive from real social practices and attitudes whose cultivation and preservation enrich the texture of daily life. These practices are also carefully cultivated, and in a few cases invented, to serve commercial and political interests. Thanks to careful packaging and marketing, the tourist and export trades are notable beneficiaries. Inevitably, in the push and pull of daily life, the habitual practices and the self-consciously elaborated ones overlap and become closely intertwined. As a result, authenticity in the culinary domain has become a more than usually vexed question. Specialty producers such as fine wine makers have long appreciated and often instigated the demand for distinguishing marks of authenticity, useful for business. For many people, the prevailing response is pride in the culture, a sense of belonging and participation. For others, a feeling of alienation results, or the sense of being compelled to live in a museum. The process of *patrimonialisation*, or identifying elements of culture as part of the heritage and then fulfilling the corresponding obligations to preserve them, can be felt to inhibit freedom, creativity, and innovation.

The restaurant is, by association, a site of culture if not historical preservation. Eating dinner in a typical, traditional, or regional restaurant reifies and affirms one's very Frenchness. Chefs in elite restaurants (*restaurants gastronomiques*) may make special efforts to incorporate local and AOC items into their menus. There is great sympathy for this gesture. Beyond the appreciation for what is fresh, the effort to identify foodstuffs and thus to render transparent the links in the food chain responds to the general sense that it is better to know exactly what one is eating. With trenchant wit and insight, the sociologist Claude Fischler has named the alternative the *OCNI: objet comestible non identifié* or Unidentified Comestible Object.[9] By this is meant the generic, heavily commercialized, highly processed "product" with no visible history or origin, that passes for food. The appreciation for local, identifiable, and AOC products can take extreme forms. During the 1990s, a group of prominent chefs published a manifesto protesting "alien" and "exotic" combinations of flavors and foods. These chefs called for a return to *terroir* and presumably to some sort of ideal state of absolute Frenchness. The position is exaggerated, yet has a clear resonance.

RESTAURANT RHYMES AND REASONS

Few people today go out to eat because they lack facilities to cook at home. The motivations lie elsewhere. Busy work schedules make the option of being served dinner at the end of the day attractive. Those traveling for business or having a long daily commute cannot eat at home. In a country where eating well is a passion shared by so many, one may return repeatedly to a restaurant to enjoy a favorite *création de la maison* (house specialty) or to test the latest invention of a particular chef. Sampling a cuisine from another nation allows one to traverse continents simply by walking down the street. Restaurants and cafés are moreover much appreciated as settings for social interaction. Eating dinner weekly at a neighborhood bistro provides a sense of continuity and social connectedness. Gregariousness and conviviality are characteristic social traits. Yet close friendships require time to develop, and the home is viewed as an intimate, private space. Eating out with a new acquaintance or a friend allows social bonds to deepen in a neutral yet comfortable and inviting setting.

Because of the longstanding customs of eating out and the pervasive culture of socializing outside the home, it is easy to find relatively inexpensive

A typical Parisian brasserie with café-style tables for sitting outside. Courtesy of Arnold Matthews.

places where one can eat a good meal in pleasant surroundings. Currently the most common terms for eating and drinking establishments are *restaurant, bistro, brasserie,* and *café.* These are often used interchangeably. Legally, the sale of beverages is regulated by licenses that specify a maximum allowed alcohol content per beverage. To serve food, restaurants must register the types of items to be served, the degree of involvement of personnel in food preparation and service, and so on. With the appropriate licenses, the various establishments may serve both food and alcoholic beverages. In practice, when one goes out, one goes to a "restaurant" to eat a full meal at noon or in the evening. Of course, some cafés serve food, and most bistros and brasseries serve full meals. On the other hand, it is only in a café that one may order as little as a coffee (i.e., only a beverage) and do so between meals. However, this is also possible in some bistros and brasseries, although the beverage will more likely be a glass of wine or a beer. A *café-restaurant* stays open all day and perhaps into the late evening, serving coffee and drinks between and after meals. A *café-tabac* marked with the *carrotte* (a red, diamond-shaped label reading *tabac* that is stuck on the window) is licensed to serve as a tobacconist and sells cigarettes.

Whether in a fancy restaurant or in a local café or bistro, eating out has rituals all its own. Especially in smaller restaurants, it is common to order what is referred to as a *menu* or *formule*. A selection of dishes is offered for each of two or three courses at a fixed price for the full meal; the sum is usually less than an *à la carte* total. Within families or groups of friends, people discuss what they are thinking of ordering and from which *menu* they will choose. This is partially a matter of practicality. It is considered courteous to order a similar sequence as one's dinner companions (i.e., items from within the three-course menu choices), so that the meal progresses according to a similar rhythm for everybody at the table. Similarly, there is discussion as to the choice of wine. It is considered sociable to all drink the same thing and egotistical not to follow the general wishes of the group. After the meal, *l'addition* (the check) is not brought to the table right away. This would be viewed as quite rude. It is assumed that people will take their time to eat, enjoy the pauses between courses, and continue talking after the meal. When one is ready to leave the restaurant, one requests the check from the waiter.

BARS AND WINE BARS

Restaurants and most cafés serve wine; many also serve beer and a selection of alcohols. As a result, bars are not particularly central to social life for most people. Nonetheless, the word *bar* owes its derivation to the French term (*une barre de comptoir*) for the foot-rest close to the floor near a counter where one stands to take a drink or to eat. Bars enjoyed a surge in popularity at the end of the nineteenth century, when alcohol was temporarily deregulated, but they declined as an institution during the Vichy period. Today, bars that are so called (*un bar*) serving only wine, beer, and drinks can be found in discos or nightclubs, in large hotels, and sometimes in large restaurants. Some cafés that remain open late at night function then as *bars de nuit* and tend to serve almost exclusively wine, beer, and alcohols during the evening hours. With the recent fashion for drinking high-quality wines, a new type of *bar à vin* or wine bar is in vogue. Much like the specialized *brasseries* that serve many varieties of beer, the wine bar offers a broad selection of bottles and is designed for sampling good wines. The focus here is on tasting wine, and the ambience is fairly sophisticated. Food, which may be served in small portions in the style of Spanish *tapas* or Turkish *mezes*, takes a secondary role as an accompaniment to the wine.

TEA SHOPS

Salons de thé (tea rooms) are few in number but enjoy a faithful clientele. Today, more women than men drink tea; tea is drunk by a few anglophiles, by the highly educated, and by the health-conscious or those seeking to avoid the larger amounts of caffeine in coffee. Among tea drinkers there is much admiration for the variety of Asian and Indian teas, for the austere ritual elegance of Japanese customs of taking tea, and for the British tradition of high tea. Most tea shops have the distinctively French touch of the exquisite. One orders a small pot of tea, choosing from a list of different kinds of leaves; some plain black teas may be flavored from the addition of bergamot oil or extract of violet or rose. A selection of *tisanes* or herbal infusions is usually available as well. The complement for tea is a pastry, a slice of tart, or one of the more refined forms of cookie. Macaroons are well liked, as are *madeleines*, the tea cakes having a scallop shape and that launched thousands of words. Dipping one in a fragrant glass of lime (linden) tea, the author Marcel Proust was overwhelmed with strong memories of his childhood and proceeded to write the lengthy semiautobiographical novel *À la recherche du temps perdu* (*In Search of Time Past*, 1913–1927).

Madeleines
- 1 1/2 cups sifted cake flour
- 1/2 teaspoon baking powder
- pinch salt

- 3 large eggs
- 2/3 cup granulated sugar
- 2 teaspoons grated lemon zest
- 3/4 cup (1 1/2 sticks) unsalted butter, melted and allowed to cool

Note: Madeleines are baked in special forms that give them their distinctive shape.

Preheat the oven to 350° F.

Sift together the flour, baking powder, and salt, and set aside.

Beat the eggs in a mixing bowl until they are fluffy and turn a pale, lemony yellow. Add the vanilla. While continuing to beat the eggs, gradually add the granulated sugar. Continue beating until the mixture doubles in volume. Add the lemon zest.

Gradually fold in the flour mixture, then stir in the melted butter.

With additional melted butter, lightly brush the madeleine pans. Spoon in the batter, filling each shell to two-thirds full.

Bake for 12 minutes or until a toothpick inserted into the fat part of the little cakes comes clean. Remove the cookies from the pans, and let them cool on a wire rack.

Makes about 3 dozen.

"EXOTIC" RESTAURANTS AND GLOBAL CUISINES

The terms exotique (exotic) and sometimes éthnique (ethnic) are used for any kind of food, cooking, or restaurant cuisine that is not traditionally French, and they are often applied to foreign cuisines associated with immigrants. The use of these terms reflects the longstanding expectation that integration into French society is effected through assimilation into the culture; however, assimilation has also worked in the other direction or not at all. North African couscous, familiar since the mid-twentieth century through the presence of immigrants from former colonies, is not typically referred to as exotique. Indeed, couscous is perceived as an everyday food. It ranks just behind steak-frites (steak and French fried potatoes) and gigot d'agneau (roast leg of lamb) as a familiar, reliable favorite. At present, the large population of citizens and residents whose national or ethnic origins are not French makes the use of a term such as exotique unclear. Clearly, the sense of the exotic varies according to perspective. Changes in eating habits as a result of dietary concerns and issues of convenience, and familiarity with a variety of foods as a result of travel and the global market, make the term even more confusing. A specialist in the sociology and anthropology of consumption points out that for some, whether of French or other national origin, traditional regional dishes such as *cassoulet* or *cuisses de grenouilles* (frogs' legs) are quite exotic, because they are not an accustomed part of the daily diet.[10] It is useful to remember that foods such as tomatoes and potatoes that are now typical and essential in the regional cuisines are not native to French territory or even to Europe.

Restaurants serving cuisines from outside the French territory are reasonably popular. Italian restaurants in France tend to specialize in pasta dishes and to serve individual, thin-crusted pizzas taken as a main course dish. Chinese restaurants are quite familiar in suburban areas and small towns, as well as cities. They usually serve Cantonese and Hong Kong–style foods and organize menus according to the French sequence of *entrée, plat,* and *dessert.* Although the complexity, variety, sophistication, and rich history of the Chinese regional and provincial cuisines are comparable to those of France, this is not apparent in the restaurants, by and large undistinguished. Indian restaurants and Japanese restaurants that mainly serve sushi rather than cooked dishes are found in the large cities. Greek and Turkish restaurants are often informal, having open counters that double as kebab and sandwich stands; in the Turkish restaurants, the nuances of Ottoman cuisine are hardly in evidence. The establishment of Algerian, Moroccan, Tunisian, Lebanese, and Vietnamese restaurants date to the independence of the respective colonies and protectorates. Varieties of North African restaurants and tea houses are relatively common and sometimes quite refined. Thai restaurants are a relatively new addition and usually have carefully annotated menus to warn against spicy dishes, to which most French eaters are not accustomed. Recently, new imports have further expanded the choices especially in the larger cities, to include Tibetan food and the cuisines of South American nations, in particular Columbia and Brazil. British or Irish pubs and Tex-Mex restaurants can be found in the large cities and in some university towns. Typical, if practically unknown beyond the reaches of the urban working-class neighborhoods where they are found, are *cafés sahéliens*. These are working-class cafés operated and frequented by immigrants from Senegal, Mali, and Mauritania who came to France starting in the 1960s and 1970s, and also by populations from Congo, Cameroon, and Burkina.[11]

FAST-FOOD AND RESTAURANT CHAINS

The rapid expansion of fast-food and chain restaurants began in the 1960s. These establishments are distinguished by a formulaic list of choices, the use of industrially prepared ingredients, and the practice of a highly rationalized *cuisine d'assemblage* ("assembly cooking" rather than preparing food from scratch, from raw ingredients). Following the principles borrowed from the United States of Frederick Taylor and Henry Ford, the cooking processes are broken down into simple procedures that are standardized and designed for maximum efficiency. The goal is to create products of consistent quality and that vary as little as possible from one outlet or franchise to the next. Ingredients have been industrially processed and prepared, freeze-dried, and vacuum packed. In the restaurant, they undergo final stages of preparation, cooking (or heating), and assembly. Initially, the restaurants were not popular, as the service was brusque and impersonal or else one had to serve oneself at a counter, and there were no real cooks. The impact and initial strangeness of the phenomenon to French eaters can be measured in Claude Zidi's film *L'Aile ou la cuisse* (1976), a parody of the industrialist Jacques Borel, founder of the hospitality firm now called Accor. American chains including McDonald's began opening stores in France in the early 1970s, with some adjustments to the menu including the availability of wine and beer. There are numerous French chains and fast food restaurants, such as Quick and Flunch.

Despite the culture of gastronomy and despite widely publicized and occasionally violent protests against the fast food restaurants, these eating establishments flourish. Today, fast food restaurants are ubiquitous, with just under one for every eight traditional cafés or restaurants. As of 1998, chains represented 2.5 percent of commercial restaurants, but accounted for 20 percent of sales.[12] One researcher points out that this may be in part precisely because the fast-food chain restaurants allow one to flaunt conventions of good taste and eating well.[13] The use of industrially prepared foods in *cuisine d'assemblage* has penetrated to many traditional commercial restaurants and has led to hybrids. Restaurants dating to the 1960s such as the Courtepaille chain found in roadside service areas on the national highways serve full, three-course meals with traditional menus, on the principle that one will want to eat a decent meal as a break from a long trip. The dishes are based on preassembled ingredients, and the service is efficient. Fast-food pizza, or pizzeria chains, enjoy mixed success. The largest share of the market is divided between two American concerns, Pizza Hut and Dominos; the success of individual franchises varies by region and adaptation to the local population. *Livraison à domicile* (delivery) for pizza, introduced by the American chains, is a late-blooming phenomenon,[14] but one that has French imitators such as Speed Rabbit Pizza.

Readying cooked carrots and peas for service. A degree of standardization is essential in nearly any professional kitchen, whether in a cafeteria, a fine dining establishment, or a fast food restaurant. Courtesy of Philippe Bornier.

LE FOODING AND NOVELTY RESTAURANTS

The semiologist and astute interpreter of culture Roland Barthes observed that food can be a situation or an event. As if taking Barthes's observation for advice, a small but growing number of restaurants have turned to creating establishments whose primary attraction is a nontraditional ambience of one sort or another. For the last few years, *Nova* magazine has been publishing a guide to *fooding,* a term coined by two journalists in 1999. The noun is manufactured from the English words "food" and "feeling." The awkwardness of the word well conveys the extremely unusual nature of these restaurants, in an eating culture that has long privileged tradition, quality, and norms. Notable is the effort to translate the primary appeal of the new establishments to one's individual sensations, to one's personal experience and reactions, to one's emotional state. The guide to *fooding* does not rate for price and quality according to the recognized grids of classical cuisine and mid–twentieth century nouvelle cuisine. Rather, it lists nontraditional restaurants in categories that have more to do with personal identity or lifestyle. Its categories include *restaus* that are *gay*, *bio-végét* (*biologique-végétarien* or organic and vegetarian), or that serve a "world food" cuisine, or perhaps some variety of fusion food. The interest here is ambience and novelty. *Le fooding* appeals in particular to younger people open to seeking a social experience or the experience of a place for its own sake, as much as eating the food.

EATING OUTSIDE

The French love to eat outdoors. An unobstructed view of the sky and a fresh breeze on the face are thought to enhance the meal, adding an extra dimension of enjoyment. In the preindustrial era, workers such as agricultural laborers often had to eat outdoors. The aristocratic classes, on the other hand, could make a party by having tables set up in a meadow, a shady glade, or a landscaped garden. Today, eating outside or in an attractive natural setting is a matter of choice. Outdoor meals have a special appeal given that the contemporary lifestyle is primarily urban and that jobs keep people indoors and relatively sedentary. Eating outside is felt to offer a break from the routine and doing so gives even a simple, everyday meal a festive feeling. Terrace or courtyard tables are selling points for restaurants and cafés during mild weather. People who have gardens or terraces set up tables even in tiny spaces, for the pleasure of being able to *manger au dehors* (eat outside). In the seventeenth century, *manger en pique-nique* (to eat picnic style) meant pooling money to share the expense of an improvised meal; the association with an outdoor meal stabilized only in the mid-twentieth century.[15] Now, during the summer, picnics in parks are popular, as is camping, as an inexpensive mode of taking a vacation. A picnic may be an impromptu lunch consisting of no more than a *jambon-beurre* (slice of ham in buttered baguette) eaten outdoors. Alternatively, especially in the middle and upper classes, picnics may be quite elaborate affairs. Extensive coordination and planning are required to unite large numbers of family members and friends in natural locations considered to be beautiful and offering good air to breathe and an attractive view to admire, such as in the mountains, near a river, or on the ocean. Cooking outside usually involves grilling or barbecuing fresh sausages and *merguez*. Other portable picnic foods are made in advance or bought already prepared. Favorites include roasted or rotisserie chickens;

hard sausages to be sliced and eaten with chunks of bread; flats of summer fruits in season such as peaches, apricots, or cherries; and bottles of wine and mineral water. These items will be carefully packed and carried to the ideal spot in backpacks, bags, baskets, and coolers.

During the summer on the hot, heavily frequented Mediterranean beaches, vendors stroll up and down musically chanting the wares they carry on flat trays: *boissons fraîches* (cool drinks, usually bottles of mineral water, juice, and soda), *café chaud* (hot coffee), *thé à la menthe* (mint tea). There are also vendors for *choux-choux* or peanuts made crunchy with a praline coating, *glaces* (ice cream), and *beignets* or round jam-filled dough-nuts covered with glinting granulated sugar. From stands set up at the edge of the beach, one can usually buy *frites* and meat kebabs served in a piece of baguette as a sandwich, with the popular option of getting the fries right in the sandwich.

NOTES

1. Sylvie-Anne Mériot, *Nostalgic Cooks: Another French Paradox*, trans. Trevor Cox and Chanelle Paul (Leiden and Boston: Brill, 2006), 47.

2. Sandrine Blanchard, "Les Français consomment moins d'alcool et de tabac," *Le Monde* (March 9, 2006) and John Tagliabue, "The Ash May Finally Be Falling from the Gauloise," *The New York Times* (September 8, 2005).

3. Martin Breugel, "'Un sacrifice de plus à demander au soldat:' L'armée et l'introduction de la boîte de conserve dans l'alimentation française," *Revue historique* 596 (October-December 1995): 260–83 and "Du temps annuel au temps quotidien: la conserve appertisée à la conquête du marché, 1810–1920," *Revue d'histoire moderne et contemporaine* (January-March 1997): 40–67.

4. Bruno Laurioux, *Manger au Moyen Âge* (Paris: Hachette, 2002), 158.

5. Aude de Saint-Loup, Yves Delaporte, and Marc Renard, *Gestes des moines, regard des sourds* (Nantes: Siloë, 1997).

6. Mériot, 36.

7. Fabrice Laroulandière, *Les Ouvriers de Paris au XIXe siècle* (Paris: Christian, 1997), 115–16.

8. Julia Csergo, "La constitution de la spécialité gastronomique comme objet patrimonial en France, fin XVIIIe-XXe siècle," pp. 183–93 in Daniel J. Grange and Dominique Poulot, eds., *L'Esprit des lieux* (Grenoble: Presses Universitaires de Grenoble, 1997).

9. Claude Fischler, *L'Homnivore* (Paris: Odile Jacob, 1990), 209.

10. Isabelle Garabuau-Moussaoui, "L'exotique est-il quotidien? Dynamiques de l'exotique et générations," pp. 281–306 in Isabelle Garabuau-Moussaoui, Elise Palomares, and Dominique Desjeux, eds., *Alimentations contemporaines* (Paris: L'Harmattan, 2002).

11. Pascal Hug, "Cafés sahéliens de Paris: Stratégies de 'gestions du ventre' dans un espace de manducation," pp. 145–71 in Garabuau-Moussaoui, Palomares, and Desjeux.

12. B. Boutboul and A. Lacourtiade, "Étude chaînes 1998" (Paris: GIRA-SIC Conseil, April 1999), 2.

13. Olivier Badot, "Esquisse de la fonction sociale de McDonald's à partir d'une étude éthnographique," pp. 83–121 in Garabuau-Moussaoui, Palomares, and Desjeux.

14. Sylvia Sanchez, "'La pizza dans le pays des autres,'" pp. 123–41 in Garabuau-Moussaoui, Palomares, and Desjeux.

15. Julia Csergo, "The Picnic in Nineteenth-Century France," pp. 139–59 in Marc Jacobs and Peter Scholliers, eds., *Eating Out in Europe* (Oxford: Berg, 2003).

6

Special Occasions

The care, interest, and enjoyment that so many people bring every day to cooking and eating bring a bit of holiday reverence and revelry to nearly any meal. This is typical *savoir-vivre* (knowing how to live well) applied at the table, on a daily basis. A holiday atmosphere certainly prevails for the Sunday lunch with family and at the dinner party given on a Friday or Saturday evening for a few close friends. Of the 11 days mandated as federal holidays, a few are secular commemorations such as Bastille Day (July 14). The rest, such as Christmas (December 24–25), derive from Catholic religious observances historically connected with fasting. These holidays are now feasts, and most people celebrate them in a secular fashion. Within families and circles of friends, there is a strong emphasis on celebrating personal days such as birthdays. Parties, of course, are simply fun, but it is also recognized that participation in shared festivities socializes children, sustains family relationships, and ensures the integration of individuals into communities. Since the 1990s a trend to revive traditional agricultural and regional celebrations has served to affirm local identity and preserve the sense of history.

RELIGIOUS HOLIDAYS AND FESTIVALS

The holidays having a religious origin and that are observed by the greatest number of people in France derive from the Catholic liturgical calendar. That said, most people today celebrate holidays such as *Noël* (Christmas), observed on December 24 with the next day a holiday from work, in a secular fashion. The family celebration is a treat much anticipated by children, who like the *sapin* or tree decorated with lights that is mounted in the living room, as well as the festive foods and gifts. December 24 was a fasting day in the Catholic calendar. Abstinence from all food was in principle required until after the midnight mass. One broke the fast at the *réveillon* (late meal after mass; from *réveiller*, to wake up) with fish, vegetables, and grains, but no meat. From the ecclesiastical requirement for a lean meal, and because of seasonal availability, baked or roasted salmon, *stockfisch* (dried cod) for modest tables, or turbot for the wealthy were typical. Fish, especially salmon, is now eaten throughout the year, and the former fasts have become secular feasts. People refer to the Christmas Eve meal as *le gros souper* (the big dinner). The old lean dishes are thus replaced on the holiday table by festive foods that suggest prosperity but are now within reach of many wallets. Oysters and *foie gras* are favorite appetizers. Roasted turkey stuffed with chestnuts is a standard main course. Good wines are saved for the occasion, and Champagne accompanies dessert.

Almost nothing is more typical than drinking sparkling wine for festive occasions, although the tradition is of recent vintage. Through the

Platters of raw oysters and steamed mussels, clams, and shrimp set out for the first course of the Christmas meal. Courtesy of Hervé Depoil.

end of the eighteenth century, sparkling wine was rare and drunk by the very wealthy. The carbonation was not sought (nor added by the monk Dom Perignon, whose aptitude as a vintner is mythical) but was rather the result of a happy accident in wine-making.[1] Cold weather halted fermentation of the sugars before it was complete. In the spring, chemical changes resumed with warm weather, producing carbon dioxide, as well as alcohol. During the nineteenth century, careful cultivation and scientific modes of production made sparkling wines more plentiful. Clever marketing transformed Champagne into an essential feature of important celebrations. Sparkling wines can be made wherever wine grapes are grown, but the greatest prestige attaches to the finest bottles from the Champagne region.

Since the late nineteenth century, the Christmas meal finishes with a *bûche de Noël* or cake in the shape of the fruit-wood Yule log that was placed on the fire as a symbol of plenty. The cake for the *bûche* starts as a flat rectangle made from a light batter containing eggs but little or no butter. The baked sponge is spread with a jam glaze, rolled, then frosted with chocolate butter-cream. Chocolate shavings resembling tree bark, baked meringue toadstools, a sprinkling of powdered sugar to suggest snow, and a few holly leaves imaginatively transform the cake into a log plucked from the woods. The adventurous make their own *bûches*, but it is common to order one from a *pâtissier*. Other winter desserts that appear around Christmas and New Year's are chocolate truffles, fruit pastes, and regional specialties such as the Germanic *Christollen* (Stollen)—a dry, buttery yeasted cake studded with candied fruits and decorated with powdered sugar eaten in Alsace—and *Spéculoos* (spice cookies of Flemish origin) common in Picardie and Pas-de-Calais. Those who do attend the midnight service on Christmas Eve often divide up the meal, saving only cake and wine for the *réveillon* after mass. Children put out their shoes near a fireplace or a *crèche* (nativity scene) in the hopes that they will be filled with gifts. As in the United States, Christmas is heavily commercialized, and children now expect toys, electronic games, bicycles, and so on, as presents. For this reason the old tradition of giving gifts to children for *la Saint-Nicolas* (the feast of St. Nicholas, patron saint of children, on December 6) has been somewhat eclipsed. For St. Nicholas's Day the traditional gifts were *pains d'épices* or spice bread flavored with honey, cloves, and cinnamon; marzipan confections; and oranges and nuts.

In Provence, foods for Christmas Eve dinner may still reflect the regional staples and the custom of eating a *repas maigre* or meatless lean meal. Snails, *aïoli* (garlicky mayonnaise) or *anchoïade* (anchovies pounded with bread crumbs, olive oil, and lemon juice) with artichoke hearts; salt cod; and winter vegetables including chard and cardoons figure on the Christmas table. The meal often begins with a simple, flavorful *aïgo-boulido* (Occitan for "boiled water," actually a far more tasty garlic soup). The soup is also recommended as a cure-all for colds and aches and as a soothing restorative in case of gastronomic excess or hangover at any time of year.

Garlic Soup (Aïgo-boulido)

- 8 cloves garlic
- 5 cups water
- 1 sprig fresh sage
- 1 bay leaf
- 4 tablespoons olive oil
- salt
- 3 very fresh egg yolks
- pepper
- 4 slices of bread, lightly grilled or toasted
- 3/4 cup of grated hard cheese such as Gruyère, aged Cantal, or Parmesan

Crush the garlic with your hand or with the side of a knife and peel it. If the garlic is at all dry, slice it in half lengthwise and remove the green germ, using the tip of a knife.

Put the garlic, water, sage, bay leaf, salt to taste, and water in a pot. Bring the mixture to the boil, and cook for 10 minutes. Turn off the heat. Pour in the olive oil.

In the bottom of a soup tureen or large serving bowl, gently beat the egg yolks with a wooden spoon, just to mix.

Pour a ladleful of the boiled broth and garlic mixture onto the eggs and whisk together, then pour on the rest of the broth. Grind fresh black pepper to taste onto the soup.

To serve, place a slice of toasted bread in the bottom of each soup bowl. Divide the cheese among the four bowls, sprinkling it on top of the bread. Ladle on the soup and serve piping hot.

The Provençal Christmas meal concludes with 13 desserts, thought to symbolize the 12 months of the year plus the *petit mois* (little month) composed of the 12 days from Christmas to Epiphany. Another explanation matches a dessert each to Christ and the 12 apostles. Either *vin cuit* (wine with macerated fruit such as oranges) or chilled sweet wine accompanies the selection of desserts: fresh fruits such as oranges, tangerines, or apples;

dried fruits and nuts such as raisins, dates, figs, almonds, hazelnuts, and walnuts; confections such as candied chestnuts, candied almonds, and light and dark nougats with nuts; and pastries such as spinach tart made with olive oil or butter, sugar and lemon peel, or a lightly sweetened chard tart. A whole melon carefully candied in syrup over two weeks at the end of summer may appear as the crown jewel of the holiday sweet spread. An indispensable element is the plain *pompe à l'huile*, *gibassier*, or *fougasse*, a lightly sweetened bread enriched with olive oil and flavored with orange flower water or anise. The name *pompe à l'huile* for the festive bread evokes the pomp and circumstance of the holiday celebration. With a pun it also literally means "oil pump," a description that is not inaccurate.

Christmas Bread (Pompe à l'huile, Pompe de Noël)

- 2 teaspoons active dry yeast
- 1 cup lukewarm water
- 5 cups bread flour
- 1 teaspoon salt
- 1/2 cup sugar
- grated zest of 1 orange
- 3 tablespoons orange flower water
- 6 tablespoons olive oil

In a medium-size mixing bowl, stir together the yeast and warm water. Using a wire whisk, mix in 1 cup of the flour to make a smooth batter. Cover the bowl tightly with plastic wrap. Let the sponge batter sit overnight, up to 24 hours.

The next day, mix 3 cups flour, salt, sugar, and orange zest together in a large bowl. Make a well in the center, then pour in the orange flower water, olive oil, and the sponge from the previous day. Using a spatula or wooden spoon, stir the flour into the liquids, incorporating it gradually first from the center and then from the edge of the bowl, until the mixture is fairly uniform.

Lightly flour a work surface, turn the dough out from the bowl, and knead for a few minutes until the dough is smoothly elastic and no longer sticky. As you knead, sprinkle on a bit of additional flour, as necessary, if the dough is sticky.

Form the kneaded dough into a ball. Place it back in the mixing bowl. Cover the bowl with a clean dish towel. Place the bowl in a warm spot in your kitchen, and allow to rise for about 2 hours, until doubled in volume.

Punch the dough down, then turn it out of the bowl onto the work surface, and divide it into four. Use your hands to flatten, turn over, and pull the dough, shaping each piece into a flat, round disk. If necessary, use a rolling pin to flatten the dough, so that the disks are about 1/2-inch thick.

Lightly grease two baking sheets, then place the disks two by two on the sheets. Use a clean razor blade or very thin, sharp, pointed knife to score the surface of the breads in a checkerboard pattern. Cut parallel lines into the dough about 1/4-inch deep and at intervals of 1 inch, then make perpendicular cuts. Cover the breads with towels, and leave for the final rise in a warm place for about 1 hour.

Preheat the oven to 400° F.

Bake the loaves for 20 minutes, until golden brown and crusty. When they are done, they will sound hollow if you tap the bottom with your fingers. Cool completely on wire racks before eating.

To serve, bring the breads whole to the table and break off square chunks where they are scored.

Makes four loaves about 8 inches in diameter.

Épiphanie or *la fête des Rois* commemorates the manifestation (*épiphanie*) of the infant Jesus to the Magi. To mark the day people eat the *galette des Rois* or *gâteau des Rois* ("kings' cake" or Twelfth Night pastry), which is in the shape of a crown. The simplest version is plain flat puff pastry glazed with egg. A lightly sweetened, thick almond custard is usually spread between two layers of puff paste. In the South, the *galette* can be a yeast-leavened *pain brioché* or dough enriched with eggs and also butter. This is baked into a round disk or a ring whose center is filled with cherries or prunes. A *fève* (dried bean), whole almond, or porcelain trinket is tucked into the paste or dough before it is baked. While the cake is being served, the youngest child in the room gets to hide under the table and to ask the question: Who will be the king? The evening requires having a gilt cardboard *couronne* (crown) in reserve. The person whose piece of pastry contains the *fève*—referred to as such even if the object is not a bean—is crowned king or queen. Near the winter solstice, Epiphany occasioned festival debauchery, and noisy bibbers chose a king from among their own numbers. Today, January 6 is given as a holiday. It is a quiet family gathering or a good excuse to get together with friends for a more relaxed evening than the rigorous celebrations of the preceding couple of weeks. As with most holidays, customs for Epiphany are now largely secular and family-oriented. Throughout January, bakeries supply *galette* to the steady stream of buyers. People eat several *galettes* through the course of the month with family groups and with friends.

Rich pancakes and pastries feature in the end-of-winter holidays that preceded the Lenten fast in the Catholic calendar. *Crêpes* are traditional for *la Chandeleur* (Candlemas or Candle Festival) observed on February 2. In recollection of the presentation of Christ in the temple and the purification of the Virgin Mary, people went to church to have a candle blessed; the candle was lighted at auspicious moments during the rest of year for good luck. In rural areas, February 2 was also the day for attempting to predict how long winter weather would continue. This was done by observing animals in their lairs, to see whether they showed any signs of emerging from hibernation. Today, little ceremony outside of regular family meal customs marks the day. The *crêpes* are eaten rolled up with a bit of sugar, spread with jam such as apricot or cherry, or filled with a *purée* of fresh fruit. In the port city of Marseille, people eat golden-brown butter cookies called *navettes* (boats), shaped as their name suggests. The dough is patted into large, fat, almond shapes that are scored down the middle, so the cookies puff out while baking.

For *mardi gras* (Fat or Shrove Tuesday), the last day before the start of *Carême* (Lent) on *mercredi saint* (Ash Wednesday), people eat rich desserts made with milk and eggs, and plenty of butter or oil. *Beignets* (doughnuts), *bugnes* or *oreillettes* (knotted or twisted strips of dough that are fried), pancakes, and *crêpes* are typical. Historically, not only rich foods but also an orgiastic period of revelry directly preceded Lent. *Carnaval* (from the Latin *carnem levare*, i.e., *enlever les viandes* or to take away meats) lasted the weekend or entire week, ending with *mardi gras*. Through the mid-twentieth century, Carnival parades and processions were often quite elaborate. The celebration in Nice was especially famous. For months beforehand, people prepared floats and masks for the festive procession, which was accompanied by showers of flower petals. Carnival included the ludic selection of a king and queen who presided over a Feast of Fools, and the ritual battle between *Carnaval* and *Carême*—or standoff between the Fat and the Lean—was a big food fight pitting sausages, meats, and fowl against the fish and vegetables. The medieval fable *Aucassin et Nicolette* (ca. 1225) has a mild version in a topsy-turvy carnival atmosphere, with the characters slinging rotten crab apples, large prairie mushrooms, and fresh cheeses.[2] The wild, sometimes violent play and the disguises for Carnival made free with the usual social order. The commoner king and queen were an invented, festival aristocracy that mocked the exclusions based on bloodlines long key to privilege in the everyday world. Social theorists and historians have observed that turning *le monde à l'envers* (the world upside-down) through festivals such as Carnival doubtless released tensions that might otherwise manifest in a much more destructive fashion. The extraordinary scenes of parades and costumes, eating and drinking, in the pictures of the Niçois artist Gustav-Adolf Mossa suggest the months of careful preparation that went into Carnival. They also show just how big the blowout was.

After Carnival one was probably only too glad to withdraw into the asceticism of the *sainte quarantaine* or *Carême* (from the Latin *quadragesima* or fortieth day). The 40 lean days anticipating Easter recall Christ's fast in the desert and struggle against diabolical temptation. The period also resonates with the 40 days of the flood, the 40 years of the reign of King David, and so on, in the Old Testament. In today's secular, democratic society, with its paid holidays and personal celebrations, Carnival has declined to the status of a minor tourist attraction, and few people observe the old Lenten dietary restrictions, much less for the full 40 days. However, people enjoy the rich desserts on Fat Tuesday, and some eat fish on Ash Wednesday and on Lenten Fridays.

Pâques (Easter), marking the resurrection of Christ and symbolized by a spring lamb, is celebrated with roast lamb, *blanquette d'agneau* (white stew made with lamb), or, on Corsica and in some southern cities, roasted or stewed kid goat. Children receive chocolates and candies in the shape of fish, eggs, chickens, and rabbits to suggest life and seasonal renewal. Hard boiled eggs are put in salads and baked whole in dishes finished in the oven; eggs are mixed up into omelets, and they enrich breads and cakes such as the rich *pain de Pâques* (Easter bread) from the Vendée called *alise pacaude*.

November 11, *la Saint-Martin*, traditionally closed the harvest season and marked the end of agricultural work for the year, with a thanksgiving meal of roast goose and new wine. Today, the federal holiday on the same day, *la fête de l'Armistice* commemorating the armistice of 1918, is as likely to be in people's thoughts.

NEW YEAR'S

If Christmas and the winter religious holidays are spent with family, *la fête de Saint-Sylvestre* or New Year's Eve is usually spent with friends. The meal is as elegant as possible, with many of the festive foods typical for Christmas: oysters, *foie gras*, a roast goose or turkey, a roast beef, a ham. The *réveillon* (late meal) usually lasts at least until midnight, when corks pop and people drink a glass of Champagne to bring in the New Year. Municipal *feux d'artifices* (fireworks) are common, and people set off noisy *pétards* (firecrackers) and light sparklers. On the *jour de l'An*

(New Year's Day), a holiday from work, friends exchange *étrennes* or little gifts to inaugurate the coming year. January 1 is also the day for tipping mail carriers, merchants, and other people whom one sees throughout the year, but who are outside the close circles of family and friends.

PERSONAL EVENTS

Even among the large population of nonbelievers, it is fairly common to observe the sacramental rituals of church christenings for babies and first communions for older children. After the church ceremonies, the parents offer a festive lunch or dinner to family members, the godparents, and close friends. Essential for both occasions and also for weddings are a *pièce montée* and *dragées*. The *pièce montée* or pastry "set piece" is a carefully constructed dessert designed to dazzle the eyes as well as the palate. The classic pastry set piece is the conical *croquembouche* ("crunches in the mouth"). *Choux fourrés,* profiteroles or round pastry puffs filled with vanilla custard, are layered and stacked up (*montés*) into a tall pyramid. The pastry tower is drizzled with caramel that hardens to a shiny gleam and adds texture contrast. The cone shape is always considered appropriate and attractive, but imaginative *pâtissiers* also make puff pastry swans, flowers, cars, and so on, which can then be filled with cream.

The festive pastry set pieces, along with sugar sculptures, can be traced to the aristocratic tables of the medieval and renaissance eras. The showy desserts—*tours de force* that required a large kitchen staff and luxury ingredients including sugar—were status symbols that accrued prestige to the host. In the early nineteenth century, the chef Marie-Antoine Carême, who first trained as a *pâtissier* and was fascinated by architecture, found great play for his creativity in the *pièce montée*, treated in his illustrated books *Le pâtissier royal parisien* (1815) and *Le pâtissier pittoresque* (1815 and 1854). Even for the most complex design, such as an elegantly realized shady grotto or neoclassical façade, Carême insisted that all parts be edible. Now a *pièce montée* made out of puff pastry is an integral element to middle class and upper middle class celebrations. They are fairly costly and almost always ordered from a baker.

Distributing sachets of *dragées* (from the Greek *tragêmata*, sweetmeats) or sugar-coated almonds as favors to guests at weddings and baptisms is a custom with ancient roots. The Greeks and Romans ate honey-coated nuts, understood as symbols of fecundity. Medieval apothecaries distributed honey-coated spices such as coriander and fennel as medicinal breath fresheners and aids to digestion. Since the Renaissance, sugar has been used to coat spices for comfits and nuts for *dragées*. Today the *pièce*

Caterer Farnier's shop window in Blanzy advertises cooking for "All Receptions: Family Meals, Anniversaries, Baptisms, Communions, Marriages, Banquets, Buffets, Cocktails, Apéritifs, Business Meals, Inaugurations." Courtesy of Janine Depoil.

montée is often decorated with a few *dragées*, usually white or silver for a wedding or baptism.

Weddings, also traditionally a religious sacrament, are today usually secular family occasions. In either case, as in the United States, middle class and upper middle class wedding parties are carefully choreographed affairs that may involve a weekend-long party and great expense. The bride selects a gown. The couple chooses rings. A site for the party must be found and rented. Formal invitations must be printed and sent. There are meetings with florists and caterers to plan the decorations and meals. Although most couples live together before marrying and have fully functioning households, people sign up for the *listes de mariage* (registry) to orchestrate the gifts that are given, with the most common requests being new sets of plates, glasses, and cutlery along with additions for the kitchen. The wedding meal is designed according to the couples' tastes, but is on the scope of a banquet. A series of four or five or six courses includes *potage, entrée, plat* (or sometimes two, with fish and then meat), salad, and cheese. Wedding foods tend to be high-status items that are presented as elegantly as possible, even for a so-called *menu champêtre* (rustic or country menu). Menus often include *foie gras*, lobster, roasted monkfish, boned and stuffed fowl such as Guinea hen or capon. Dessert is the obligatory *coupe de Champagne* and spectacular *pièce montée*, although some couples choose a *gâteau à étages* or layer cake.

In addition to full-on weddings, parties to celebrate personal relationships assume many forms, from a gathering of friends and family at a favorite restaurant, to an evening party given at the home that already has been established. It is quite common for couples to live together without marrying and to start families. About 30 percent of children are born outside of wedlock; sometimes the parents decide to marry later on. Some marry at the local town hall but forego the religious celebration and traditional wedding. Since 1999, others marry through the PACS or *pacte civil de solidarité*, a civil alliance available both to heterosexual and to homosexual couples. Couples celebrate anniversaries with each other, perhaps with a romantic dinner out, but give large parties for important milestones such as the 25th and 50th anniversaries.

After a funeral, the bereaved family traditionally offers a *collation* or luncheon to their guests.

BIRTHDAYS

Before the 1950s, individuals quietly observed their name days according to the Catholic calendar with its commemorations of the deaths and ascensions of the various saints. Now the Anglo-Saxon custom of celebrating one's own *anniversaire* or *jour anniversaire* (birthday) prevails. For children, afternoon parties announced with written invitations enlarge on the four o'clock *goûter*, the regular afternoon snack. Entertaining savories such as *oeufs durs farcis* (stuffed hard-cooked eggs), stuffed tomatoes, *crêpes* garnished with an egg or piece of ham, or *croque-monsieur* (hot ham sandwiches pressed flat in an iron) may be offered first. The birthday cake is usually a plain cake that will appeal to children, such as a white or chocolate cake with chocolate icing. The cake is brought to the table studded with lit candles that the birthday person tries to blow out in one great breath. Avoided by many parents because of the sugar content, soft drinks are considered a great treat by children, and they are served for the exceptional occasion of the birthday. Sparkling apple juice called *champomi* (from *Champagne* and *pomme* for "apple champagne") is also popular. Family members and the child's godparents attend, along with other children, and all bring a gift. For the family meal, the favorite foods of the birthday person often figure on the menu.

Adults give their own birthday parties, and there is strong social pressure to stage parties for friends and family, who reciprocate by giving gifts. Since 1974, when the *majorité* was lowered from 21, the eighteenth

Carrying the birthday cake from
kitchen into dining room. Courtesy
of Nadine Leick.

birthday marks the passage into adulthood. At 18 one can vote, drive,
and drink alcoholic beverages legally. Older teenagers are usually quite
accustomed to drinking small amounts of wine as a part of the family meal
and alcohols in the form of an *apéritif*. The right to purchase alcohol at
age 18 is essentially a formality, rather than a rite of passage. Other important birthdays are the 25th, for the quarter-century, and then the decade
markers. The 60th birthday often coincides with a retirement party, an
occasion to celebrate an entire career.

ACADEMIC AND PROFESSIONAL ACHIEVEMENTS

To mark achievements at school and work, people invite colleagues
and teachers, family and friends, to a ceremonial *apéritif* or *pot* (drink).
A vernissage or gallery opening, or a gathering of business partners and
colleagues, may be the occasion for a *cocktail*, whose name borrows from the
American cocktail party. Since the 1970s, a *vin d'honneur*, with speeches
and toasts to accompany the lifting of glasses, takes place at weddings
before the dinner. At business or academic conferences, a *vin d'honneur*

may be drunk in tribute to an important speaker or guest, with *canapés* (light appetizers) to accompany the glass of wine, Champagne, or kir, before dinner. The verb *arroser* means "to water" or "to sprinkle" and by metaphorical, argotic extension to celebrate with a drink. A person who has just passed an important examination, defended a doctoral thesis, or even bought a new car invites family and friends to an *arrosage*.

HOUSE-WARMING PARTIES

People who have just moved into a new house or apartment invite guests to *pendre la crémaillère*. The phrase recalls the ceremony of hanging a rack or trammel in the chimney to hold the stock-pot over the fire. This done, one could cook, making the house inhabitable. People usually give parties with a buffet for the *pendaison de la crémaillère*, both to inaugurate the new place, and to make family and friends feel welcome. Foods are selected according to personal taste and the ease with which they can be served and then eaten from small plates as people circulate around the party. Common buffet items include platters of artfully arranged *crudités* or *charcuterie*, *bouchées de fromage* or savory baked puffs filled with a bit of cheese, salads of greens or grated carrots, *hachis parmentier* or shepherd's pie, slices of roast beef served at room temperature, a stew such as a southern *daube* or North African *tagine*, fruit salad, wedges of apple tart, and slices of *quatre quarts* (pound cake) or chocolate cake.

BASTILLE DAY

Le Quatorze juillet, or *le jour de la Bastille* (July 14), is the national holiday commemorating the storming of the Bastille prison in Paris at the start of the Revolution of 1789. Only a handful of prisoners were found, but the riot symbolized release from the oppressive shackles of the ancien régime social and political orders. Bastille Day brings tremendous collective celebrations. Cities and towns organize fireworks, *défilés* (parades), and outdoor concerts and dancing. The immense Paris parade is always televised. Other spectacular events include the fireworks off the picturesque Pont d'Avignon, which dramatically breaks off halfway across the Rhône River. Families and community groups such as volunteer firemen, military veterans, and hunting clubs set up the outdoor barbecue for *une grillade*, a mixed grill that might include *merguez*, steaks, and lamb chops. For fun, people improvise foods with the *bleu blanc rouge* (blue, white, and red) of the flag: cocktails made with layers of strawberry syrup on the bottom, and then mixed vodka and anisette, and finally Curaçao; scallops garnished with reddish-orange salmon eggs to be served on a bright blue plate; and desserts of blueberries, *fruits rouges* (raspberries, strawberries, cherries), and cream or *fromage blanc*.

Since the 1980s, events now staged annually such as Youth Day, Gay Pride (also called Euro-Pride or *la Marche des fiertés*), and the Techno Parade have the proportions and feelings of civic festivals, with parades, music, and plenty of eating, drinking, and revelry out of doors. As in many countries, sporting events such as soccer matches—a national passion— the Tour de France bicycle race, and marathons similarly offer something of the collective holiday experience.

TRADITIONAL LOCAL AND REGIONAL FESTIVALS

In recent years a great effort has been made to continue or revive traditional regional and agricultural celebrations. Most villages and small towns have a *fête votive*, *fête patronale*, *fête du pays*, or *kermesse* celebrating the town's patron saint. The festivals usually take place during the warm months, from May through October. They are fixed to a Sunday closest to the saint's day, and last a weekend or three days. The festivals often were tied to a communal activity for farming, such as planting, harvesting, or threshing, and many have ancient pagan roots. Today, there is great appreciation for the *fêtes votives* and also *fêtes folkloriques*, as they are thought to preserve and teach about local customs including dress, regional styles of dancing, and gastronomic specialties. For a *fête patronale* or other local occasion, a special mass may be observed in the town church, and vendors set up outdoor markets and flea markets in the main street or square.

Other festivals revived largely since the early 1990s are the May and December *fêtes de la transhumance*. It was customary to drive cows, sheep, and goats up to high ground for summer grazing. The descent back down to lower meadows and plains then followed the harvests. Today, trucks usually move the cattle, but the transhumance festivals are popular again especially in the late fall, when local cheeses made with the summer's rich milk can be sold. The *fêtes des vendanges* or *des moissons* or *d'abondance* were feasts offered to harvesters to thank them for their work and celebrate the year's bounty. New versions commemorate the old agricultural calendar and artisanal methods of work. The festivals are of great historical interest and are good for tourism. In recent years, they have also become vehicles for a certain revivalist, nationalist sentiment nostalgic for *la vieille France;* "old" here means Catholic France.

Demonstrating the mechanics of a wine press, in Grimaud. Courtesy of Janine Depoil.

On a larger scale, city or regional *fêtes* are often associated with a special cultural practice, although some of these are of modern vintage. Highlights of the festivals vary according to region. In Nîmes there is bull-fighting, although the bull is never killed, as in Spain. The international film festival takes place each May at Cannes, the theater festival in July in Avignon, and operas are staged throughout the summer in the Roman theatre at Orange. Organized on the model of these cultural festivals, newer *fêtes gourmandes* organized to promote the *patrimoine* have flourished in recent years. Local restaurateurs, producers, and the municipal authorities collaborate to stage fairs that focus on local produce, from chestnuts to wine. *Manifestations gastronomiques* or gastronomic events take many forms, such as a *tournée des restaurants* where people make the rounds of participating restaurants to sample local dishes.

Foires (fairs) have a carnival atmosphere like that of an amusement park. *Foires* or *fêtes foraines* formerly were associated with yearly outdoor markets (*marchés forains*) visited by itinerant merchants and traders. Today, the *foires* are heavily commercialized. Itinerant carnival workers set up lotteries, games, and rides. Vendors sell grilled *merguez* placed lengthwise in a piece of baguette, *barbes à papa* ("dad's beard" i.e., spun sugar cotton

Alain Gontard's restaurant in La Pacaudière announces an "open table" as part of the local gastronomic festival. The restaurant specializes in duck cookery including *foie gras de canard*. Courtesy of Christian Verdet/regard public-unpact.

candy), nougats, spice bread, waffles, *guimauves* (marshmallows), and the adored *chichi*, a long, flat *beignet* made of yeast dough flavored with orange-flower water and sprinkled with granulated sugar.

The mercantile aspect of the old *foires* is recalled in today's *salons* and *expositions* for producers of wine and brandies. These can be quite fancy affairs with a busy boutique atmosphere. Their attraction is increased by the fact that an invitation card is required for entry and tasting.

NEW HOLIDAYS AND FESTIVALS

Since the 1990s, American customs associated with Halloween on October 31 have been heavily commercialized, and Halloween is now quite popular among children. Adults have had mixed reactions, finding the macabre emphasis on ghosts and skeletons unappealing, but children love wearing costumes and masks, carving *citrouilles* (pumpkins), and receiving sweets. Halloween celebrations have for the moment overshadowed *la Toussaint* (All Saints' Day, November 1), a traditional religious holiday, today one of the federal holidays.

Also modeled after American counterparts are the *fête des Pères* (Father's Day), instituted in 1949 as the third Sunday in June, and the *fête des Mères* (Mother's Day), the last Sunday in May. These days are celebrated with a festive family meal. The other spouse and the children offer gifts and either do the cooking or treat everybody to an evening out.

NOTES

1. Kolleen M. Guy, *When Champagne Became French: Wine and the Making of a National Identity* (Baltimore: The Johns Hopkins University Press, 2003), 28–9.

2. "Il avoient aportés/des fromage[s] fres assés/et puns de bos waumonés/et grans canpegneus canpés." *Aucassin et Nicolette* (ca. 1225), ed. Jean Dufournet (Paris: Flammarion, 1984), canto 31.

7

Diet and Health

Abundance and variety have characterized the diet in France since the end of the Second World War. Across economic classes, the French associate taking the full three-course meal with a sense of well-being and with being in good health. The structured family meal provides nutritional balance and conditions daily eating for most people, while contributing to the quality of life that is so highly valued. As in other affluent nations, how-ever, abundance, the modern lifestyle, and contemporary agricultural and manufacturing practices also create dietary dilemmas. For some, *grignotage* (snacking) replaces or augments the cycle of three daily meals. Problems related to overconsumption, such as obesity, are on the rise. Genetically modified foods and agribusiness practices are perceived as threats to a healthy diet. At present, the widely felt need for precautionary and protective measures shapes the response to matters of diet and health.

BALANCE, MODERATION, AND PLEASURE

The variety of foods that is now available to the broadest swathe of the population has not always been a feature of the diet. In rural areas, bread, legumes, and vegetables from the kitchen garden had been the building blocks of daily meals. Animal protein was likely to be in the form of eggs, milk, or cheese, although meat consumption varied by region. In cities, meat consumption increased substantially during the nineteenth century, but prices fluctuated and the best cuts were quite expensive. During the

Occupation of the 1940s, farmers sent their best meat and dairy products off to the German Reich. Rationing at home allowed for only 1,200 calories per day by 1943, and life expectancy dropped drastically during the Vichy years. As recently as the mid-twentieth century, hunger and diseases that result from dietary deficiencies had not been eradicated. Affluence and modernization associated with the *Trente glorieuses* or Thirty Glorious Years of rebuilding after the war resulted in significant changes. In 1962, under the PAC or *Politique agricole commune* (CAP or Common Agricultural Policy), the European Union began giving massive subventions to French grain, dairy, and beef farmers. The purpose of the assistance was to guarantee a stable food supply. Using PAC funds, farmers adopted modern industrial techniques. Overproduction and a reliable, inexpensive supply of beef, dairy products, and grains made the earlier shortages and fluctuations a thing of the past.

Today the centerpiece of most middle class meals in France is meat, whether beef, pork, *charcuterie*, lamb, or fowl. Dairy products, including milk, eggs, and fresh and aged cheeses are very important. Yogurt, which has been heavily marketed as a healthy way to "eat milk," is popular. A wide variety of fruits and vegetables are eaten, including raw salads and *crudités*. Bread retains a strong symbolic importance, but consumption has declined in favor of animal proteins and fresh produce. The use of butter, animal fats such as lard and goose fat, and vegetable oils used to vary largely by region. At present, the broad preference for cooking with vegetable oils such as sunflower oil stems from their lower prices, on the one hand, and information about health benefits associated with unsaturated vegetable oils and the Mediterranean diet, on the other. Wine was long viewed as a healthy, strengthening beverage and in this sense was seen as quite distinct from distilled alcohols. Despite this perception, rates of alcoholism and diseases such as cirrhosis of the liver were high through the mid-twentieth century. The view that wine is healthful has not disappeared, but consumption of wine has declined.[1]

The benefits of eating the full three-course family meal are thought of in a holistic fashion. The American practices of counting calories and weighing portions would seem quite strange to most people. Eating a variety of fresh foods is more generally understood as key to *une bonne nutrition* or *une alimentation saine* (good nutrition, a diet that is healthy), and variety is precisely what characterizes the full meal with its complement of three or four different dishes. Nutrition is only part of the recipe, however. Culinary quality and sensual appreciation of food are essential to the perception that one is eating well. Conviviality and social connection, eating in the company of friends or family, are equally necessary ingredients. Similarly, the respite from the activities of the day imposed by the slow rhythm of the full meal, cannot be discounted.[2] Spending time at table and taking pleasure in eating are as important as what is eaten. People use the terms *équilibre* (balance), *modération* (moderation), and *plaisir* (enjoyment) to name the salient features of eating well and *harmonieuses* (harmonious) to describe the ensemble of practices that go into eating well. The sense of pleasure and balance guide the practical aspects of cooking and serving daily meals, such as determining the relatively small portion sizes for individual components of a meal.

THE FRENCH PARADOX

In the late 1980s and early 1990s, American and French researchers identified a phenomenon they named the French Paradox, which received extensive coverage in the media. The French, it was observed, regularly drank wine and ate all sorts of foods rich in animal fats, such as cheeses and butter. Relative to Americans, northern Europeans, and the British, they had comparable or higher cholesterol levels, yet lower mortality rates from cardiovascular and coronary diseases. The very lowest rates of coronary disease were measured in the southwestern Languedoc region, famous for *foie gras* and rib-sticking *cassoulet*, the baked meat and

Enjoying a good meal and a glass of wine with friends contributes to quality of life and good health *à la française*. Courtesy of Christian Verdet/regard public-unpact.

bean stew that is generously enriched with goose or duck fat.³ Here, then, was a people eating a dangerously delicious diet, yet enjoying good health. How was this contradiction to be explained?

Various answers have been proposed to explain the so-called paradox. Moderate consumption of wine or other alcohols can play a role in counteracting the effects of cholesterol. Other factors are important, as well. The French diet is varied. It includes relatively high proportions of fruits, vegetables, grains, and legumes, in addition to meats, cheese, and wine. Compared with their American equivalents, portion sizes in restaurants, homes, stores, and recipes are small. People spend more time at table for meals, yet they eat less. The rituals of serving and sharing food and of politeness such as finishing up at about the same time as one's table companions, tend to prevent one from eating too much. Mealtime is strongly associated with relaxation, socializing, and enjoyment.⁴ Physical activities such as walking have a larger place in people's daily routines. Nearly universal access to high quality health care through the national *sécurité sociale* (social security) and emphasis on preventive care contribute to the health of the population. (Lifespan for women is more than 83 years, the longest in Europe.) Each of these elements in the diet and lifestyle plays a role in maintaining health.

PREGNANCY, BIRTH, AND BREASTFEEDING

Women expecting babies are notorious for having sudden, strong *envies* (cravings), but a *régime équilibré* (balanced diet) is the order of the day. The health insurance system guarantees women prenatal care, including a minimum of five required prenatal visits to the doctor, a hospital stay that lasts four to five days under normal circumstances at the time of the birth, and 10 weeks of paid maternity leave from their jobs. Midwives commonly deliver babies. In case of any complication, a doctor is called. Pregnancy is not seen as an infirmity, but rather as an enhanced state of health and femininity. Doctors discourage women from putting on too much extra weight during pregnancy, as this is seen as self-indulgent and quite unnecessary. Making minor adjustments to the diet in response to the changing state of the body during pregnancy is recommended, however. Mineral waters with a high magnesium content are useful against the common problem of constipation, for instance. Beyond the constant admonition to drink as much plain "pure" (i.e., lacking trace minerals) water as possible, moderation in all things is recommended. Most women reduce the amount of coffee and wine during pregnancy to avoid excessive caffeine and alcohol. At the same time, few cut these items out of their diet entirely, continuing to sip a *café au lait* in the morning, if it continues to appeal, and perhaps a small glass of wine with dinner. Except in the case of a specific health problem or intolerance, a more extreme approach is perceived as fanatical. The exception is raw salads and raw vegetables that cannot be peeled. These are strictly *déconseillés* (recommended against), because in France they bring the risk of toxoplasmosis.

The birth of the child is, naturally, an occasion for celebration. Family and friends visiting the new mother and child after they have left the *maternité* (maternity ward or room) bring gifts for the mother, such as flowers and bottles of Champagne, in addition to useful items for the baby, such as clothing.

The attitude toward feeding infants is practical. It is recognized that breastfeeding a newborn is highly beneficial to the child. At the same time, there is little stigma attached to choosing against breastfeeding. If the mother does not want to or cannot, it is thought that there is no use asking her to act *à contrecoeur* (against her wishes). In this case, there is recourse to the wide variety of formulas for infants in every stage of development, available in the *supermarchés*. About half of women breast-feed their babies, and doctors recommend that they stop at three months. At three months, the baby has received the essential nutrients and antibodies from the mother. There is also a good deal of generalized social pressure to stop at this point. It is widely felt that to extend breastfeeding any longer is unseemly, as if to do so might hold back the infant in the earliest stages of development. To continue to breast-feed an infant after three months may also be impractical if the mother must return to work after the 10-week paid maternity leave.

BABIES AND CHILDREN

Initiating children into the rites of the table is essential to their education, socialization, and health. Babies and very young children often eat separately from the parents, who take their meals a bit later. At about three to four months, babies are offered *purées de fruits,* then cooked puréed vegetables, in addition to breast milk or formula. As the baby begins to eat solid food, people buy *petits pots* (jars of baby food) or make food at home, relying on the simplest cooking methods that avoid the use of fats, such as steaming, boiling, and poaching. At about six months, a greater variety of vegetable purées are proposed, then cereals such as semolina and rice, honey, yogurt and *fromage blanc,* and tiny quantities of meat or fish: first *viande blanche* or white meats (chicken, veal) and *poisson blanc* or *maigre* or white fish that is low in fat (sole, cod, hake), then beef, and eventually ham. At about nine months or so, children are offered bread, then eggs. At about one year, fattier fish such as sardines, tuna, and salmon may be incorporated into the diet, along with raw vegetable such as peeled grated carrots and cooked dried legumes such as lentils and *haricots*. By about a year to 15 months, when the baby can drink cow's milk, it is thought that the child can eat a full variety of solid foods. The strong dietary prohibitions for babies are against added salt and sugar, foods that are too fatty or strong in flavor, and foods that present extra risks of bacteria or allergens: no pork, horsemeat, game, shellfish, fried foods, peanuts, or spices, and no sweets.

To young children (ages three to six years) parents give simple foods seen as easy to digest and appealing to the still-developing palette. The classic child's meal begins with a *potage* (soup) made of vegetables boiled in lightly salted water or plain broth, then passed through a *moulinette* (food mill) or puréed with the hand-held *mixeur-plongeant*. Potatoes, broccoli, turnips, leeks, spinach, carrots, pumpkin, and artichokes are common soup ingredients. A bit of pasta may be cooked in the soup and a spoon of grated Gruyère added for garnish. *Jambon-coquillettes* is a favorite children's meal: boiled pasta such as small shells or elbow macaroni with a bit of butter and mild grated cheese and a slice of *jambon blanc* (fresh ham, more meaty and less salty than the aged hams). Meat, especially red meat, and beef in particular, is considered important, as it is thought to *donner des forces* (build strength). It is recommended that children eat meat once each day, and parents enjoin their child to *Mange ta viande!* ("Eat your meat!"). Small children eat meat that is thoroughly cooked; older children are taught to appreciate beef that is *saignant* ("bloody," i.e., rare), as adults do. Butchers grind to order children's portions of *steak haché* (ground or chopped beef), which is then loosely patted into a flat oval shape to be pan fried. *Escalopes de poulet* (chicken cutlets) sautéed in butter or oil are popular. Vegetable *purées*, enriched with a little milk and a tiny quantity of butter, are essential preparations, along with bread to accompany everything. Food for children is ideally to be nutritious, tasty, and well textured. Soft foods, too many sweets, and too much sugar are avoided. Sodas are viewed as empty calories and are frowned upon. The same is true of fruit juices, seen as overly sugary, and a poor substitute for fresh fruit. In the morning, children are given hot milk or hot chocolate. Later in the day they may drink *tisanes* (herbal infusions) but no coffee or tea. Older children are expected to sit at table with adults, to eat the same foods that adults are eating, and to be polite and sociable.

There is great concern among parents and at the level of the state to inculcate good eating habits in children. Parents want to raise healthy children who enjoy a good quality of life and who are equipped to be socially integrated. The state is concerned with public health, as it regulates the health care system and has the economic vitality of the country in mind. In secondary schools, the annual fall *Semaine du goût* and other initiatives teach children about the country's culinary heritage and simultaneously present alternatives to *la mal bouffe* ("bad grub"). Beginning in the 1970s, the term *mal bouffe* or *malbouffe* was used to mean fast food and junk food. Now it can refer to any food considered unhealthy, an unbalanced diet, an unreflecting mode of eating. As part of the effort to protect the health of children by encouraging good eating habits, the state has forbidden the sale of soft drinks and candies in secondary schools and mandated that lessons on nutrition and health be incorporated into the national curriculum. Similarly, the state regulates television advertising, seen as exerting a nefarious influence on children's health and eating and consumer habits. At present, for instance, commercials cannot occupy more than 12 minutes to the hour on television, and televised publicity for tobacco and for beverages containing more than 1.2 percent alcohol is forbidden.[5]

FOOD FOR THE SICK

When care of the seriously ill still was given at home and predominantly by family members, household manuals and most cookbooks included a section with recipes for the treatment of the *invalide* (invalid or sick person). Today, "pectoral" broths and home remedies such as chest plasters have disappeared, in favor of the modern commercial pharmaceuticals that professional doctors prescribe.

There remains little concept of specific foods appropriate for the ill; rather, adjustments are made to the diet overall. As in the United States, serious conditions are addressed with radical changes, such as a low-protein diet in the case of kidney problems. In a nation of wine-drinkers, the *crise de foie* ("liver crisis") was a classic complaint, extensible to nearly any malaise. Today, of course, avoiding alcohol is recommended against the more specific problems of cirrhosis or enzyme imbalance. There is, similarly, little conception of a special diet for the *troisième* and *quatrième âges* (third and fourth ages, i.e., retirement and old age: people ages 60 and older and 75 and older, respectively) outside of reducing portions to suit lower activity levels and a slower metabolism. For the minor, day-to-day complaints, smaller adjustments are made. In case of *bouffissures* or *gonflements* (swelling resulting from water retention), an effort is made to reduce the intake of wine, coffee, and salty and rich foods such as cheese. For temporary illness affecting the appetite, light and easily digested foods are recommended. Against gastric ills, plain boiled rice and cooked carrots form the menu, and doctors recommend that one avoid green vegetables and salads, until the illness has passed. *Purée de pommes* (apple sauce) may also be given, as well as broths or light soups. Mineral waters high in magnesium, salads, fresh fruits and vegetables, even a drink of *pastis* may be taken to improve digestion, and plain yogurt eaten to soothe the stomach and encourage beneficial intestinal flora. *Tisanes* or herbal infusions are enjoyed as after-dinner hot drinks or before bed, but they are also thought to have specific useful properties: rose hips against colds, chamomile to soothe the stomach, linden as a calming tea before bed. An after-dinner drink such as a Cognac or other fruit brandy is referred to as a *digestif* (digestive). The small shot of strong alcohol is thought to settle the stomach after a rich or large meal and to promote digestion.

Knowledge of the medicinal properties of foods and notions of regulating health through diet are traceable to antiquity. The holistic approach to balancing the diet has its most ancient roots in the Greek theory of the four bodily humors, which had to be balanced through the best choice of foods for an individual's constitution. Today, the view that connects health and diet through a notion of harmony and balance is completed by the conviction that adequate rest and relaxation, including proper vacations from work, are important for health.

As a complement to the maintenance of health through a balanced, harmonious diet, there is also a *cachet* (gel capsule), *comprimé* (tablet), or *pillule* (pill) designed, it seems, for every health problem, no matter how small. That France is a highly medicalized country is due in part to the provisions of the outstanding national medical care. Coverage allows patients to choose their physicians, and it gives physicians great freedom to prescribe medications and tests. Consumer awareness and the ongoing development of new pharmaceuticals, including those to treat complaints such as cardiovascular disease and hypertension that are relatively common in the aging population, further contribute to this trend.[6]

PROBLEMS OF ABUNDANCE

As in most affluent countries where people have an *embarras du choix* (a wealth of choice—or too many choices), problems related to eating too much are on the rise. Conditions associated with an overabundant diet combined with a sedentary lifestyle, notably obesity, are becoming more prevalent. In 2006, INSERM, the *Institut National de la Santé et de la Recherche Médicale* or National Institute for Health and Medical Research, estimated that 1 of every 10 children is obese by the age of 10, twice the figure measured in 1980.[7] Categorizations of weight as "normal," "excessive," and so on derive from the IMC or *indice de masse corporelle* (BMI or body mass index) established by the World Health Organization's International Obesity Task Force. The IMC is a ratio calculated to evaluate a person's weight status. It is defined as weight in kilograms, divided by the square of the height measured in meters. According to this ratio, overweight is defined as having an IMC of greater than 25; an IMC greater than 30 indicates obesity. In France as in the United States, putting on excess weight often results from the addition of snacks to the schedule of regular meals[8]; from eating for reasons such as boredom or stress, rather than hunger; from eating large quantities of sugar in sweets, processed foods, and sodas; and from a lack of adequate physical activity. Physicians and researchers observe higher incidences of gastric and intestinal disorders, diabetes, sleep apnea, and other conditions associated with excess weight. Overconsumption may bring or manifest psychological stresses, as well, especially as contemporary ideals of beauty for both men and women require a slender *ligne* (figure). Pathological behaviors related to eating and having psychological causes, such as anorexia and bulimia, slowly increase, along with the sale of weight loss products first developed in the United States and now infiltrating the French market.

The progress of afflictions related to overconsumption, although alarming, is slower in France than in many other nations. This is due to the strong traditions of the family meal, to the sense of ceremony that accompanies eating, and to the fact that many families continue to cook regular meals at home and to take regular meals when dining out. In the last decade, the state has adopted an interventionist mode, encouraging, and even requiring, preventive measures as part of regular health care. A *carnet de santé* (health notebook) is established for each child at birth. The notebook is used to monitor preventable conditions throughout childhood. Doctors note such information as the dates of required vaccinations, any instance of dental decay, and domestic accidents. Since 1995, the notebooks contain a *courbe de corpulence* (corpulence curve) to track the child's weight relative to a normal estimate for development based on the body mass index. A departure from the normal range on the curve sounds the alert. For cases of weight gain, doctors advise a modest reduction in portion size to be observed over the long term, avoidance of sweets and eating between meals, and the encouragement of physical activity such as walking and playing outdoors.

FOOD SAFETY

The safety of the food supply and the reliability of the federal and European governments in its regulation are contemporary preoccupations. Although most edibles are purchased at grocery stores, procuring fresh food directly from a farmer remains an ideal. People want the foods that they purchase and eat to be natural and unadulterated for the purpose of commerce or convenience, thus pure, as well as affordable. Ideally, they want to know the origins of what they eat, traceable to a specific place and an individual producer. *Terroir* and the AOC label, with their references to quality, artisanal methods, and regional particularity, respond well to these ideals. The notion of purity at work here should not be confused with the equally important matter of hygiene or cleanliness. The French are notorious defenders of the salubriousness and unbeatable savor of, for instance, the cheeses that they carefully craft from raw (unpasteurized) milk. The expanding market for domestic and imported *produits biologiques* (organic items) indexes the concern to eat the natural foods that are believed to be the healthiest. That people pay more for organic items suggests the additional ethical interest in supporting ecologically sustainable and nonpolluting methods of agriculture, a feature of organic farming.

The biggest bugbears are OGM or *organismes génétiquement modifiés* (GMOs or genetically modified organisms) and other corporate industrial agricultural practices such as the use of antibiotics and growth hormones in meat. Human interference with the genetic makeup of foods is traceable to prehistoric times. Long before the development of sophisticated techniques for breeding and hybridization, humans began to tinker with the natural selection of characteristics in plants and animals through hunting and gathering, herding and agriculture. Where these and later practices result in modifications within single species, however, the term OGM refers to transgenic alterations. That is, an OGM is a plant or animal that has received genetic material from a different kind of plant or animal. At present worldwide, the most common transgenic foodstuffs and crops are soybeans, corn, and cotton that contain genes from bacteria providing resistance to herbicides (allowing for or requiring the use of pesticides) or insects (providing resistance to pests). Most genetically modified crops are grown (since 1994) in the United States, where most processed foods for sale contain ingredients from a genetically modified crop. By contrast, transgenic foods are rare in Europe. France grows only a few hundred hectares of genetically modified crops, and the farmers who grow them are responsible for indemnities, should other crops accidentally be contaminated by a stray seed or by pollen.[9]

The pervasive mistrust of transgenic foods and industrial farming practices—viewed as unnatural, unhealthy, and environmentally harmful—combines with abiding suspicion of the state's commitment to protect people. Two incidents that occurred in the mid-1990s provoked extraordinary social mobilization, protest, and debate. In 1996, cargo loads of American transgenic soy arrived in France. This transpired shortly after the first known death (in 1995) in the United Kingdom from Creutzfeldt-Jacob disease, the human variant of BSE or bovine spongiform encephalopathy. As tens of thousands of cows were put to death, and as more people died including in France, the spread of the disease was traced to the cannibalistic practice in industrial agriculture of recycling animal waste as feed. That is, cows on industrial farms were being fed the remains of other slaughtered cows, such as in the form of bone meal. Some of the feed was contaminated. The strong reaction in France and Europe to these incidents and practices helps to explain regulations currently in force.

Recent statutes regarding animals and meat give a sense of the strong interest in maintaining a safe, natural food supply in a manner that is also ethical and ecologically sustainable. In 1997, the European Union included a clause in the Treaty of Amsterdam that requires member states to protect the welfare of animals as sentient beings.[10] Veterinary inspectors make regular visits to slaughterhouses, and other changes have been enacted. For instance, European Union regulations now prohibit old-fashioned methods for raising *le veau sous la mère* (milk-fed veal), designed to produce truly white, rather than pink, flesh, such as sheltering young calves from the light. In France and the European Union, administering growth hormones to animals destined to be sold for meat is illegal. In 1999, the European market closed to imported beef raised on growth hormones, and the European Union is currently financing studies to understand the harmful effects of hormones and also antibiotics in meat.[11] Laws enacted in the 1990s multiplied the quality-control labels for meat. As in the case of wine, the *AOC* label indicates a typical, regional product, as well as a standard of quality. *AB* stands for *Agriculture biologique* or organically raised meat. The *Label Rouge* (red label) and *Certificat de Conformité* (quality standards certificate) indicate high grades of meat. Since the late 1970s, animals raised for milk and meat have been carefully tracked. In 1998, the French system was modified to conform to European regulations, which in fact largely follow the French system of controls that was already in place. Since 2000, meat sold prepackaged in supermarkets carries an identifying ticket indicating the cut of meat, the date by which it is best consumed, the place of origin of the animal, and identifying information for the slaughterhouse where it was killed and processed. The year 2001 saw the creation of the AFSSA or *Agence française de sécurité sanitaire des aliments* (French Agency for Food Sanitation and Security) to protect consumer interests.[12]

The current stance regarding OGM is slightly ambiguous. France, like Europe, and unlike the United States, follows the *principe de précaution* (precautionary principle) regarding transgenic modification. According to the precautionary principle, transgenic crops and foods must be proven safe before they are made available to farmers and consumers, with the burden of proof for safety resting on producers. In 1998, seven member states, including France, implemented a ban on the sale of any new bio-engineered crops, as testing of old applications continued. In October 2003, European rules began to require that the presence even of a small quantity of transgenic organism (0.9 percent of authorized and 0.5 percent of nonauthorized OGM for the European market) be indicated on labels for food and animal feed.[13] In 2004, Europe began again to approve transgenic crops for importing, effectively putting an end to the old moratorium. The blanket bans on genetically modified foods have been superseded, then, by the labeling rules that make their presence transparent and that make transgenic products traceable. Against the rulings of other authorities such as the European Commission, however, the European Court of Justice continues to back countries that wish to ban genetically modified crops if they can demonstrate a health risk. Despite the legal ambiguity, few people are willing to buy transgenic foods. Many people, including specialized consumer interest groups, maintain a remarkably vigilant attitude. People remain aware of the sway that corporate and trading interests exert on the government, which is responsible for regulation, and keen to protect the rich traditions of agriculture and artisanal production, cooking and eating that define living well *à la française*.

NOTES

1. Sandrine Blanchard, "Les Français consomment moins d'alcool et de tabac," *Le Monde* (March 9, 2006).

2. Alexandre Lazareff, *L'exception culinaire française* (Paris: Albin Michel, 1998), 136.

3. J. L. Richard, "Les facteurs de risque coronarien: Le paradoxe français," *Archives des Maladies du Coeur et des Vaisseaux* 80 (April 1987): 17–21; Serge

Renaud and M. de Lorgeril, "Dietary lipids and their relation to ischaemic heart disease: From epidemiology to prevention," *Journal of Internal Medicine* 225 (Supplement 1, 1989): 39–46 and "Wine, alcohol, platelets, and the French paradox for coronary heart disease," *The Lancet* 339 (1992): 1523–26; and Serge Renaud, *Le Régime Santé* (Paris: Éditions Odile Jacob, 1995).

4. Paul Rozin, Kimberly Kabnick, Erin Pete, Claude Fischler, and Christy Shields, "The Ecology of Eating: Smaller Portion Sizes in France Than in the United States Help Explain the French Paradox," *Psychological Science* 14, no. 5 (September 2003): 450–54.

5. Monique Dagnaud, *Enfants, consommation et publicité télévisée. Notes et études documentaires* 5166 (Paris: La Documentation Française, 2003), 12 and 55–67.

6. Sophie Chauveau, "Malades ou consommateurs? La consommation de médicaments en France dans le second XXe siècle," pp. 182–98 in Alain Chatriot, Marie-Emmanuelle Chessel, and Matthew Hilton, eds., *Au nom du consommateur* (Paris: Découverte, 2004).

7. "Obésité des jeunes" (May 2006), http://www.inserm.fr/.

8. Jean-Pierre Poulain, *Sociologies de l'alimentation* (Paris: PUF, 2002) and *Manger aujourd'hui* (Toulouse: Privat, 2002).

9. Hervé Morin, "Monsanto élabore les OGM de demain," *Le Monde* (March 21, 2006).

10. Jo Murphy-Lawless, "Risk, Ethics, and Public Space: The Impact of BSE and Foot-and-Mouth Disease on Public Thinking," p. 225 in Barbara Herr Harthorn and Laury Oaks, eds., *Risk, Culture, and Health Ineqality* (Westport, CT: Praeger, 2003).

11. Francesca Bray, "Genetically Modified Foods: Shared Risk and Global Action," in Harthorn and Oaks, 196.

12. Alain Chatriot, "Qui défend le consommateur? Associations, institutions et politiques publiques en France (1972–2003)," p. 179 in Chatriot, Chessel, and Hilton.

13. Céline Granjou, "Traçabilité, étiquetage et émergence du 'citoyen-consommateur': l'exemple des OGM," p. 208 in Chatriot, Chessel, and Hilton.

Glossary

Amuse-bouche   Appetizer.

Apéritif   A drink taken before lunch or dinner and served with finger food such as nuts, chips, or appetizers.

Baguette   Long, slim crusty loaf of bread.

Biscuits   Cookies.

Boulangerie   Bread bakery and shop.

Bouquet garni   A bundle of fresh herbs dropped into broths and soups to lend flavor during cooking.

Café   A small, strong coffee. Also a café or coffee shop.

Café au lait   Coffee with hot milk drunk at breakfast.

Cantine   Canteen or cafeteria.

Charcuterie   Cured meat products, especially pork, such as hams and sausages.

Collation   Mid-morning snack for children.

Croissant   Buttery, flaky, crescent-shaped breakfast pastry.

Crudités   Raw vegetables, served as a composed salad for the first course of a meal.

Déjeuner   Lunch, mid-day meal.

Digestif   Drink served after a meal.

Dîner   Dinner, evening meal.

Dragée   Sugar-coated almond or Jordan almond.

Entrée   The first course of a meal, such as a cooked salad.

Foie gras   Fattened liver of a *canard* (duck) or *oie* (goose). A great delicacy.

Frites   French fried potatoes.

Fromage   Cheese; also the cheese course of a meal.

Goûter   Afternoon snack for children.

Lard   Fresh bacon used in cooking.

Merguez   Spicy beef or lamb sausage.

Pain au chocolat   Croissant filled with chocolate.

Pâtisserie   Pastry; also the pastry bakery and shop.

Petit-déjeuner   Breakfast.

Pâte   Pastry dough or bread dough.

Pâtes   Pasta, such as spaghetti or elbow macaroni.

Plat   Main course of a meal, usually meat; the *plat* is the second course, after the *entrée*.

Poisson   Fish.

Potage   Soup.

Réveillon   Late festive meal served on Christmas Eve and on New Year's Eve.

Stockfisch   Salted dried codfish.

Tarte   Tart, like a pie with a bottom crust only.

Tartine   Bread spread with something, such as butter or jam.

Tisane   Herbal tea, or infusion.

Tourte   Tart covered with a top crust and usually having a savory filling.

Viande   Meat.

Vinaigrette   Oil and vinegar dressing.

Resource Guide

WEB SITES, ORGANIZATIONS, AND OFFICES

Centre de Recherche pour l'Étude et l'Observation des Conditions de Vie (CREDOC)
Research Center for the Study and Observation of Living Conditions
http://www.credoc.fr/

Chef Simon
http://www.chefsimon.com/

Commission Européenne
European Commission
http://ec.europa.eu/

Institut Européen d'Histoire et des Cultures de l'Alimentation (IEHCA)
European Institute of Food History and Cultures
http://www.ieha.asso.fr/

Institut National des Appellations d'Origine (INAO)
National Institute of Denominations of Origin
http://www.inao.gouv.fr/

Institut National de la Recherche Agronomique (INRA)
National Institute of Agronomic Research
http://www.inra.fr/

Institut National de la Santé et de la Recherche Médicale (INSERM)
National Institute of Health and Medical Research
http://www.inserm.fr/

Institut National de la Statistique et des Études Économiques (INSEE)
National Institute of Statistics and Economic Studies
http://www.insee.fr/

Ministère de l'Agriculture et de la Pêche
Ministry of Agriculture and Fishing
http://www.agriculture.gouv.fr/

Ministère de la Culture
Ministry of Culture
http://www.culture.gouv.fr/

Ministère de l'Éducation Nationale
Ministry of National Education
http://www.education.gouv.fr/

Ministère de la Santé et de la Protection Sociale
Ministry of Health and Social Protection
http://www.sante.gouv.fr/

Recipes
http://marmiton.org/

MAGAZINES

Chefs et saveurs
L'Hôtellerie
Néorestauration
Omnivore
Papilles
60 Millions de consommateurs
Vins, saveurs et traditions

FILMS

Adieu, Philippine (1963) by Jacques Rozier.
Une affaire de goût (2000) by Bernard Rapp.
L'Aile ou la cuisse (1976) by Claude Zidi.
Alimentation générale (2005) by Chantal Briet.
Au Bon Beurre (1952) by Jean Dutourd.
Le Boucher (1970) by Claude Chabrol.
La Bûche (1999) by Danièle Thompson.
Carnages (2002) by Delphine Gleize.

Chacun cherche son chat (1996) by Cedric Klapisch.

Le Chagrin et la pitié (1972) by Marcel Ophüls.

Le Charme discret de la bourgeoisie (1972) by Luis Buñuel.

Chocolat (1988) by Claire Denis.

La Cuisine au beurre (1963) by Gilles Grangier.

Cuisine et dépendances (1993) by Philippe Muyl.

Décalage horaire (2002) by Danièle Thompson.

Delicatessen (1991) by Marc Caro and Jean-Pierre Jeunet.

La Femme du boulanger (1938) by Marcel Pagnol.

Le Festin de Babette [*Babettes Gaestebud*] (1987) by Gabriel Axel.

Les Glaneurs et la glaneuse (2000) by Agnès Varda.

La Grande bouffe (1973) by Marco Ferreri.

Jean de Florette (1986) by Claude Berri.

Le joli mai (1962) by Chris Marker.

Manon des sources (1953) by Marcel Pagnol and version of (1986) by Claude Berri.

Masculin / Féminin (1966) by Jean-Luc Godard.

Métisse (1993) by Mathieu Kassovitz.

Mille et une recettes d'un cuisinier amoureux (1996) by Nana Dzhordzadze.

Mon oncle (1958) by Jacques Tati.

Mondovino (2004) by Jonathan Nossiter.

Monsieur Ibrahim et les fleurs du Coran (2002) by François Dupeyron.

Nénette et Boni (1996) by Claire Denis.

Au Petit Marguery (1995) by Laurent Bénégui.

Les Quatre cents coups (1959) by François Truffaut.

Les Stances à Sophie (1970) by Moshé Mizrahi.

37°2 le matin (1986) by Jean-Jacques Beineix.

Touchez pas au grisbi (1954) by Jacques Becker.

La Traversée de Paris (1956) by Claude Autant-Lara.

Vatel (1990) by Roland Joffé.

Le Week-end (1967) by Jean-Luc Godard.

Selected Bibliography

GENERAL WORKS

The Cambridge World History of Food. Editors Kenneth F. Kiple and Kriemhild Coneè Ornelas. 2 vols. Cambridge, UK: Cambridge University Press, 2000.
Culinary Biographies. Editor Alice Arndt. Houston: YesPress, 2006.
Larousse gastronomique. Editors Joël Robuchon and the Gastronomic Committee. New York: Clarkson Potter, 2001.
The Oxford Companion to Food. Editor Alan Davidson. Oxford, UK: Oxford University Press, 1999.
The Oxford Companion to Wine. Editor Jancis Robinson. 2nd edition. Oxford, UK: Oxford University Press, 1999.

COOKBOOKS

Andrews, Colman, et al. *Saveur Cooks Authentic French.* San Francisco: Chronicle Books, 1999.
Blanc, Georges and Coco Jobard. *Simple French Cooking: Recipes from Our Mothers' Kitchens* (2000). London: Cassell, 2001.
Bocuse, Paul. *La Cuisine du marché* (1976). Paris: Flammarion, 1980.
Boudou, Evelyne and Jean-Marc Boudou. *Les bonnes recettes des bouchons lyonnais.* Seyssinet: Libris, 2003.
Child, Julia with Louisette Bertholle and Simone Beck. *Mastering the Art of French Cooking* (1961). Vol. 1. New York: Alfred A. Knopf, 1998.
——— with Simone Beck. *Mastering the Art of French Cooking* (1970). Vol. 2. New York: Alfred A. Knopf, 1998.

Le Cordon Bleu at Home (1991). New York: William Morrow, 2001.

Culinaria France (1998). Editor André Dominé. Cologne: Könemann, 1999.

Duplessy, Bernard. *Cuisine traditionnelle en pays niçois*. Aix-en-Provence: Édisud, 1995.

Escoffier, Auguste. *The Complete Guide to the Art of Modern Cookery* (1903). Translators H. L. Cracknell and R. J. Kaufmann. New York: John Wiley, 2001.

Fletcher, Janet and Hallie Donnelly Harron. *French Home Cooking*. San Francisco: California Culinary Academy, 1989.

Gaborieau, Stéphane. *Cuisine lyonnaise d'hier et d'aujourd'hui*. Rennes: Ouest-France, 2005.

Granoux-Lansard, Monique. *Les meilleures recettes de Provence et de Côte d'Azur*. Colmar: S.A.E.P., 1986.

Gringoire, T. and L. Saulnier. *Le Répertoire de la cuisine* (1914). Paris: Flammarion, 1986.

Guérard, Michel. *La grande cuisine minceur*. Paris: Robert Laffont, 1976.

Guillot, André. *La grande cuisine bourgeoise: Souvenirs, secrets, recettes*. Paris: Flammarion, 1976.

———. *La vraie cuisine légère*. Paris: Flammarion, 1981.

Hal, Fatéma. *Les saveurs et les gestes: Cuisines et traditions du Maroc*. Preface by Tahar ben Jelloun. Paris: Stock, 1996.

Maincent-Morel, Michel. *La cuisine de référence*. Preface by Bernard Loiseau. Paris: BPI, 2002.

Mathiot, G. *Je sais cuisiner* (1932). Paris: Albin Michel, 1990.

Olney, Richard. *Simple French Food* (1974). New York: Wiley, 1992.

Olney, Richard with Jacques Gantié. *Provence: The Beautiful Cookbook* (1993). San Francisco: HarperCollins, 1999.

Pellaprat, Henri-Paul. *The Great Book of French Cuisine* (1966). New York: Vendome Press, 2003.

Pudlowski, Gilles. *Great Women Chefs of Europe*. Paris: Flammarion, 2005.

Raphaël, Freddy. *La cuisine juive en Alsace*. Strasbourg: La Nuée Bleue, 2005.

Vié, Blandine and Henri Bouchet. *Premiers repas de bébé*. Paris: Marabout, 2003.

Wolfert, Paula. *The Cooking of Southwest France: Recipes from France's Magnificent Rustic Cuisine* (1983). Revised edition. Hoboken: John Wiley & Sons, Inc., 2005.

Yana, Martine. *Trésors de la table juive*. Aix-en-Provence: Édisud, 2005.

CHAPTER 1

Abramson, Julia. "Grimod's Debt to Mercier and the Emergence of Gastronomic Writing Reconsidered." *EMF: Studies in Early Modern France* 7 (2001): 141–62.

———. "Legitimacy and Nationalism in the *Almanach des Gourmands* (1803–1812)." *Journal for Early Modern Cultural Studies* 3, no. 2 (2003): 101–35.

Albala, Ken. *Eating Right in the Renaissance*. Berkeley: University of California Press, 2002.

Ancient France: Neolithic Societies and Their Landscapes 6000–2000 B.C. Editor Christopher Scarre. Edinburgh: Edinburgh University Press, 1984.

Barbero, Alessandro. *Charlemagne* (2002). Translator Allan Cameron. Berkeley: University of California Press, 2004.

Baumgartner, Frederic J. *France in the Sixteenth Century*. New York: St. Martin's Press, 1995.

Bérard, Laurence and Philippe Marchenay. *Les produits du terroir: Entre cultures et règlements*. Paris: Centre National de la Rercheche Scientifique, 2004.

Bober, Phyllis Pray. *Art, Culture, and Cuisine: Ancient and Medieval Gastronomy*. Chicago: University of Chicago Press, 1999.

Bynum, Caroline Walker. *Holy Feast and Holy Fast: The Religious Significance of Food to Medieval Women*. Berkeley: University of California Press, 1987.

Caesar, Gaius Julius. *The Gallic War*. Translator Carolyn Hammond. Oxford: Oxford University Press, 1996.

Clément, Alain. *Nourrir le peuple: Entre État et marché, XVIe-XIXe siècle*. Paris: L'Harmattan, 1999.

Clottes, Jean. "Twenty Thousand Years of Paleolithic Cave Art in Southern France." In *World Prehistory*, pp. 161–76. Editors J. Coles, R. Bewley, and P. Mellars. Oxford: Oxford University Press, 1999.

Crosby, Alfred W. *The Columbian Exchange* (1972). Westport: Praeger, 2003.

Dalby, Andrew. *Dangerous Tastes: The Story of Spices*. Berkeley: University of California Press, 2000.

Davidson, James. *Courtesans and Fishcakes: The Consuming Passions of Classical Athens* (1997). London: Fontana Press, 1998.

Depeyrot, Georges. *Richesses et société chez les Mérovingiens et Carolingiens*. Paris: Errance, 1994.

Detienne, Marcel and Jean-Pierre Vernant. *La Cuisine du sacrifice en pays grec*. Paris: Gallimard, 1979.

Diamond, Jared. *Guns, Germs, and Steel* (1997). New York: Norton, 1999.

Durrenmath, Gilles. "Continuity and Change in the Late Neolithic in Southern France: A Technological Point of View." In *Prehistoric Pottery: People, Pattern, and Purpose*, pp. 53–64. Editor A. Gibson. Oxford: Archaeopress, 2003.

Effros, Bonnie. *Creating Community with Food and Drink in Merovingian Gaul*. New York: Palgrave Macmillan, 2002.

Elias, Norbert. *The History of Manners* (1939). Translator Edmund Jephcott. New York: Pantheon, 1982.

Fifth-Century Gaul: A Crisis of Identity? Editors J. Drinkwater and H. Elton. Cambridge: Cambridge University Press, 1992.

Food and Drink in History. Editors Robert Forster and Orest Ranum. Baltimore: The Johns Hopkins University Press, 1979.

From Roman to Merovingian Gaul. Editor Alexander Callander Murray. Toronto: Broadview, 2000.

Galen, Claudius. *On the Powers of Food.* Translator Mark Grant. In *Galen on Food and Diet,* pp. 68–190. London: Routledge: 2000.

Garnsey, Peter. *Food and Society in Classical Antiquity.* Cambridge: Cambridge University Press, 1999.

Geary, Patrick J. *Before France and Germany.* New York: Oxford University Press, 1988.

Gowers, Emily. *The Loaded Table: Representations of Food in Roman Literature.* Oxford: Clarendon Press, 1993.

Halsall, Guy. *Settlement and Social Organization: The Merovingian Region of Metz.* New York: Cambridge University Press, 1995.

Histoire de l'alimentation. Editors Jean-Louis Flandrin and Massimo Montanari. Paris: Arthème Fayard, 1996.

Jacobs, Marc and Peter Scholliers, eds. *Eating Out in Europe: Picnics, Gourmet Dining and Snacks since the Late Eighteenth Century.* Oxford: Berg, 2003.

Kaplan, Steven L. *The Bakers of Paris and the Bread Question, 1700–1775.* Durham: Duke University Press, 1996.

———. *La fin des corporations.* Translator Béatrice Vierne. Paris: Arthème Fayard, 2001.

King, Anthony. *Roman Gaul and Germany.* Berkeley: University of California Press, 1990.

Laroulandière, Fabrice. *Les Ouvriers de Paris au XIXe siècle.* Paris: Christian, 1997.

Laurioux, Bruno. *Manger au Moyen Âge.* Paris: Hachette, 2002.

Les lieux de mémoire (1984–92). Editor Pierre Nora. 3 vols. Paris: Gallimard, 1997.

Maier, Bernhard. *The Celts* (2000). Translator Kevin Windle. Notre Dame: University of Notre Dame Press, 2003.

McCormick, Michael. *Origins of the European Economy: Communications and Commerce,* A.D. *300–900.* Cambridge: Cambridge University Press, 2001.

McGowan, Andrew. *Ascetic Eucharists: Food and Drink in Early Christian Ritual Meals.* Oxford: Clarendon Press, 1999.

Méniel, Patrice. *Les Gaulois et les animaux: Élevage, repas et sacrifices.* Paris: Errance, 2001.

Milcent, Pierre-Yves. *Le premier âge du Fer en France centrale.* 2 vols. Toulouse: Université du Mirail, 2004.

Mintz, Sidney W. *Sweetness and Power: The Place of Sugar in Modern History.* New York: Viking, 1985.

Mitford, Nancy. *The Sun King.* New York: Penguin, 1966.

Paxton, Robert O. *Vichy France: Old Guard and New Order, 1940–1944* (1972). New York: Columbia University Press, 2001.

Pearson, Kathy L. "Nutrition and the Early-Medieval Diet." *Speculum* 72, no.1 (January 1997): 1–32.

Price, T. Douglas, editor. *Europe's First Farmers*. Cambridge: Cambridge University Press, 2000.

Rambourg, Patrick. *De la cuisine à la gastronomie: Histoire de la table française*. Paris: Louis Audibert, 2005.

Scarre, Christopher. "Enclosures and related structures in Brittany and western France." *Neolithic Enclosures in Atlantic Northwest Europe*, pp. 24–42, editors Timothy Darvill and Julian Thomas. Oxford: Oxbow Books, 2001.

Schivelbusch, Wolfgang. *Tastes of Paradise* (1980). Translator David Jacobson. New York: Vintage, 1992.

Sévigné, Mme de. *Lettres*. Editor Bernard Raffalli. Paris: Garnier-Flammarion, 1976.

Society and Culture in Late Antique Gaul. Editors R. W. Mathisen and D. Shanzer. Aldershot: Ashgate, 2001.

Sokolov, Raymond A. *Why We Eat What We Eat*. New York: Summit, 1991.

Spang, Rebecca. *The Invention of the Restaurant*. Cambridge: Harvard University Press, 2000.

Stouff, L. *Ravitaillement et alimentation en Provence aux XIVe et XVe siècles*. Paris: 1970.

Ulin, Robert C. *Vintages and Traditions*. Washington: Smithsonian Institution, 1996.

Weber, Eugen. *The Hollow Years: France in the 1930s*. New York: Norton, 1994.

Wheaton, Barbara Ketcham. *Savoring the Past*. Philadelphia: University of Pennsylvania Press, 1983.

White, Stephen D. *Feuding and Peace-Making in Eleventh-Century France*. Burlington: Ashgate, 2005.

Zvelebil, Marek. "Les derniers chasseurs-collecteurs d'Europe tempérée." In *Les derniers chasseurs-cueilleurs d'Europe occidentale (13,000–5,500 av. J.-C.)*, pp. 379–406. Besançon: Presses Universitaires de Franche-Comté, 2000.

CHAPTER 2

Adams, William James. "The Political Economy of Agriculture in France's Fifth Republic." *Explorations in Economic History* 36 (1999): 1–29.

Arndt, Alice. *Seasoning Savvy*. New York: Haworth Press, 1999.

Barthes, Roland. *Mythologies* (1957). In *Oeuvres complètes*, vol. 1, pp. 561–724. Paris: Seuil, 1993.

Boisard, Pierre. *Camembert: A National Myth* (1992). Translator Richard Miller. Berkeley: University of California Press, 2003.

Crane, Eva. *The World History of Beekeeping and Honey Hunting*. New York: Routledge, 1999.

Fischler, Claude. *Du vin*. Paris: Odile Jacob, 1999.

Flandrin, Jean-Louis. "Et le beurre conquit la France." *L'Histoire* 85 (1986):108–11.

Garrier, Gilbert. *Histoire sociale et culturelle du vin* (1995). Paris: Larousse-Bordas, 1998.

Landrieu, François. *La viande*. Paris: Herscher, 2003.

Kaplan, Steven L. *Le retour du bon pain*. Paris: Perrin, 2002.

Maincent, Michel. *Technologie culinaire*. Preface by Pierre Troisgros. Paris: BPI, 1999.

Masui, Kazuko and Tomoko Yamada. *French Cheeses* (1993). London: Dorling Kindersley, 1996.

Nourrisson, Didier. *Le Buveur du XIXe siècle*. Paris: Albin Michel, 1990.

Serventi, Silvano. *Le livre du foie gras*. Paris: Flammarion, 2002.

———— and Françoise Sabban. *Pasta* (2000). Translator Antony Shugaar. New York: Columbia University Press, 2002.

Vissac, Bertrand. *Les Vaches de la République*. Paris: Institut National de la Recherche Agronomique, 2000.

CHAPTER 3

Andrews, Colman. "After *Nouvelle cuisine*." *Saveur* 67 (June–July 2003): 79–91.

————. "Back to the Basics: Jean-Pierre and Isabelle Silva Give Up a Michelin Star in Burgundy to Lead a Simple Life." *Saveur* 76 (June–July 2004): 64–73.

Ardagh, John. *France in the 1980s* (1982). New York: Penguin, 1983.

Chelminski, Rudloph. *The Perfectionist: Life and Death in Haute cuisine*. New York: Penguin, 2005.

Claflin, Kyri Watson. "Culture, Politics, and Modernization in Paris Provisioning, 1880–1920." Ph.D. dissertation, Boston University, 2006.

Csergo, Julia and Christophe Marion, eds. *Histoire de l'alimentation: Quels enjeux pour la formation?* Dijon: Educagri, 2004.

Davet, Stéphane. "La nouvelle vague de la jeune cuisine." *Le Monde* (April 17, 2006).

Drouard, Alain. *Histoire des cuisiniers en France XIXe-XXe siècle*. Paris: Centre National de la Recherche Scientifique, 2004.

Edwards, Nancy. "The Science of Domesticity: Women, Education and National Identity in Third Republic France, 1880–1914." Ph.D. dissertation, University of California at Berkeley, 1997.

Ferguson, Priscilla Parkhurst. *Accounting for Taste: The Triumph of French Cuisine*. Chicago: The University of Chicago Press, 2004.

————. "A Cultural Field in the Making: Gastronomy in 19th-Century France." *American Journal of Sociology* 104, no. 3 (November 1998): 597–641.

Ferguson, Priscilla Parkhurst and Sharon Zukin. "The Careers of Chefs: 'French' and 'American' Models of Cuisine." In *Eating Culture*, pp. 92–111, editors Ron Scapp and Bryan Seitz. Albany: State University Press of New York, 1998.

Friedberg, Susanne. *French Beans and Food Scares: Culture and Commerce in an Anxious Age*. New York: Oxford University Press, 2004.

de Gary, Marie-Noël and Gilles Plum. *Les cuisines de l'hôtel Camondo*. Paris: Musée Nissim de Camondo and Union centrale des arts décoratifs, 1999.

Hammack, William. "There's a Lot More to the Story of the Microwave Oven Than a Melted Candy Bar." *Invention and Technology Magazine* (Spring 2005) accessed at http://www.americanheritage.com/articles/magazine/it/2005/4/2005_4_48.shtml.

Mériot, Sylvie-Anne. *Nostalgic Cooks: Another French Paradox* (2002). Translators Trevor Cox and Chanelle Paul. Boston: Brill, 2006.

Neirinck, Edmond and Jean-Pierre Poulain. *Histoire de la cuisine et des cuisiniers.* Paris: J. Lanore, 1997.

Orwell, George. *Down and Out in Paris and London* (1933). New York: Harcourt Brace, 1961.

Ory, Pascal. *Le Discours gastronomique français.* Paris: Gallimard, 1998.

de la Pradelle, Michèle. *Market Day in Provence* (1996). Translator Amy Jacobs. Chicago: The University of Chicago Press, 2006.

Rambourg, Patrick. "Guerre des sexes au fourneau!" *L'Histoire* 273 (February 2003): 25–26.

Rao, Hayageeva, Philippe Monin, and Rodolphe Durand. "Border Crossings: Bricolage and the Erosion of Categorical Boundaries in French Gastronomy." *American Sociological Review* 70 (December 2005): 968–91.

Rémy, Pascal. *L'Inspecteur se met à table.* Paris: Équateur, 2004.

Ross, Kristin. *Fast Cars, Clean Bodies: Decolonization and the Reordering of French Culture.* Cambridge, MA: MIT Press, 1995.

Rowley, Anthony. *The Book of Kitchens* (1999). Translator Deke Dusinberre. Paris: Flammarion, 2000.

Shephard, Sue. *Pickled, Potted, and Canned: How the Art and Science of Food Processing Changed the World.* New York: Simon and Schuster, 2000.

Trubek, Amy. *Haute Cuisine: How the French Invented the Culinary Profession.* Philadelphia: University of Pennsylvania Press, 2000.

CHAPTER 4

Aymard, Maurice, Claude Grignon, and Françoise Sabban, eds. *Le Temps de manger: Alimentation, emploi du temps et rythmes sociaux.* Paris: Éditions de la Maison des sciences de l'homme and Institut National de la Recherche Agronomique, 1993.

de Certeau, Michel, Luce Giard, and Pierre Mayol. *The Practice of Everyday Life: Living and Cooking* (1994). Translator T. J. Tomasik. Minneapolis: University of Minnesota Press, 1998.

Csergo, Julia, ed. *Pot-au-feu. Convivial, familial: Histoires d'un mythe.* Paris: Autrement, 1999.

Demossier, Marion. "Consuming Wine in France: The 'Wandering' Drinker and the *Vin-anomie*." In *Drinking Cultures: Alcohol and Identity,* pp. 129–54, editor Thomas M. Wilson. Oxford: Berg, 2005.

Grignon, Claude. *Les conditions de vie des étudiants.* Paris: Presses Universitaires de France, 2000.

Shields-Argelès, Christy. "Imagining the Self and the Other: Food and Identity in France and the United States." *Food, Culture and Society* 7, no. 2 (Fall 2004): 13–28.

CHAPTER 5

Aron, Jean-Paul. *Essai sur la sensibilité alimentaire à Paris au 19 e siècle.* Paris: Armand Colin, 1967.

Ascher, François. *Le mangeur hypermoderne.* Paris: Odile Jacob, 2005.

Blowen, Sarah, Marion Demossier, and Jeanine Picard, eds. *Recollections of France: Memories, Identities and Heritage in Contemporary France.* Oxford: Bergahn, 2000.

Chatriot, Alain, Marie-Emmanuelle Chessel, and Matthew Hilton, eds. *Au nom du consommateur: Consommation et politique en Europe et aux États-Unis au XXe siècle.* Paris: Découverte, 2004.

Conord, Sylvaine, Yasmine Mouhid, Elsa Gisquet, and Charlotte Deprée. *Regards anthropologiques sur les bars de nuit.* Paris: L'Harmattan, 1999.

Garabuau-Moussaoui, Isabelle, Elise Palomares, and Dominique Desjeux, eds. *Alimentations contemporaines.* Paris: L'Harmattan, 2002.

Gopnik, Adam. *Paris to the Moon.* New York: Random House, 2000.

Grange, Daniel J. and Dominique Poulot, eds. *L'esprit des lieux: Le patrimoine et la cité.* Grenoble: Presses Universitaires de Grenoble, 1997.

Jacobs, Marc and Peter Scholliers, eds. *Eating Out in Europe: Picnics, Gourmet Dining and Snacks since the Late Eighteenth Century.* Oxford: Berg, 2003.

Mériot, Sylvie-Anne. *Nostalgic Cooks: Another French Paradox* (2002). Translators Trevor Cox and Chanelle Paul. Leiden and Boston: Brill, 2006.

Tardieu, Marc. *Les Auvergnats de Paris.* Paris: Rocher, 2001.

CHAPTER 6

Corbin, Alain, Noëlle Gérôme, and Danielle Tartakowsky, eds. *Les usages politiques des fêtes aux XIXe-XXe siècles.* Paris: Sorbonne, 1994.

Cretin, Nadine. *Inventaire des fêtes de France d'hier et d'aujourd'hui.* Paris: Larousse, 2003.

Graham, Peter. *Mourjou: The Life and Food of an Auvergne Village* (1998). Totnes, Devon: Prospect Books, 2004.

Guy, Kolleen M. *When Champagne Became French: Wine and the Making of a National Identity.* Baltimore: The Johns Hopkins University Press, 2003.

Pleij, Herman. *Dreaming of Cockaigne: Medieval Fantasies of the Perfect Life* (1997). Translator Diane Webb. New York: Columbia University Press, 2001.

Segalen, Martine. *Rites et rituels contemporains.* Paris: Nathan, 1998.

Vovelle, Michel. *Les métamorphoses de la fête en Provence de 1750 à 1820.* Paris: Flammarion, 1976.

Wylie, Laurence. *Village in the Vaucluse* (1957). Cambridge: Harvard University Press, 1974.

CHAPTER 7

Ariès, Paul. *La fin des mangeurs*. Paris: Desclée de Brouwer, 1997.

Blanchet, Jacques and Alain Revel. *L'agriculture européenne face aux enjeux internationaux*. Paris: Économica, 1999.

Bourdelais, Patrice. "Improving Public Health in France: The Local Political Mobilization in the Nineteenth Century." *Hygiea Internationalis* 4, no. 4 (2004): 229–53.

Bové, José and François Dufour. *The World Is Not for Sale* (2000). London: Verso, 2001.

Chatriot, Alain, Marie-Emmanuelle Chessel, and Matthew Hilton, eds. *Au nom du consommateur: Consommation et politique en Europe et aux États-Unis au XXe siècle*. Paris: Découverte, 2004.

Dagnaud, Monique. *Enfants, consommation et publicité télévisée. Notes et études documentaires* 5166. Paris: La Documentation Française, 2003.

Fischler, Claude. *L'Homnivore*. Paris: Odile Jacob, 1990.

Forum on Functional Food. Proceedings, Council of Europe, December 1–2, 1998, Strasbourg. Strasbourg: Council of Europe, 1999.

Freeman, Richard. *The Politics of Health in Europe*. Manchester: Manchester University Press, 2000.

Garabuau-Moussaoui, Isabelle, Elise Palomares, and Dominique Desjeux, eds. *Alimentations contemporaines*. Paris: L'Harmattan, 2002.

Harthorn, Barbara Herr and Laury Oaks, eds. *Risk, Culture, and Health Inequality*. Westport, CT: Praeger, 2003.

Joly, P. B., G. Assouline, D. Kréziak, J. Lemarié, C. Marris, and A. Roy. *L'innovation controversée: Le débat public sur les OGM en France*. Grenoble: Collectif sur les Risques, la Décision et l'Expertise-Institut National de la Recherche Agronomique, 2000.

Lambert, Jean-Louis. *L'évolution des modèles de consommation alimentaire en France*. Paris: Technique et Documentation-Lavoisier, 1987.

Lazareff, Alexandre. *L'exception culinaire française*. Paris: Albin Michel, 1998.

Pernoud, Laurence and Agnès Grison. *J'élève mon enfant*. Paris: Pierre Horay, 2006.

Poulain, Jean-Pierre. *Manger aujourd'hui: Attitudes, normes et pratiques*. Toulouse: Privat, 2002.

———. *Sociologies de l'alimentation: Les mangeurs et l'espace social alimentaire*. Paris: Presses Universitaires de France, 2002.

Pour une politique nutritionnelle de santé publique en France. Rennes: École nationale de la santé publique, 2000.

Ramsey, Matthew. "Public Health in France." In *The History of Public Health and the Modern State*, pp. 45–118, editor Dorothy Porter. Amsterdam: Rodopi, 1994.

Rollet, Catherine. "Histoire de l'allaitement en France: Pratiques et représentations." Laboratoire Printemps, Centre National de la Recherche Scientifique. May 2006. http://www.co-naitre.net/articles/histoire_allaitement_CR_mai2006.pdf

de Rosnay, Stella and Joël de Rosnay. *La mal bouffe*. Paris: Orban, 1979.

Rozin, Paul, Kimberly Kabnick, Erin Pete, Claude Fischler, and Christy Shields. "The Ecology of Eating: Smaller Portion Sizes in France Than in the United States Help Explain the French Paradox." *Psychological Science* 14, no. 5 (September 2003): 450–54.

Sorum, Paul Clay. "France Tries to Save Its Ailing National Health Insurance System." *Journal of Public Health Policy* 26 (2005): 231–45.

Stanziani, Alessandro. *Histoire de la qualité alimentaire (XIXe-XXe siècle)*. Paris: Seuil, 2005.

Index

ABOUT THE AUTHOR

JULIA ABRAMSON is Associate Professor of French at the University of Oklahoma, Norman.